The Perennial Philosophy

Series

World Wisdom
The Library of Perennial Philosophy

The Library of Perennial Philosophy is dedicated to the exposition of the timeless Truth underlying the diverse religions. This Truth, often referred to as the *Sophia Perennis*—or Perennial Wisdom—finds its expression in the revealed Scriptures as well as the writings of the great sages and the artistic creations of the traditional worlds.

The Perennial Philosophy provides the intellectual principles capable of explaining both the formal contradictions and the underlying unity of the great religions.

Ranging from the writings of the great sages who have expressed the *Sophia Perennis* in the past, to the perennialist authors of our time, each series of our Library has a different focus. As a whole, they express the inner unanimity, transforming radiance, and irreplaceable values of the great spiritual traditions. *Paths to the Heart: Sufism and the Christian East* appears as one of our selections in The Perennial Philosophy series.

The Perennial Philosophy Series

In the beginning of the Twentieth Century, a school of thought arose which has focused on the enunciation and explanation of the Perennial Philosophy. Deeply rooted in the sense of the sacred, the writings of its leading exponents establish an indispensable foundation for understanding the timeless Truth and spiritual practices which live in the heart of all religions. Some of these titles are companion volumes to the Treasures of the World's Religions series, which allows a comparison of the writings of the great sages of the past with the perennialist authors of our time.

Paths to the Heart

Sufism and the Christian East

Edited by
James S. Cutsinger

Paths to the Heart
Sufism and the Christian East

Library of Congress Cataloging-in-Publication Data

Paths to the heart : Sufism and the Christian East / edited by James S. Cutsinger.
p. cm. — (Perennial philosophy series)
Includes bibliographical references.
ISBN 0-941532-43-7 (alk. paper)
1. Islam—Relations—Orthodox Eastern Church. 2. Orthodox Eastern Church—Relations—Islam. 3. Islam—Relations—Christianity. 4. Christianity and other religions—Islam. I. Cutsinger, James S., 1953- II. Series.
BP172.5.O77 P38 2002
261.2'7—dc21

2002005226

Cover art courtesy of the following:
"Ascent of the Prophet Muhammad" (OR2265.f.195r)
by permission of the British Library.
"Virgin of the Sign" by the hand of T. Anne Mancuso.

Printed on acid-free paper in Canada

For information address World Wisdom, Inc.
P.O. Box 2682, Bloomington, Indiana 47402-2682

www.worldwisdom.com

Contents

In grateful memory of

Frithjof Schuon

Spiritual Guide to both Christians and Muslims

Foreword

The essays collected in this book, written by some of the world's leading authorities on the mystical and contemplative dimensions of Islam and Eastern Christianity, were prepared for a major international conference, held on the campus of the University of South Carolina, October 18-20, 2001. Attended by nearly three hundred people, this important and most timely gathering included both academics and students, clergy and laity, spiritual leaders and seekers. To our knowledge, a symposium of this kind—on such a topic and on such a scale—was without precedent, and so also is this resulting volume of proceedings.

The aim of the conference was to do something new. Interfaith gatherings are common enough, but dialogue is almost always confined to the outward or exoteric level of doctrines and practices, and at this level, given the considerable differences among the teachings of the world's religions, contradiction or compromise often appear to be the only alternatives. This is particularly so in the case of Christianity and Islam. It seems that Jesus must either be God or not, and that the Quran is either the final and uniquely perfect revelation of God, or not—to mention only two of the more obvious "contradictions" between these traditions. It is therefore inevitable that Christians and Muslims who limit their approach to the dogmatic letter of their religions will find their perspectives to be mutually exclusive, and their "dialogue"—if and when they discuss their beliefs at all, and do not resort instead to conflict and violence—will be reduced to two parallel monologues.

Religions, however, are not just systems of exoteric beliefs and behaviors deployed on a plane, to be accepted (or rejected) by the reason and will. Each of the great traditions also has a third "dimension", a spiritual heart, in which the deeper meaning of those beliefs and practices comes alive, and where the spiritual pilgrim may discover, beyond the level of seemingly contradictory forms, an inner commonality with those who follow other paths.

This is certainly true of the two religions here in question. Despite the long and well-known history of conflict between Christians and Muslims, one finds that their mystical traditions, especially in the Christian East and in Sufism, have for centuries shared many of the same spiritual methods and goals, and in certain exceptional cases Sufi *shaykh*s and their Christian counterparts have even accepted disciples in the others' tradition. The anonymous Russian classic *The Way of a Pilgrim* is quite explicit in teaching that in the absence of a *starets* or spiritual father, the Christian seeker may receive spiritual instruction "even from a Saracen", and evidence of the reverse relationship can be found in the spiritual friendship of the Sufi Ibrahim ibn Adham and the Orthodox monk Symeon. One also recalls that the oldest continuously existing Christian monastery in the world, St Catherine's on Mt Sinai, contains a mosque within its precincts, constructed by the monks for the local Bedouins. These and other commonalities and historical contacts suggest the possibility for a deeper and more inward kind of conversation between Christians and Muslims than has been customary in our day. Our aim in organizing this conference was to lay the foundation for just such a dialogue in hopes that spiritual travelers in both religions might come to realize what the great Sufi teacher Ibn Arabi meant in saying, "My heart has opened unto every form: it is . . . a cloister for Christian monks . . . and the *Ka'ba* of the pilgrim."

Of course, whatever the commonalities between these traditions and no matter the fruitfulness of the occasional contacts between them, it is clear historically that most masters in the Christian East and in Sufi Islam would nonetheless have stopped short of embracing so explicitly universalist a point of view, insisting instead on the superiority of their own religions. As the reader will discover in the following pages, this same insistence was by no means absent from our conference. Some of the Christian contributors in particular, while readily expressing their appreciation for the teachings of mystical Islam, preferred to accentuate the insights of their own Hesychast tradition, and were considerably less willing than Ibn Arabi to concede the premise that the Divine Son of God might be equally "incarnate" in more than one saving path to the heart. The conference was therefore not without its controversial moments.

On the other hand, other speakers, both Muslim and Christian, were very open to the idea of searching for a unified truth beneath their dogmatic differences, and in undertaking this search, several acknowledged their indebtedness to the perennial philosopher and spiritual authority Frithjof Schuon (1907-1998), whose perspective has shaped their contributions to this volume, and to whom the editor has offered a grateful dedication. Schuon, who was a teacher and guide for many people, including both Muslims and Christians, throughout the world, was one of the most forceful and influential voices in our day in describing what he referred to as the "transcendent unity of religions" and in underscoring the importance of an "esoteric ecumenism", a form of interfaith dialogue which, while fully respecting the integrity of traditional dogmas and rites, "calls into play the wisdom which can discern the one sole Truth under the veil of different forms". The chapters that follow, which range from studies focused on major figures and themes in one of the two traditions to more explicitly dialogical and perennialist essays, have been organized in such a way as to lead the reader toward a clearer and deeper appreciation of Schuon's perspective.

But whatever one's opinion of the perennial philosophy, there is little doubt that explorations of the kind collected in this book are of greater importance now than ever before. Meeting just five weeks after the tragic events of September 11, the speakers and other conference guests were all keenly aware of the precariousness, but also the potential, of the present moment for the relationship between Christians and Muslims. Some who had intended to come to the symposium, including one invited speaker, were obliged to cancel their plans in view of concerns about air travel, but many others made the decision to attend precisely because of their heightened sense that a new level of understanding simply must be reached, and reached soon. Not surprisingly, however, a few participants wondered aloud what good could come from the reflections of a few scholars and mystics. How could discourse in the rarified atmosphere of contemplative vision ever reach the "solid ground" of actual human events? But a ready answer was supplied in the famous apothegm of St Seraphim of Sarov, quoted by several speakers: "Acquire inner peace, and thousands around you will find their salvation."

We could not but recall as well the words of Socrates spoken near the end of Plato's *Republic*, historically one of the most decisive texts for both Eastern Christians and Sufis, and deeply influential in shaping the vocabularies and trajectories of these two great traditions. Having described in considerable detail the ideal spiritual commonwealth—a "republic" ordered toward man's vision of the Divine Sun—Socrates finds himself faced with the criticism that a state of this kind "can be found nowhere on earth". He quickly responds to the objection, however, by explaining that "it makes no difference whether such a commonwealth exists now or will ever come into being, for there is a pattern of it laid up in Heaven for him who wishes to contemplate it and, so beholding, to constitute himself its citizen" (592b). Our prayer is that the readers of this book, whatever the course of future events may bring, will find their own sights lifted to precisely this contemplation.

The editor gratefully acknowledges the assistance of all who contributed to the conference and to helping prepare this volume, especially: Wight Martindale and the Aurora Institute, the University of South Carolina Bicentennial Commission, and the University of South Carolina departments of Religious Studies and Philosophy for their welcome financial support; my wife, Carol, for her usual indefatigable support and indispensable, last-minute help with registration and logistics; Daniel Wilson, for his beautiful design of the conference flyer and the cover of this volume; my department's administrative assistant, Anne Lucht, for her many hours of organization and planning; the directors and their staffs at World Wisdom and Fons Vitae presses, in particular Michael Fitzgerald, Barry McDonald, Mary-Kathryne Nason, and Gray Henry; Sabra Vidali for her help with transcription; Father Mark Mancuso, Joshua Robinson, Michael Allen, Carl Still, Louise Wilson, Deborah Casey, and Leslie Cadavid for their painstaking efforts in proofreading; and, of course, the conference speakers themselves, all of them wise and generous friends, for their contributions to the present book.

James S. Cutsinger
Feast of the Theophany, 2002

Dimensions of the Heart

Chapter 1

How Do We Enter the Heart?

Kallistos Ware, Bishop of Diokleia

Within the heart is an unfathomable depth.
—The Macarian Homilies

Le Point Vierge

In the experience of almost everyone there have surely been certain texts—passages in poetry or prose—which, once heard or read, have never been forgotten. For most of us, these decisive texts are probably few in number; but, rare though they may be, they have permanently altered our lives, and they have helped to make us what we are. One such text, so far as my own life journey is concerned, is a paragraph on *le point vierge*, "the virgin point", in Thomas Merton's *Conjectures of a Guilty Bystander* (definitely my firm favorite among his many books):

> At the center of our being is a point of nothingness which is untouched by sin and by illusion, a point of pure truth, a point or spark which belongs entirely to God, which is never at our disposal, from which God disposes of our lives, which is inaccessible to the fantasies of our own mind or the brutalities of our own will. This little point of nothingness and of absolute poverty is the pure glory of God in us. It is so to speak his name written in us, as our poverty, as our indigence, as our dependence, as our sonship. It is like a pure diamond, blazing with the invisible light of heaven. It is in everybody, and if we could see it we would see these billions of points of light coming together in the face and blaze of a sun that would make all the darkness and cruelty of life vanish completely. . . . I have no program for this seeing. It is only given. But the gate of heaven is everywhere.[1]

Here Thomas Merton is seeking to elucidate the moment of disclosure which came to him on 18 March 1958, and which he

1. *Conjectures of a Guilty Bystander* (New York: Doubleday, 1966), p. 142.

recorded in his journal on the following day: "Yesterday, in Louisville, at the corner of 4th and Walnut, suddenly realized that I loved all the people and that none of them were or could be totally alien to me. As if waking from a dream—the dream of my separateness."[2] It is noteworthy that, when attempting later on in his *Conjectures* to understand what was clearly for him an experience of intense visionary insight, Merton makes use of a term, *le point vierge*, which he had derived from Sufi sources. He had come across this phrase in the writings of the renowned French Orientalist Louis Massignon, with whom he had been in correspondence during the year 1960. Massignon in his turn employed the phrase when expounding the mystical psychology of the tenth-century Muslim saint and martyr al-Hallâj, whose custom it was to say, "Our hearts are a virgin that God's truth alone opens."[3]

Significantly al-Hallâj refers in this context to the heart. This word does not actually occur in the passage quoted above from *Conjectures of a Guilty Bystander*, but Merton is in fact describing precisely what the Christian East has in view when it speaks in its ascetic and mystical theology about the "deep heart" (see Psalm 63:7 [64:6]). By "the virgin point" Massignon, interpreting al-Hallâj, means "the last, irreducible, secret center of the heart", "the latent personality, the deep subconscious, the secret cell walled up [and hidden] to every creature, the 'inviolate virgin'", which "remains unformed" until visited by God; to discover this virgin point is to return to our origin.[4] Thus *le point vierge* or the innermost heart is, in the words of Dorothy C. Buck, the place "where God alone has access and human and Divine meet"; it embodies "the sacredness hidden in the depth of every human soul".[5]

This is exactly what is signified by the "deep heart" in the neptic[6] theology of the Orthodox Church. St Mark the Monk (? fifth cen-

2. *The Intimate Merton: His Life from His Journals*, ed. Patrick Hart and Jonathan Montaldo (San Francisco: Harper Collins, 2001), p. 124.
3. See Sidney H. Griffith, "Merton, Massignon, and the Challenge of Islam", in *Merton and Sufism: The Untold Story: A Complete Compendium*, ed. Rob Baker and Gray Henry (Louisville: Fons Vitae, 1999), pp. 63-64.
4. Griffith, p. 65.
5. "Mary and the Virgin Heart: A Reflection on the Writings of Louis Massignon and Hallaj", *Sufi*, 24 (1994-95), p. 8; *Sufi*, 28 (1995-96), p. 8.
6. "Neptic": from the word *nepsis*, meaning sobriety, vigilance, spiritual insight. "Neptic theology", in the Eastern Orthodox Church, includes the realms of both "ascetical theology" and "mystical theology", as these are understood in

tury), for example, speaks of "the innermost, secret and uncontaminated chamber of the heart . . . the innermost and untroubled treasury of the heart, where the winds of evil spirits do not blow". According to Mark the Monk, it is to this hidden *temenos* that Christ is alluding when he states, "The Kingdom of God is within you" (Luke 17:21), and when he talks about "the good treasure of the heart" (Luke 6:45).[7] A similar understanding of the heart is beautifully expressed by the Roman Catholic Benedictine Henri le Saux, who wrote under the name Swami Abishiktananda, when he terms it "the place of our origin . . . in which the soul is, as it were, coming from the hands of God and waking up to itself".[8] In the words of another Roman Catholic author, the Dominican Richard Kehoe, "The 'heart' is the very deepest and truest self, not attained except through sacrifice, through death."[9]

It is immediately apparent that St Mark the Monk, al-Hallâj, and Merton share in common an all-important conviction concerning the character of this deep or innermost heart. For all three of them it is something pure, inviolate, inaccessible to evil; and specifically for this reason it can rightly be described as "the virgin point". Thus Mark says of the "secret chamber of the heart" that it is "uncontaminated", "untroubled", a hidden sanctuary "where the winds of evil spirits do not blow". For al-Hallâj it is opened by "God's truth alone". Likewise Merton insists that it is "untouched by sin and by illusion, a point of pure truth, a point or spark which belongs entirely to God". While the outer levels of the heart are a battleground between the forces of good and evil, this is not true of the innermost depth of the heart. As "the virgin point" the deep heart belongs only to God. It is pre-eminently the place of Divine immanence, the locus of God's indwelling.

the Roman Catholic tradition. For the importance of the term *nepsis,* note the Greek title of *The Philokalia,* a classic collection of Orthodox spiritual writings from the fourth to the fifteenth centuries: "The Philokalia of the Holy Neptic [Fathers]".

7. Mark the Monk (alias Mark the Ascetic or Marcus Eremita), "On Baptism", §§4, 5, 11 (*Patrologia Graeca* [PG] 65: 996C, 1005 BCD, 1016 D), ed. Georges-Matthieu de Durand, *Sources chrétiennes* 445 (Paris: Cerf, 1999), pp. 322, 342-43, 368.
8. Abishiktananda, *Prayer* (London: SPCK, 1972), p. 54.
9. "The Scriptures as Word of God", in *The Eastern Churches Quarterly,* VII, Supplementary Issue on "Tradition and Scripture" (1947), p. 78.

It is, then, at the level of the deep heart that we experience our human personhood as fashioned in the image and likeness of God (Genesis 1:26-27); it is at the level of the deep heart that we become "partakers of the Divine Nature" (2 Peter 1:4), that we encounter the Uncreated in a meeting face-to-face, that we are "oned" with the living God in a transforming union of love. When the Fathers of the Christian Church, both Greek and Latin, understand salvation in terms of *theosis* or "deification", they are referring to a process which certainly embraces the totality of our personhood, yet which comes to its ultimate fulfillment only within the "virgin point" of the deep heart.

The heart is in this way a pivotal concept in the spiritual teaching both of Sufism and of Christianity. As Thomas Merton correctly observes, "Sufism looks at man as a heart. . . . The heart is the faculty by which man knows God", and so the supreme aim in Sufism is nothing else than "to develop a heart that knows God".[10] In the words of Rumi, "I have looked into my own heart; it is there that I have seen Him; He was nowhere else."[11] This leads Martin Lings to observe in his book *What is Sufism?*, "What indeed is Sufism, subjectively speaking, if not 'heart-wakefulness'?". Illustrating this, he quotes al-Hallâj: "I saw my Lord with the Eye of the Heart."[12] The Hesychast tradition of the Orthodox Church, for its part, speaks repeatedly of "prayer of the heart", of the "discovery of the place of the heart", of the "descent from the head to the heart", and of the "union of the intellect (*nous*) with the heart".

"The heart's a wonder", exclaims J. M. Synge in *The Playboy of the Western World.* But the time has come to ask more specifically what is meant by the heart. Are we speaking literally about the physical organ in our chest, or is the heart a symbol of certain spiritual realities? Is it perhaps both these things at once? Moreover, how do we enter into the deep heart, and what do we find when we have entered?

10. Cited by Rob Baker, "Merton, Marco Pallis, and the Traditionalists", in *Merton and Sufism*, p. 256.
11. Cited by Frithjof Schuon, *Christianity/Islam: Essays on Esoteric Ecumenicism* (Bloomington, Indiana: World Wisdom Books, 1985), p. 89. Schuon goes on to quote the striking words of the Hindu Lalla Yogishwari: "My guru gave me but a single precept. He told me: 'From without, enter into the most inward place'" (p. 91).
12. *What is Sufism?* (London: George Allen & Unwin, 1975), pp. 48-49.

The Fox, Ochwiay Biano, and the Bible

Some years ago the Duchess of Windsor—Wallace Simpson, the wife of King Edward VIII—issued her memoirs under the title *The Heart has its Reasons*. This was of course a quotation from Pascal: "The heart has its reasons, which the reason knows nothing of."[13] What Pascal meant by the heart is a complex question; but it is clear from the memoirs of the Duchess of Windsor that she understood the heart to denote the feelings, emotions, and affections—in her case, I fear, somewhat wayward emotions and affections.

Is this in fact the true and full meaning of the heart, or should we look further? A vital clue is provided by a book much loved by my own spiritual father, a priest of the Russian emigration, Fr George Cheremetiev. He used to repeat the farewell words of the fox in *Le Petit Prince* by Antoine de Saint-Exupéry: "'Goodbye,' said the fox. 'And now here is my secret. It is very simple. It is only with the heart that one can see rightly. What is essential is invisible to the eye.'"[14] *On ne voit bien qu'avec le coeur*: here the heart no longer signifies merely the emotions and affections, but it is regarded as the organ of inner vision, the place of insight and understanding.

Let us turn from France to North America. With the remark of the fox, let us compare the words of an American Indian, Ochwiay Biano, recorded by C. G. Jung in his book *Memories, Dreams, Reflections*:

> "See," Ochwiay Biano said, "how cruel the whites look. Their lips are thin, their noses sharp, their faces furrowed and distorted by folds. Their eyes have a staring expression; they are always seeking something. What are they seeking? The whites always want something; they are always uneasy and restless. We do not know what they want. We do not understand them. We think that they are mad."
>
> I asked him why he thought the whites were all mad.
>
> "They say that they think with their heads," he replied.
>
> "Why, of course. What do you think with?", I asked him in surprise.

13. *Pensées*, iv, 277, ed. A. J. Krailsheimer (Harmondsworth: Penguin Books, 1966), § 423 (p. 154).
14. *Le Petit Prince* (London: Heinemann Educational Books, 1981), p. 72.

"We think here," he said, indicating his heart.[15]

Evidently Ochwiay Biano agrees with the fox. In his conception of the human person there is no contrast between head and heart. The heart is not only, and not primarily, the locus of the feelings and emotions, but it is the place where we think, the focal point of wisdom.

Coming now to the Bible, we find that beyond any shadow of doubt it agrees with the fox and with Ochwiay Biano rather than with the Duchess of Windsor. In the Old and New Testaments there is no head/heart dichotomy. In Hebrew anthropology, as in that of the American Indians, the heart is the organ with which we think. For Biblical authors, the heart does not signify the feelings and emotions; for these are located lower down, in the guts and the entrails. The heart designates, on the contrary, the inwardness of our human personhood in its full spiritual depth. The word is to be interpreted in a wide-ranging sense: the heart is the primary center of the total person, the ground of our being, the root and source of all our inner truth. It is in this way a symbol of the unity and wholeness of our personhood in God.

In Ephesians 3:16-17, for example, the "heart" is treated as equivalent to the "inner man" (*ho esô anthropos*) or "inner being": "May God grant that you may be strengthened in your inner being with power through his Spirit, and that Christ may dwell in your hearts through faith." Here "heart", as the inner self in its totality, is manifestly far more than merely the affections and feelings. It denotes the human person viewed as a spiritual subject, as is clear from the often-quoted words of Christ in the Sermon on the Mount: "Where your treasure is, there will your heart be also" (Matthew 6:21). The heart is in this way the place where we formulate our primary hope, where we express our sense of direction, our purpose in life. It is the moral center, the determinant of action, and so it corresponds in part to what we mean today by the conscience. It is the seat of the memory, understood not just as the recollection of things past but as deep self-awareness at the present moment. So it is said of the Holy Virgin, after the birth of Christ, "Mary treasured all these words and pondered them in her heart" (Luke 2:19; cf.

15. *Memories, Dreams, Reflections* (London & Glasgow: The Fontana Library, Collins, 1967), p. 276.

2:51). The heart, then, is the faculty with which we ponder, the place of reflection and self-knowledge.

Throughout the Bible, the heart is generally understood in an inclusive sense. Just as there is no head/heart contrast in Scripture, so there is no separation between body and soul. The heart does not denote the body to the exclusion of the soul or the soul to the exclusion of the body, but it embraces both of them together. "Cardiac anthropology" is in this way holistic: the human being is envisaged as a psychosomatic totality, an undivided unity. The heart, that is to say, is at one and the same time a physical reality—the bodily organ located in our chest—and also a psychic and spiritual symbol. Above all it signifies integration and relationship: the integration and unification of the total person within itself, and at the same time the centering and focusing of the total person upon God.

Interpreting the heart in this comprehensive sense, we are enabled to give a fuller meaning to many familiar Biblical sayings. When the prophet Ezekiel speaks of the "stony heart" within us that is to be replaced by a "new heart" or a "heart of flesh" (Ezekiel 11:9, 18:31), he is referring to the conversion of our entire self, to a fundamental spiritual renewal and reorientation. When our Lord exhorts us, "You shall love the Lord your God with all your heart" (Matthew 22:37; compare Deuteronomy 6:5), he means "with the totality of yourself". When it is said by God, "My son, give me your heart" (Proverbs 23:26), this implies "give me your whole self". Likewise, when we are told, in a text constantly repeated in Orthodox spiritual writings, "Guard your heart with all vigilance" (Proverbs 4:23), this is to be interpreted, "Keep watch over the entirety of your inner life."

Because of our personal sinfulness, and dwelling as we do in a fallen world, the human heart is deeply ambivalent, a battle-field between good and evil forces. The heart is thus the arena in which we come face to face with the power of sin. "Out of the heart come evil intentions, murder, adultery, fornication, theft, false witness, slander", Christ warns us (Matthew 15:19); and, referring to the contemporary pagan world, St Paul states: "God gave them up to uncleanness through the lusts of their hearts" (Romans 1: 24). At the same time, however, the heart is the place where we come face to face with the Divine: "God searches the hearts" (Romans 8:27). It is more specifically the locus of the indwelling presence of God the Holy Trinity: "God has sent the Spirit of his Son into our hearts, crying, 'Abba! Father!'" (Galatians 4:6; compare Romans 8:15-16). The heart is in this way the point of self-transcendence, where my human personhood is taken up into the Divine life; it is the meeting-place of the created and the Uncreated. It is in and through the heart that the believer is enabled to affirm, not in a sentimental and imaginary fashion but with strict literalness, "It is no longer I who live, but it is Christ who lives in me" (Galatians 2:20).

It is now possible for us to appreciate more fully the true dimensions of the saying that we have already quoted from the Psalms, "The heart is deep" (63:7 [64:6]). Along with Proverbs 4:23, this is another key text in Orthodox neptic theology. It means that the human person is a profound mystery, that I understand only a very small part of myself, that my conscious ego-awareness is far from exhausting the total reality of my authentic Self. But it signifies more than that. It implies that in the innermost depths of my heart I transcend the bounds of my created personhood and discover within myself the direct unmediated presence of the living God. Entry into the deep heart means that I experience myself as God-sourced, God-enfolded, God-transfigured. Although sinful and unworthy, I am yet enabled to say with humble confidence, "His life is mine".[16]

This brings us back to the theme with which we began, Massignon's and Mertons's "virgin point", *le point vierge*, the "point of nothingness" which "belongs entirely to God" and which is his "pure glory" within us. This is precisely what Orthodox spirituality means by the "deep heart", understood as the place of Divine indwelling. There are two ways in which this indwelling is interpreted in the theology of the Christian East. Some authors, such as St Mark the Monk (already cited),[17] hold that it is specifically through the sacrament of Baptism that Christ and the Holy Spirit come to dwell within "the innermost, secret, and uncontaminated chamber of the heart". This presence, according to Mark, is inalienable: however careless and sinful our subsequent life may be, the baptismal indwelling of Christ and the Spirit continues to remain "secretly" (*mystikôs*) within us,

16. Compare the book of that title by Archimandrite Sophrony (Sakharov), disciple of St Silouan of Mount Athos and founder of the Orthodox Monastery of St John the Baptist at Tolleshunt Knights, Essex, England: *His Life is Mine* (London & Oxford: Mowbrays, 1977).

17. See note 7.

but if we do not fulfill the Divine commandments we shall not become consciously aware of their presence.[18]

There is, however, a second approach, which insists that this secret presence of God in the "deep heart" is to be found in every human person, whether baptized or not, for all alike are created in the Divine image and likeness (Genesis 1:26-27); as Merton says, "It is in everybody." Support for this "universalist" standpoint can be found in St Paul's speech to the Athenians on the Areopagus, as recorded by St Luke in the Book of Acts. Speaking to the unbaptized, who as yet know nothing of Christ, Paul affirms: "God is not far from each one of us, for in him we live and move and in him we exist; as even some of your own poets have said, 'For we too are his offspring'" (Acts 17:27-28). It is significant, however, that having affirmed this universal presence of the Divine in every human heart, Paul then goes on at once to speak specifically of the Resurrection of Jesus Christ.

The same "universalism" is expressed in the prologue to the Fourth Gospel, which refers to Christ the *Logos* as "the true light that enlightens everyone who comes into the world" (John 1:9). In similar terms, the second-century Apologist Justin Martyr sees Christ as the cosmic Sower who has implanted *logoi spermatikoi,* seeds of the truth, in the hearts of all human persons without exception; thus Socrates is a Christian before Christ.[19] It was this "universalist" vision of Justin which inspired and guided the nineteenth-century Russian Orthodox mission in Alaska under St Innocent (Veniaminov). In his preaching of Christ to the native peoples, he always sought points of contact between the Christian message and their existing beliefs. In so doing he never fell into any syncretistic compromise, but displayed on the contrary a true spirit of catholicity.[20]

The two approaches can perhaps be combined together. Christian believers may affirm, with Justin Martyr, that Christ the *Logos* is present in every human heart; and then they may go on to maintain, with St Mark the Monk, that this universal indwelling of the

18. See "On Those Who Think That They are Justified by Their Works", §56 (PG 65:937 D); "On Baptism", §4[993 C], ed. de Durand, pp. 146, 316-18.
19. See Justin, *1 Apology*, 44, 46; *2 Apology*, 6, 8, 10.
20. See Kallistos Ware, "'The Light that Enlightens Everyone': The Knowledge of God Among Non-Christians according to the Greek Fathers and St Innocent", *The Greek Orthodox Theological Review*, 44:1-4 (1999), pp. 557-64.

Divine is confirmed and deepened through sacramental Baptism in the Church.

Such in brief outline is the Biblical understanding of the heart. It is an all-embracing concept, a symbol of wholeness and integration. The heart includes the body, for it is a physical organ; but it is also the spiritual center of our personhood, the means whereby we think, make moral decisions, and attain wisdom. But this is not all. Advancing inward, penetrating through the many different levels of the heart where good and evil confront each other in conflict, eventually by God's grace and mercy the seeker attains the "deep heart", which is the Divine spark within us, the innermost sanctuary where God the Trinity dwells, the point of encounter between time and eternity, between space and infinity, between the created and the Uncreated.

"All Things are There"

How far is this rich and many-sided Biblical understanding of the heart preserved and developed in the Early Church, especially in the Christian East?[21] There are certainly many Greek Fathers from whose writings the distinctive Hebraic meaning of the heart is largely absent. Such authors tend to adopt a Platonist scheme, contrasting heart and head. They make little use of the term "heart"; when it does occur, it is either associated with the feelings or else treated as an equivalent to "intellect" (*nous*), but in both cases the fullness of the Biblical usage is lost. This is broadly true of writers such as Origen (d. c. 254), Evagrios of Pontus (d. 399), and St Dionysios the Areopagite (*fl.* c. 500).

There are, however, other Patristic authors who continue to use the word "heart" in its strong Scriptural sense, as denoting the spiritual center of the total person. This is the case, for example, with St Mark the Monk, St Diadochos of Photiki, and Abba Isaias in the fifth century, with St Barsanuphios and St John of Gaza in the early sixth century, with St John Klimakos and St Isaac of Nineveh in the

21. On the meaning of the heart in the Greek Fathers, the best treatment is still the two articles by André Guillaumont, "Les sens des noms du coeur dans l'antiquité", *Le Coeur,* Études Carmélitaines 29 (Paris, 1950), pp. 41-81; "Le 'coeur' chez les spirituels grecs à l'époque ancienne", *Dictionnaire de Spiritualité* 2 (1952), cols. 2281-8.

seventh century, and with St Hesychios of Batos in the eighth-ninth century. Typical of the standpoint of this second group of writers is the concise affirmation of St John Klimakos, ascribing to the heart the inclusive significance that it possesses in the Bible: "'I cried out with my whole heart,' says the Psalmist (Psalm 118 [119]:145): that is to say, with my body, soul, and spirit."[22] Typical also is the statement of St Isaac of Nineveh (Isaac the Syrian), assigning to the heart a focal and mediating position in our personhood: "The heart is placed as the mediator between the soul's senses and those of the body"; it is "in the middle".[23]

A particularly eloquent expression of the full meaning of the heart is to be found in the "Spiritual Homilies" of Makarios, a Greek text dating from around 370-390, traditionally attributed to the Coptic monk Makarios of Egypt, but in fact Syriac in background. Here the heart is most emphatically regarded as the axial point and the center of unity within the human person as a whole:

> The heart governs and reigns over the whole bodily organism; and when grace possesses the pasturages of the heart, it rules over all the members and the thoughts. For there, in the heart, is the intellect (*nous*), and all the thoughts of the soul and its expectation; and in this way grace penetrates also to all the members of the body.[24]

Let us try to spell out the implications of this key passage. First of all, when the Macarian Homilies speak here of the "pasturages" or "prairies" (*tas nomas*) of the heart, it has to be kept in mind that the circulation of the blood was not clearly understood in the ancient world. Patristic authors did not think of the heart as a kind of pump, in the way that we might do today, but they viewed it as a container

22. *The Ladder of Divine Ascent*, § 28 (PG 88:1140 B), trans. Colm Luibheid and Norman Russell, *The Classics of Western Spirituality* (New York/Ramsey/Toronto: Paulist Press, 1982), p. 281.
23. *Mystic Treatises* 33, trans. A. J. Wensinck (Amsterdama: Koninklijke Akademie van Wetenschappen te Amsterdam Afdeeling Letterkunde, 1923), p. 148; *Ascetical Homilies* 35, trans. Dana Miller (Boston: Holy Transfiguration Monastery, 1984), p. 158.
24. *Homilies* 15:20, ed. Hermann Dörries, Erich Klostermann, and Matthias Kroeger, *Patristische Texte und Studien* 4 (Berlin: Walter de Gruyter, 1964), p. 139, trans. George A. Maloney, *The Classics of Western Spirituality* (New York/Mahwah: Paulist Press, 1992), p. 116. All my quotations from the Macarian Homilies are taken from Collection II, but the same understanding of the heart is to be found in the other collections.

or empty vessel, full of space and air. This needs to be remembered whenever we come across such phrases as "finding the place of the heart" or "entering the heart".

"The heart governs and reigns", state the Macarian Homilies: it is the dominant element in our total human structure, the controlling power. It governs and reigns, more specifically, "over the whole bodily organism": it is in the first place a corporeal organ, located in the chest, which acts as the physical center of the human being; when our heart stops beating, we die. Yet this is not all. The Homilies go on to say that the heart rules also over the "thoughts", and that "there in the heart is the intellect". The heart is not only the physical but the psychic and spiritual center. The Greek word used here for "intellect", *nous*, signifies not only the reasoning brain but also, more fundamentally, a higher faculty of intuitive insight and mystical vision. Elsewhere in the Macarian Homilies it is stated that the *nous* within the heart is like the eye within the body;[25] in other words, through the use of the intellect within the heart we do not merely reach conclusions by means of discursive argumentation, but the intellect enables us to see the truth in a direct and unmediated manner. The heart in which the intellect dwells is thus the faculty with which we think, both in a rational and a suprarational way. It is both the seat of reasoning intelligence and also, on a higher or deeper level, the place of wisdom and spiritual knowledge (*gnosis*).

As the passage that we have quoted from the Macarian Homilies makes clear, the heart is not only the center of the human person considered on a natural plane, not only the point of convergence and union between body, soul, and spirit, but it is also the means whereby the human person is initiated into the Divine realm and enters into communion with God. It is through the heart that we

25. *Homilies* 43:7, ed. Dörries, p. 289, trans. Maloney, p. 222. On the relationship between *nous* and heart, see Kallistos Ware, "*Nous* and *noesis* in Plato, Aristotle, and Evagrius of Pontus", *Diotima* 13 (Athens, 1985), pp. 158-63; and by the same author, "Prayer in Evagrius of Pontus and the Macarian Homilies", in *An Introduction to Christian Spirituality*, ed. Ralph Waller and Benedicta Ward (London: SPCK, 1999), pp. 14-30. Some "neptic" writers, following Plato, draw a distinction between *dianoia* and *nous*: the first term denotes discursive reasoning, while the second indicates intuitive insight. But in other Patristic texts this distinction is not found, so that *nous* sometimes includes rational argumentation as well as mystical understanding.

experience uncreated grace "when grace possesses the pasturages of the heart". The heart in this way fulfils a mediatorial function, transmitting God's grace not only to the intellect and soul but also to the body: "in this way grace penetrates also to all the members of the body".

Developing this idea of the heart as the meeting-place between the Divine and the human, the Macarian Homilies continue:

> Within the heart is an unfathomable depth. There are reception rooms and bedchambers in it, doors and porches, and many offices and passages. In it is the workshop of righteousness and of wickedness. In it is death, in it is life. . . . The heart is Christ's palace. . . . There Christ the King comes to take his rest, with the angels and the spirits of the saints, and he dwells there, walking within it and placing his Kingdom there.[26]

In affirming here that there is within the heart "an unfathomable depth", the Homilies presumably mean in the first place that the heart includes what we today tend to describe as "the unconscious". The heart, that is to say, includes those aspects of myself which I do not as yet understand, the potentialities within myself of which I am at present largely or totally unaware. At the same time the Homilies underline the ambivalence that exists in this "depth" of the heart. As the moral center of the human person, it is the battleground between God and Satan, between good and evil; it is "the workshop of righteousness and of wickedness", containing within itself both "life" and "death". But, despite the presence of evil within the heart, it remains in its fundamental essence "Christ's palace", the place of Divine indwelling. Beyond the battleground there is *le point vierge*, the innermost *temenos*, "where the winds of evil spirits do not blow": "there Christ the King comes to take his rest".

Emphasizing the ambivalence of the heart, the Macarian Homilies state in another passage:

> The heart is but a small vessel; and yet dragons and lions are there, and there likewise are poisonous creatures and all the treasures of wickedness; rough, uneven paths are there, and gaping chasms. There also is God, there are the angels, there life and the Kingdom, there light and the apostles, the heavenly cities and the treasures of grace: all things are there.[27]

26. *Homilies* 15:32-33, ed. Dörries, p. 146, trans. Maloney, p. 120.
27. *Homilies* 43:7, ed. Dörries, p. 289, trans. Maloney, p. 222.

"Rough, uneven paths are there, and gaping chasms": here again we may think of the modern concept of the unconscious. "All the treasures of wickedness" are there, but so also are "the treasures of grace": the heart is at the cross-roads, at the storm-center of the cosmic conflict between good and evil; the heart determines our eternal destiny. "There also is God": the heart is the place where created personhood becomes transparent to the Divine, where God the Holy Trinity is at work within me. "All things are there": the heart is all-inclusive, all-embracing, a symbol of wholeness, integration, and totality, signifying the human person as an undivided unity. The standpoint of "cardiac" anthropology, as we have already emphasized, rejects any dichotomy between mind and matter, between soul and body, between head and heart. It views the human being in holistic terms.

Summarizing the Macarian teaching, we may say that the heart is open both below and above: below, to the abyss of the subconscious; above, to the abyss of the mystical supraconscious—below, to the forces of evil; above, to the Divine Light. In the words of the Russian philosopher Boris Vysheslavtsev, it is "the absolute center": "the center not only of consciousness but of the unconscious, not only of the soul but of the spirit, not only of the spirit but of the body, not only of the comprehensible but of the incomprehensible; in one word, it is the absolute center".[28] The heart is the point of meeting between human freedom and Divine grace, between image and Archetype, between the created and the Uncreated.

At the end of the Byzantine era, the great Hesychast master St Gregory Palamas (1296-1359) sums up the earlier Patristic teaching on the heart in words that directly recall the teaching of the Macarian Homilies, written nearly a thousand years earlier. The heart, says Palamas, is "the innermost body within the body . . . the shrine of the intelligence and the chief intellectual organ of the body". The intellect (*nous*), the visionary faculty whereby we apprehend the Transcendent and the Eternal, is located within the heart, although in an incorporeal and non-spatial sense. When we pray, our aim is precisely to "collect our intellect, outwardly dispersed

28. Quoted in John B. Dunlop, *Staretz Amvrosy: Model for Dostoevsky's Staretz Zossima* (Belmont, Massachusetts: Nordland,1972), p. 22.

through the senses, and bring it back within ourselves—back to the heart itself, the shrine of the thoughts".[29]

Such is the wealth of meaning, the complexity of content, that the term "heart" possesses in Scripture and in many of the Fathers. Once the word is interpreted in this inclusive way, many key phrases in the Hesychast tradition suddenly acquire a much more profound meaning. The phrase "prayer of the heart", for example, when used in an Orthodox source such as *The Philokalia*, does not signify solely "affective prayer" in the modern Western sense, that is to say, prayer of the feelings and emotions, but it denotes prayer of the total person. Since the heart is a bodily organ it means prayer in which the body participates, as well as the soul and spirit.[30] But, since the heart is also the place of Divine indwelling, "prayer of the heart" indicates at the same time those levels at which it is not merely I who pray, but at which Christ and the Holy Spirit are praying within me. It signifies the experience of being "prayed in": "not I, but Christ in me". The Hesychast injunctions: "discover the place of the heart", "descend into the heart", "unite your intellect with your heart", are to be interpreted in a similar way. They mean: enter into relationship with your deep self, find God in the profundity of your being, discover the true dimensions of your personhood in God, realize yourself as created in the Divine image and likeness.

The Heart and the Jesus Prayer

If this is what is meant by the heart, and if this is what we discover when we enter, then we may well feel both encouraged and daunted. How, we ask, is such an entry possible? What shall we do to find the pathway into the deep heart? What is the key that opens the door?

Among human beings there is an inexhaustible variety. Because we are each endowed with free will, we are all of us different; each

29. *Triads in Defence of the Holy Hesychasts*, 1:2:3, ed. Jean Meyendorff, Spicilegium Sacrum Lovaniense 30-31 (Louvain: Université Catholique, 1959), p. 80, trans. G. E. H. Palmer, Philip Sherrard, and Kallistos Ware, *The Philokalia*, Vol. 4 (London: Faber and Faber, 1995), p. 334.

30. On the physical techniques used by the Byzantine Hesychasts and on the parallels in yoga and Sufism, see Jacques-Albert Cuttat, *The Encounter of Religions: A Dialogue between the West and the Orient, with an Essay on the Prayer of Jesus* (New York/Tournai: Desclée, 1960), especially pp. 89-97; Kallistos Ware, "Praying with the Body: The Hesychast Method and Non-Christian Parallels", *Sobornost*, incorporating *Eastern Churches Review*, 14:2 (1992), pp. 6-35.

is unique, and each expresses the Divine image in his or her distinctive and unrepeatable way. This is emphasized in a saying by the Hasidic master Rabbi Zusya: at the Last Judgment, he insisted, I shall not be asked, "Why were you not Moses?" I shall be asked, "Why were you not Zusya?"[31] Such is the question of all questions that will be put by God to each one of us at the *Parousia*: Why did you not become your own true self? Such is exactly the purpose of obedience to a spiritual guide: his or her aim is to enable us to discover who we truly are.

By virtue of this inexhaustible human variety, it follows that there is no single, uniform way of praying that is automatically imposed upon all. Since we each possess free will, there is within prayer a wide-ranging freedom. As a personal dialogue with the personal God, prayer has as many different forms as there are human persons. Yet, while allowing full scope for this freedom in prayer, most Orthodox teachers—when asked, "How may I enter the heart?"—would give the same answer: through the use of the Jesus Prayer.[32] By the "Jesus Prayer" is meant a short invocation to Christ, frequently repeated, most commonly in the form "Lord Jesus Christ, Son of God, have mercy on me". But there are many variants. It is possible to say only "Lord Jesus", "My Jesus", or even nothing more than the one word "Jesus", although in the Christian East it is not usual to invoke the Holy Name entirely on its own.

The Jesus Prayer may be used in two complementary ways. First, it may be said in a "free" manner, as we go about our daily tasks, when we are performing some piece of repetitive work, or during the passing moments of time when we are not doing anything spe-

31. Martin Buber, *Tales of the Hasidim*, Vol. 1, *The Early Masters* (New York: Schocken, 1968), p. 251.
32. For a brief and practical introduction to the Jesus Prayer, see Kallistos Ware, *The Power of the Name: The Jesus Prayer in Orthodox Spirituality*, Fairacres Publication 43 (Fairacres, Oxford: SLG Press, Convent of the Incarnation, revised edition, 1986). For the historical background, see "A Monk of the Eastern Church" [Archimandrite Lev Gillet], *The Jesus Prayer*, new edition revised by Kallistos Ware (New York: St Vladimir's Seminary Press, 1987); and Irénée Hausherr, S.J., *Noms du Christ et voies d'oraison*, in the series Orientalia Christiana Analecta 157 (Rome, 1960); English translation, *The Name of Jesus*, in Cistercian Studies Series 44 (Kalamazoo, 1978). The works of Gillet and Hausherr are both in need of updating. On the Western usage see Rama Coomaraswamy, *The Invocation of the Name of Jesus as Practiced in the Western Church* (Louisville: Fons Vitae, 1999).

cific and which would otherwise be wasted. It may be the first words that we speak as we wake in the morning and our last words as we fall asleep at night. We can say it, once or many times, as we clean our room, as we do the washing-up, as we walk from place to place, as we wait for the bus or are delayed in a traffic jam. It is particularly valuable at moments of temptation, tension, and anxiety, or at times of acute physical pain, when more complex forms of prayer are all but impossible. The aim of this "free" use is to break down the false dichotomy between "sacred" and "secular", and to bring the Divine presence into every aspect of our daily life. Through the frequent Invocation of the Name we are enabled, wherever we look, to see Christ everywhere and to rejoice in him. The whole world becomes a sacrament. In the words of the Gospel of Thomas, "Split a piece of wood, and there am I; lift up the stone, and you will find Me there."[33]

In the second place, there is what may be termed the "fixed" use of the Jesus Prayer, when it is recited during the periods of time that we have set aside exclusively for the remembrance of God, and when we endeavor to pray without doing anything else. Usually in the Orthodox practice on these occasions the Prayer is said seated, although it may also be said standing, accompanied by deep bows or prostrations. Normally it is said alone, although occasionally it is recited in groups, in which case it is the practice for one person at a time to say the Prayer aloud, while the others invoke the Name inwardly. When we say the Prayer alone, the words may be recited aloud, or else they may be expressed silently but with a definite inner articulation. A prayer rope (*komvoschoinion*) of knotted wool or twine may be employed, to enhance the unbroken regularity of the Invocation. It is also possible to co-ordinate the rhythm of the Prayer with the tempo of the breathing; there are various ways of doing this, but they should only be attempted under the personal guidance of an experienced spiritual father or mother. In general, whether or not someone intends to use the physical technique, the Orthodox tradition insists upon the need for direct spiritual direction, person to person, if we wish to journey in a seriously committed manner upon the Way of the Name.

The primary aim of this second or "fixed" use of the Jesus Prayer is to establish within ourselves, through the Divine mercy, the inner

33. Gospel of Thomas, logion 77.

stillness and creative silence that is known in Orthodoxy as *hesychia* (hence the term "hesychast", meaning one who practices interior prayer). In itself, the Jesus Prayer is an oral prayer, a prayer in words. But because the words are exceedingly simple, because they are repeated over and over again in the same form, it is a prayer which leads us through words into silence; or, more precisely, which enables us to discover the dimension of silence that is hidden within the words. We speak, but at the same time we listen. Silence in this context should be understood not in negative but in supremely positive terms. It is not merely a cessation of sound, a pause between words, but an attitude of openness, receptivity, of attentive waiting upon God. It is not isolation but relationship, not emptiness but fullness, not an absence but a presence: at the core of it is God. Significantly the Psalmist says, not just "Be still", but "Be still, and know that I am God" (Psalm 45:11 [46:10]). True silence is nothing else than God-awareness. Thus the one who seeks to be silent, in this affirmative sense, is actually saying to God, in the words of the child Samuel: "Speak, Lord, for thy servant hears" (1 Kingdoms [I Samuel] 3:9).

The Jesus Prayer—understood in this manner as a means of entry into silent communion with God—is at the same time precisely a means of entry into the deep heart. If we say, "Silence is a presence: at the core of it is God", what we are in fact talking about is nothing else than the heart. For, as we have found both in Scripture and in the Greek Fathers, the heart is the meeting-point between God and the human person, the place of Divine indwelling and of loving union between Creator and creature. To encounter God in silence is therefore to encounter God in the heart.

Here, then, in simple terms is the beginning of an answer to the question: How do we enter the heart? One way of entry—certainly not the only way, but a way which many Orthodox Christians follow with gratitude and joy—is through the Invocation of the Holy Name of Jesus. This will lead us to the place of inner stillness and of God-awareness, which is also the place of the heart.

What does the Hesychast find when, by God's grace, he has in this way entered the heart? The practice of the Jesus Prayer, so it is affirmed in works such as *The Philokalia,* leads to a vision of Divine Light. The saints in prayer behold the Light that shone from Christ at his Transfiguration on Mount Tabor (see Matthew 17:1-8; Luke 9:28-36), and that we shall all of us behold, whether righteous or sinners, at the Last Day when Christ comes again in glory. This Taboric and eschatological splendor is not a created, physical light of the senses, but it is a revelation of the eternal and uncreated Energies of God. Gazing upon the Light and entering into union with it, the saints become that which they contemplate, and are themselves transformed into Light—on most occasions inwardly, but sometimes also in a visible and bodily fashion. Without losing their created identity, they undergo "deification" (*theosis*) and are "oned" with God the Holy Trinity in a union without confusion. In the words of the Macarian Homilies, "The soul becomes all light, all face, all eye. . . . Peter is still Peter, Paul is Paul, Philip is Philip. Each one retains his own unique nature and personality, but they are all filled with the Spirit."[34] Such is the journey's end on the pilgrimage of the Jesus Prayer; to quote Seyyed Hossein Nasr, "The invoker becomes the invocation and the invocation, the invoked."[35]

Parallels and Differences

Enough has been said about the Hesychast understanding of the heart and about the practice of the Jesus Prayer to suggest many parallels between Eastern Orthodoxy and Sufism. In particular there are striking similarities between the physical techniques of the Byzantine Hesychasts, with the regulation of breathing, and the bodily exercises that accompany *dhikr* among the Sufis. So close are the points of resemblance as to render it highly probable that there has been some direct contact between the two traditions. But, to the best of my knowledge, no one has so far discovered specific evidence indicating when and where this contact took place. Has Sufism influenced Hesychasm, or vice-versa? Or was the influence mutual? Here is a challenging area for future research.

Yet, having noted the parallels, it would not be honest for me as a Christian to pass over what I am bound to regards as a crucial point of difference. The Jesus Prayer is an invocation, not simply of God, but specifically of Jesus Christ, the second person of the Holy Trinity. We are not calling upon the Supreme Being in general terms, but we are speaking precisely to God incarnate, the Son of the eternal

34. *Homilies* 1:2 and 15:10, ed. Dörries, pp. 2, 132-33, trans. Maloney, pp. 37, 112.
35. Quoted by Bonnie Thurston, "Thomas Merton's Interest in Islam: the Example of *Dhikr*", in *Merton and Sufism*, p. 45.

Father who is also Son of Mary. Without overlooking the universality of Christ the *Logos*, "the true light that enlightens everyone who comes into the world" (John 1:9), we cannot but emphasize the historicity of the Jesus Prayer. We are invoking Christ by the human name "Jesus", which was given to him by his Mother and his foster-father Joseph at his earthly birth in Bethlehem (see Matthew 1:21).

Here I would like to recall an analogy that I have used elsewhere.[36] Most pictures have frames, and all picture-frames have certain characteristics in common; yet the pictures within the frames may be altogether diverse. What has primary significance is the picture, not the frame. In the case of the Jesus Prayer, the use of physical techniques—as an optional aid, not as an indispensable part of the Prayer—along with the discipline of repetition represents as it were the frame, while the Name of Jesus Christ constitutes the picture within the frame. The "frame" of the Jesus Prayer undoubtedly resembles various non-Christian "frames", but this should not lead us to underestimate the uniqueness of the picture within, that is to say, the distinctively Christian content of the actual Prayer itself. The essential point of the Jesus Prayer is not how we pray, not the exterior techniques, but to whom we are speaking. In the case of the Jesus Prayer, our words are addressed unambiguously to the Incarnate Savior Jesus Christ, Son of God and Son of Mary.

If it seems that I am placing undue emphasis upon the contrast between the Hesychast use of the Jesus Prayer and the Sufi use of *dhikr*, then I ask your forgiveness; but I cannot in conscience speak otherwise. There can be no true dialogue that does not acknowledge the distinctiveness of each side in the interchange. Let me add, however, a story told by the Desert Fathers of fourth-century Christian Egypt, which applies to all of us, whatever our religious affiliation. A monk came to see Abba Joseph of Panepho and said to him, "Abba, as far as I can I say my little office, I observe my little fast, I pray and meditate and maintain stillness, and as far as I can I keep my thoughts pure. What more can I do?" Then the old man stood up and stretched out his hands towards heaven, and his fingers became like ten burning lamps of fire. "If you wish," he said, "you can become all flame."[37]

36. Kallistos Ware, *The Power of the Name* (see n. 32), p. 23.

37. *Apophthegmata Patrum*, alphabetical collection, Joseph of Panepho, 7 (PG 65:229 CD).

That is what this suffering and broken world needs most of all: not people who say prayers from time to time but people who are prayer all the time—a living flame of adoration.

This brings us to a final question that we cannot afford to neglect. Is it not selfish, it may be objected, to close the door of our room, to pray in solitude, to say repeatedly with our eyes closed "have mercy on me", and so to seek a way of entry into the hidden sanctuary of our own heart? Is not such prayer anti-social and world-denying? Are we not turning our back upon the anguish of a despairing and tormented humanity? What relationship does inward-looking prayer of this kind have with, for instance, the aftermath of the tragedy on 11 September 2001 or the deadly crisis existing at present in the Holy Land?

By way of answer, I would like to recall two sayings. The first is from a Russian *starets* ("elder") of the nineteenth century, St Seraphim of Sarov: "Acquire inner peace and thousands around you will find salvation."[38] The second is from the one-time Secretary General of the United Nations, Dag Hammarskjöld (d. 1961): "Understand—through the stillness, act—out of the stillness, conquer—in the stillness."[39] "Acquire inner peace": the aim of the Jesus Prayer, and equally of all forms of contemplative prayer that seek the path of entry into the heart, is exactly to acquire inner peace. But this is in no way selfish or anti-social, for such prayer makes us, under the Divine mercy, into an instrument of peace for others. The impetus for social healing has always to be, in the direction of its movement, from within outwards. As Professor Nasr has reminded us, we cannot do good unless we are good. We cannot bring peace to the sorrowful world around us unless there is peace in our own hearts. Because we have prayed alone, with the door shut, "in secret" (Matthew 6:6)—perhaps for no more than fifteen or thirty minutes each day—then, throughout all the other minutes and hours of the day, we shall be available to others, open to their concerns, Christ-like, lovingly compassionate, in a way that would otherwise be impossible. True prayer of the heart turns each one of us into a man or woman for others, in a way that nothing else can.

38. See Archimandrite Lazarus (Moore), *St Seraphim of Sarov: A Spiritual Biography* (Blanco, Texas: New Sarov Press,1994), p. 126.
39. *Markings* (New York: Alfred A. Knopf, 1964), p. 127.

"Understand—through the stillness": the aim of all forms of contemplative prayer is indeed to enable us to understand through the stillness, so that we can then act out of the stillness and conquer in the stillness. St Ignatios of Antioch (d. c. 107), in a pregnant phrase, describes Jesus Christ as "the Word that came forth from silence".[40] Unless, by God's grace, our words and acts in some measure come forth from *hesychia,* silence of the heart, then they will remain superficial and ineffective. But if they do indeed have their source in creative silence, then they will prove words of fire and light, acts of healing and transfiguration.

"Beauty will save the world", said Dostoevsky. With equal and indeed greater truth it may be said: Prayer of the heart will save the world.

40. "To the Magnesians", 8:2.

Chapter 2

St Seraphim of Sarov in Sufic Perspective

Gray Henry

In the Name of God, the Merciful, the Compassionate.

I dedicate this lecture to Bishop Kallistos, for were it not for his open heart to me in the late 1980s, I would never have had my own heart expanded with love for the Eastern Church and its Hesychast tradition. I asked him to be my supervisor, along with Dr Martin Lings, for a doctoral dissertation entitled "The Rosary and the Remembrance in Hesychasm and Sufism—The Hidden Martyrdom". His Grace gave me a reading list, and I obediently read everything on it, but my parents needed me home in Kentucky. I returned. But what I learned from him still rings in my heart.

This morning I shall very simply mention a number of the parallels to be found in these two great methodologies for realization. Then I propose to make a few brief remarks on the subject of light, particularly in regard to my beloved St Seraphim of Sarov.

In his book *The Orthodox Way*, Bishop Kallistos states, "We are on a journey through the inward space of our heart, a journey not measured by the hours of our watch or the days of the calendar, for it is a journey out of time into eternity,"[1] and he points out that one of the most ancient names for Christianity is the Way. Similarly, a Sufi order is called a *tarîqah,* which is also translated as a way, and the aim of both ways is *theosis* or divinization. We are asked to become who we already are—beings made in God's image. Neither way envisions this transmutation as a substitute for the rites or sacraments enjoined by the exoteric frameworks of Christianity and Islam, but each of them deepens and intensifies the spiritual life through specific additional practices. Central to both is the invocation of a sacred name—usually Jesus or Allah—which is either used on its own or is found contained within other formulations. In both traditions, the efforts which we make against our soul's lower, dis-

1. Kallistos Ware, *The Orthodox Way* (Crestwood, NY: St Vladimir's Seminary Press, 1986), pp. 7-8.

ruptive tendencies are understood to involve an arduous struggle, which is referred to in the Christian East as "the hidden martyrdom", and in Islam as "the greater *jihad*", with Paradise as the reward.

A seeker wishing to undertake this most serious and noble of pursuits takes guidance from a master. The words *starets* in Russian, *geron* in Greek, and *shaykh* in Arabic all refer to an elder capable of guiding an aspirant, someone who knows the Way and its pitfalls. In both traditions there have been women and men as both masters and disciples. It occurred to me when reading *Early Sufi Women* by as-Sulami,[2] a record of the lives of Sufi women around the 10th century, that the austerities they sought to imitate were those practiced by the Virgin Mary.[3] For those who may not be familiar with Islam, Mary figures highly and is considered the highest woman in all creation and is considered an example for both men and women in regard to her piety and purity.

In both Hesychasm and Sufism, it is usual for the disciple to receive a second name, symbolic of his second birth upon entering the Way. The master gives the disciple instructions according to the degree of his or her experience and progress. The postures and breathing exercises which may accompany the Jesus Prayer are permitted in stages, as are the recitations or ritual participations in Sufism. In each methodology, there is both the free and formal use of the practices, which are used both alone and in groups. Regular retreats and the rosary provide further support. Most Eastern Orthodox prayer rosaries have one hundred woolen beads, and the Muslim prayer beads also number one hundred—ninety-nine representing the Divine attributes, and a single longer bead called an *alif* or "a" stands for the Divine Essence. There is also a parallel here, for the Eastern Christian distinction between God's essence and energies is similar to the distinction in Sufism between the essence of God or *Dhât* and the ninety-nine names of Allah. In his study of St Gregory Palamas, John Meyendorff notes, "As God (Essence) is completely present in each of the divine energies, each serves as his name." St Gregory writes, "Manifesting the personal being of God, the Divine energies reflect the unity of the Divine

2. Rkia Cornell, *Early Sufi Women* (Louisville, KY: Fons Vitae, 1999).
3. Aliah Schliefer, *Mary the Blessed Virgin of Islam* (Louisville, KY: Fons Vitae, 1998).

essence and are inseparable from the essence, but not identical with it."

In his *Ways of Prayer and Contemplation*, Bishop Kallistos describes three stages of the spiritual journey, as follows:

1) *Praktiki*, which involves repentance, *metanoia*, and change of mind. One's aim is to purify the heart. In Sufism the term for this is *tawbah*, or turning, with the intention not just of asking forgiveness, but literally of turning one's life completely around. The Hesychast redirects his passions, rather than attempting to suppress or mortify them, and the result is called *apatheia.*

2) *Physiki*, which involves contemplation, first of the natural world and then of the angelic and other realms of immateriality. "To see all things in God, and God in all things . . . treat each thing as a sacrament." According to Evagrius, someone came to the righteous St Anthony, asking how he could manage without the consolation of books. "My book," the inquirer was told, "is the nature of created things, and it is at hand whenever I wish to read the words of God." For the Muslim, too, natural forms are seen as the *ayat* or signs of God.

3) *Theologia*, which represents knowledge of God beyond all concepts and images. According to Evagrius, "When you pray, do not shape within yourself any image of the deity." The aim here is God's immediate presence.

In his symbolic interpretation of the first of the Ten Commandments, which prohibits graven images, St Gregory of Nyssa says, "Every concept grasped by the mind becomes an obstacle. Our aim is to attain beyond all words and concepts a contained presence." Bishop Kallistos comments, "This non-iconic, non-discursive consciousness of God's presence—often referred to in Greek as *hesychia*, that is, tranquility and inner stillness—is not an emptiness or a void but a *Presence.*" The word for this same presence in Arabic is *hadrah*, and a Sufi spiritual gathering to invoke God's name is also called a *hadrah.*

The Hesychast idea of quietude and presence appears in a Quranic verse recited at Sufi *hadrahs*: "He it is Who has caused the Spirit of Peace (*sakina*) to descend into the Heart of the believers—that they may increase in faith." The etymological root of the term *Sakina* has different levels of related meaning: *sakan*—dwelling; *sakana*—to be quiet; *sukûn*—pause; *sakînah*—the indwelling distillation of grace and presence. In the third stage of the journey, where both the Hesychast and the Sufi aim at union or knowledge of God beyond all concepts, the Sufi apophatically recites upon his rosary *Lâ ilâha illâ 'Llâh*: "There is no divinity save the Divinity."

Lord have mercy upon us—*Kyrie Eleison* in Greek. Here we come to yet another parallel, for the word *Eleison* shares the same root with the word for olive oil, and in this regard Metropolitan Anthony Bloom mentions that the dove returning to Noah bearing an olive branch conveys a healing mercy, "that we should be able to live and become that which we are called to be". In the "light verse" of the Quran, we hear of this same olive oil and tree, and an identical mercy:

> "Allah is the Light of the heavens and the earth; the likeness of His Light is as a niche wherein is a lamp—the lamp is in a glass, the glass as it were a brightly shining star kindled from a blessed Olive Tree that is neither of the East nor of the West, whose oil well-nigh would shine, though fire does not touch it; Light upon Light; Allah guides to His Light whom He wills."

The verse concludes: "God strikes similitudes for man, and God is all knowing."

A similitude He struck for me was this. I came down the hill from my home in Kentucky to our river and was walking along the banks of the Ohio, and ahead in the mud I saw something shining brightly like a star. I found it was an empty shell, whose emptiness exposed its pearl-like lustrous interior. Not a fleck of the former inhabitant remained, so it totally reflected the light. I saw it as a sign or *ayat* in Nature, and an indication of the way I should be. Only in total emptiness, humility, and the corresponding silence can I too shine forth with light.

And this leads me to Saint Seraphim of Sarov—whose emptiness shone—and then on to a Sufic perspective bearing on his luminosity.

In my readings for the Bishop, I came across a book called *The Flame in the Snow*, the life of Saint Seraphim (1759-1833), who entered a monastery in the Taiga Siberian Forest at age nineteen and after sixteen years in the community spent a further twenty-six years in seclusion in a hut in the forest. He endured extraordinary hardship as he fiercely wrestled with his soul. His feet became swollen from illness. He carried stones on his back to remind himself of the burdens of others he could not relieve. He even despaired of God. But throughout his struggles, he repeated the

Jesus Prayer incessantly, and at last his body was transfused with Light, a Light that would shine into the darkness and destroy it. At age sixty-seven, he had attained a perfect blend of spirit and body.

Having withdrawn for purification, in 1815 he returned to society and received all who came, in much the same way as the early Desert Father St Anthony. After his austerities and night vigils, he was granted a vision of the Divine and Uncreated Light, which outwardly transformed him. I have an image of him moving, laden down with stones, in the deep snow and gloom, glowing. A woman who came for consolation bends her head, unable to endure the brightness of his face.

When a certain man named Motovilov asked Saint Seraphim how a man could be sure of being in the Spirit of God, the following occurred:

"Father Seraphim replied: 'I have already told you, your godliness, that it is very simple, and I have related in detail how people come to be in the Spirit of God and how we can recognize His presence in us. So what do you want, my son?'

"'I want to understand it well,' I said.

"Then father Seraphim took me very firmly by the shoulders and said: 'We are both in the Spirit of God now, my son. Why don't you look at me?'

"I replied: 'I cannot look, father, because your eyes are flashing like lightning. Your face has become brighter than the sun, and my eyes ache with pain.'

"Father Seraphim said: 'Don't be alarmed, your godliness! Now you yourself have become as bright as I am. You are now in the fullness of the Spirit of God yourself; otherwise you would not be able to see me as I am.'

"Then bending his head towards me, he whispered softly in my ear: 'Thank the Lord God for His unutterable mercy to us! You saw that I did not even cross myself; and only in my heart I prayed mentally to the Lord and said within myself: "Lord, grant him to see clearly with his bodily eyes that descent of Thy Spirit which Thou grantest to Thy servants when Thou art pleased to appear in the light of Thy majestic glory."'

"After these words I glanced at his face, and there came over me an even greater sense of reverent awe. Imagine in the center of the sun, in the dazzling light of its midday rays, the face of a man talking to you. You see the movement of his lips and the changing expression of his eyes, you hear his voice, you feel someone holding your shoulders; yet you do not see his hands; you do not even see yourself or his figure, but only a blinding light spreading far around for several yards and illumining with its glaring sheen both the snow-blanket which covered the forest glade and the snow-flakes which besprinkled me and the great elder."[4]

According to Bishop Kallistos, this passage is important for our understanding of the Orthodox doctrine of deification and union with God, which is the goal of the whole Eastern Orthodox Church. He says, "It shows how the Orthodox idea of sanctification includes the body: it is not Seraphim's or Motovilov's soul only—but the whole body which is transfigured by the Grace of God. We may note that neither Seraphim nor Motivilov is in a state of ecstasy—both can talk in a coherent way and are still conscious of the outside world—but both are filled with the Holy Spirit and surrounded by the Light of the Age to come." This recalls Moses, who shone with such extraordinary light people could not bear to look at him.

In his book *In the Image and Likeness of God,* Vladimir Lossky quotes from St Gregory's *Homily on the Transfiguration* in a chapter entitled "The Theology of Light in the Thought of St Gregory Palamas". "The light of the Lord's transfiguration had no beginning and no end; it remained uncircumscribed and imperceptible to the senses although it was contemplated with corporeal eyes. By a transmutation of their senses the disciples of the Lord passed from the flesh to the Spirit." Lossky explains, "In order to see the Divine Light with corporeal eyes, as the disciples did on Mt Tabor, one must participate in this Light, one must become transformed by it—to a greater or lesser degree." In another homily, St Gregory of Thessalonica says of the mystical experience that "he who participates in the Divine energy, becomes himself, in a sense, *Light*".

The tradition of Sufism is also filled with references to light, but it is to the Sufi school of illumination that I turn for now, and to the writings of a 13th century poet, Fakhruddin Iraqi, whose central concern was the purification of the heart, elucidated in a treatise called *Divine Flashes.* In his introduction to the volume, William Chittick describes how the various schools of Islamic thought employ a variety of terms when referring to Ultimate Reality:

4. *A Conversation of St Seraphim of Sarov* (Resaca, GA: Ascension Monastery).

- Theologians speak of God/Allah and explain His attributes in Quranic terms.
- The peripatetic philosophers speak of Necessary Being, *wajib al wujud.*
- The Illuminist philosophers refer to Ultimate Reality as Light or *Nur.*[5]

As an illuminist, Iraqi identifies Being with Light. When we refer to Being as *Light,* a creature or entity whose nature is darkness can be luminous only when it participates in and reflects Divine Being. Darkness mixed with Light results in the "brightness or the dimming of the Light". Professor Chittick writes, "By acting as a veil over sheer light, darkness allows the myriad colors to be perceived, that is, the possibilities and perfections of outward manifestation *latent* within the very nature of Light to be perceived. But what becomes outward and visible is never anything other than Light—for darkness has no positive reality and thus can never itself be seen. The nature of the varying degrees of 'brightness' that are perceived is not determined by *darkness* but by the Essence of light itself"—like God's grace to Saint Seraphim.

Being is none other than sheer light. Only humans have the capacity to attain a station where they can act as reflectors or transmitters for this Light. Iraqi says that "one needs Thy light to see Thee", and Chittick explains that "only through the preparedness He (God) has already bestowed on the entity can the entity act as a receptacle for His Being." In Iraqi's flashes or *lama'at* we read that Light has no color: "A sun shining through a thousand bits of glass beaming to plain sight through each a ray of color—why should any difference appear between this one and that? All light is one, but colors a thousand-fold." This reminds us of Rumi's metaphor of the sun being One even when its light is broken up into the many courtyards of homes. Professor Chittick says of these lines: "When the door is open, truly open, we shall retreat into the cell of our non-existence and behold ourselves and our Beloved in the mirror of each-otherness. We shall travel no farther." Returning to Iraqi: "This mirror form has no need of wayfaring, for it receives its form

5. In her *Mystical Dimensions of Islam,* A. M. Schimmel states that "what is conceived metaphysically as existence (*wujûd*) coincides with what is grasped in terms of root experience as Light. In this context existence *is* Light".

from Light. I shall not leave this luminous house nor depart from this blessed city." Of this, Chittick says, "No one ever leaves this cell, so where are you going?" Iraqi's words are not unlike those in the Psalm which declares, "I shall dwell in the Holy House of the Lord forever."

So I am thinking that the haloes we find in Christianity and Islamic art must indicate this Light of God, able to shine through due to sanctity. In the Islamic world one always hears the term *munawar,* meaning "lit up". Thus he or she is *munawar,* and this is inevitably said of one truly pious. You can *see* it with the heart's eye and even the physical eye. We should, each one of us, through increasing our contentment, humility, and emptiness, permit our true natures, our theomorphic essences—our Light—to shine through, and in this way mercifully to increase God's Infinite Luminous Being in this brief span of existence. If we do not take ourselves below sea level, how can the Ocean pour in? Just as the Jews were slaves in Egypt, we too are enslaved to our diversions, and we too can be saved from this duality only by "I AM THAT I AM".

We all depend on God's Mercy in this life and in the next, and of all the virtues Mercy, though the grandest, is the easiest to assume. It must become our very nature, or *fitra.* May He draw us all back into His Divine Presence with hearts purified. *Ameen ya Rab.*

Chapter 3

The Heart of the Faithful is the Throne of the All-Merciful

Seyyed Hossein Nasr

> Among [the human] faculties, the heart (*al-qalb*) is central, for it is the "place" where the Transcendent Realities enter into contact with man; it is the organ of intuition and of Divine Revelation (*at-tajallî*).
>
> Titus Burckhardt[1]

The heart is the center of the human microcosm, at once the center of the physical body, the vital energies, the emotions, and the soul, as well as the meeting place between the human and the celestial realms where the spirit resides. How remarkable is this reality of the heart, that mysterious center which from the point of view of our earthly existence seems so small, and yet as the Prophet has said it is the Throne (*al-'arsh*) of God the All-Merciful (*ar-Rahmân*), the Throne that encompasses the whole universe. Or as he uttered in another saying, "My Heaven containeth Me not, nor My Earth, but the heart of My faithful servant doth contain Me."

It is the heart, the realm of interiority, to which Christ referred when he said, "The kingdom of God is within you" (Lk 17:21), and it is the heart which the founders of all religions and the sacred scriptures advise man to keep pure as a condition for his salvation and deliverance. We need only recall the words of Gospel, "Blessed are the pure in heart, for they shall see God" (Mt 5:8). But this supreme reality of the human state is veiled from us. We have fallen into such a state that the heart has become a hidden crypt, at the center of our being and yet so inaccessible that the itinerary of the spiritual life may be said to be none other than the re-discovery of the heart and penetration into it.

The doctrine of the centrality of the heart to the human state is universal, as is its relation to intellection, sapience, and union. The

1. *De l'homme universel* (Lyon: P. Derain, 1953), p. 20.

Bible and the Quran speak often of heart-knowledge. In Christianity the Desert Fathers articulated the spiritual, mystical, and symbolic meanings of the reality of the heart, and these teachings led to a long tradition in the Eastern Orthodox Church known as Hesychasm, culminating with St Gregory Palamas, which is focused on the "prayer of the heart" and which includes the exposition of the significance of the heart and the elaboration of the mysticism and theology of the heart. In Catholicism another development took place, in which the heart of the faithful became in a sense replaced by the heart of Christ, and a new spirituality developed on the basis of devotion to the Sacred Heart of Jesus. Reference to His bleeding heart became common in the writings of such figures as St Bernard of Clairvaux and St Catherine of Sienna.

The Christian doctrines of the heart, based as they are on the Bible, present certain universal theses to be seen also in Judaism, the most important of which is the association of the heart with the inner soul of man and the center of the human state. In Jewish mysticism the spirituality of the heart was further developed, and some Jewish mystics emphasized the idea of the "broken or contrite heart" (*levnichbar*) and wrote that to reach the Divine Majesty one had to "tear one's heart" and that the "broken heart" mentioned in the Psalms sufficed.

To make clear the universality of the spiritual significance of the heart across religious boundaries, while also emphasizing the development of the "theology of the heart" and methods of "prayer of the heart" particular to each tradition, one may recall that the name of Horus, the Egyptian god, meant the "heart of the world". In Sanskrit the term for heart, *hridaya*, means also the center of the world, since, by virtue of the analogy between the macrocosm and the microcosm, the center of man is also the center of the universe. Furthermore, in Sanskrit the term *shraddha*, meaning faith, also signifies knowledge of the heart, and the same is true in Arabic, where the word *îmân* means faith when used for man and knowledge when used for God, as in the Divine Name *al-Mu'min.* As for the Far Eastern tradition, in Chinese the term *xin* means both heart and mind or consciousness.

One could go on almost indefinitely pointing out the remarkably universal doctrine of the heart as both the center which relates man to the spiritual world and to the higher levels of being and as the means of approach to that inner knowledge which makes access to those levels and finally to the Divine abode possible. There are, moreover, specific developments of the doctrine of the heart which are related to the particular characteristics of a given religion, as one sees clearly in the case of Christianity, where there is in fact more than one tradition dealing with this subject, namely, the Orthodox and the Roman Catholic, not to speak of the special case of St Juan de la Cruz, who develops a theology and mysticism of the heart very similar to that of Islam. In any case, our goal here has been to point only briefly to the significance of the heart and the theology and spiritual practices related to it on a global scale and across religious boundaries before turning to the Islamic tradition, with which we shall be particularly concerned.

There is a vast literature in Islam dealing with the heart and its intellectual and spiritual significance. Already in the Quran there are over one hundred thirty references to the heart (*qalb*; pl. *qulûb*), and numerous traditions of the Prophet (*ahâdîth*) also refer to this central subject. Likewise there is hardly a Sufi treatise that does not refer to the heart and what Sufis call "matters pertaining to the heart" (*al-umûr al-qalbiyyah*). One often finds titles of Islamic metaphysical and spiritual writings containing the term "heart", such as *Qût al-qulûb* ("Nourishment for Hearts"), *Shifâ' al-qulûb* ("Healing of Hearts"), and *Nûr al-fu'âd* ("Light of the Heart"). Moreover, there is not one but a series of terms referring to the heart on various levels of its reality, including, besides *qalb*, the terms *fu'âd*, *sirr*, and *lubb*, not to mention the Persian term *dil*.

To delineate the Islamic understanding of the heart on both a metaphysical and an operative level, it is best to start with the basic term in Arabic for heart, namely *qalb*. The root meaning of this term means change and transformation. The term *inqilâb*, which is used in modern Persian as a translation for the European concept of revolution, meant originally a change of state. One of the Names of God is in fact *Muqallib al-qulûb*, that is, the Transformer of Hearts, and Ibn Arabi uses the term *taqallub*, derived from the same root as *qalb*, to mean the constant transformative power inherent in the heart, a power which brings about integration in a dynamic mode. The root *QLB* also means to turn upside down. The heart on its corporeal level is in a sense suspended upside down, its traditional symbol being an inverted triangle. It has also the root meaning of mold (the Arabic word for mold being *qâlib*), that is, what holds together the inner reality of man. There is here also an inversion of the "positive" and "negative" elements since the heart is moreover the isthmus (*barzakh*) and the principle of the microcosmic domain. The mutation of the root *QLB*, often carried out in the traditional Islamic science of *jafr*, gives *QBL*, which is the root of the word *qiblah* or point, to which one orients oneself during the daily canonical prayers, the *qiblah* (which is related in its root meaning to Kabbalah) being the direction pointing to where the *Ka'bah*, the House of God, is located. Esoterically the heart is the *Ka'bah*, where the All-Merciful (*ar-Rahmân*) resides. That is why Rumi, in reference to this inner identification between the *qalb* and the *Ka'bah*, hence the *qiblah*, which is also the supreme goal of pilgrimage to Mecca, sings:

> O People who have gone to pilgrimage, where are you,
> where are you?
> The Beloved is here, come here, come here.[2]

The expression "the *Ka'bah* of the heart"—*Ka'ba-yi dil* in Persian—is very commonly used in Sufi literature. The root *QBL* also possesses the meaning of acceptance and receptivity, which are basic characteristics of the heart. The *qalb* is receiving evermore the theophanies which reach it from above and within, and it possesses not only the power of transformation or *taqallub*, but also receptivity, that is *qabûl* or *qâbil*. It is to this reality that Ibn Arabi refers in his famous poem *Tarjumân al-ashwâq* ("The Interpreter of Desires") when he says, "My heart is capable of taking on any form" (*laqad sâra qalbî qâbilan li kulli sûratin*), using the terms *qalb* and *qâbil* in the verse.

The Quran, like other sacred scriptures, associates knowledge and understanding with the heart and the blindness of the heart with loss of understanding, as for example when God, after complaining of man's not learning the appropriate lessons from earlier sacred history, asserts, "For indeed it is not the eyes that grow blind, but it is the hearts, which are within the bosoms, that grow blind"

2. *Kulliyât-i Shams*, ed. B. Forouzanfar, Vol. 2 (Tehran: Sipihr Press, 1984), *ghazal* 648, p. 65.

(22:46, Pickthall translation). This blindness of the heart so characteristic of fallen man is also described by the Quran as a hardening of the heart. "But their hearts were hardened, and the devil made all that they used to do seem fair unto them!" (6:43). Also, "Woe unto those whose hearts are hardened against remembrance of Allah. Such are in plain error" (39:22). Furthermore, the Quran identifies this hardening of the heart with a veil that God has cast over the heart of those who have turned away from the truth. "We have placed upon their hearts veils, lest they should understand, and in their ears a deafness" (6:25); also, "And We place upon their hearts veils lest they should understand it, and in their ears a deafness" (17:46).

The heart can, however, be softened and the veil removed with the help of God Himself, who has knowledge of our hearts, for "Allah knoweth what is in your hearts" (33:51), and "He knew what was in their [the believers'] hearts" (48:18). This melting or softening of the hardened heart can be achieved only with God's help through what He has revealed in His sacred scriptures and the grace that emanates from revelation. "Allah hath (now) revealed the fairest of statements, a Scripture consistent . . . so that their flesh and their hearts soften to Allah's reminder" (39:23). God wants man's heart to be at peace and rest, and although from one point of view God as *ar-Rahmân* resides in the heart of the faithful, from another point of view He comes between man and his heart. "Allah cometh in between the man and his own heart" (8:24), and it is only with the help of God that fallen man can gain access to his own heart. It is in this context that the famous Sufi description of the spiritual path as *takhliyah* (emptying), *tahliyah* (embellishing), and *tajliyah* (receiving theophanies of and in the heart) must be understood.

Once one turns to God for help, He provides man with the possibility of having tranquility and peace in his heart. "Allah appointed it only as good tidings, and that your hearts thereby might be at rest" (8:10); also, "Verily in the remembrance (*adh-dhikr*) of Allah do hearts find rest!" (13:28), a verse which relates peace and rest in the heart directly to *adh-dhikr* or quintessential prayer, this verse serving as the scriptural basis for invocation in its relation to the heart. When God softens the heart and removes its veils, the heart becomes worthy of being the receptacle of the Divine Peace or *as-sakînah* (*shekinah* in Hebrew), for as the Quran says, "He it is who sends down peace of reassurance (*as-sakînah*) into the hearts of believers" (48:4).

On the basis of these Quranic teachings and the prophetic *sunnah* and *ahadîth*, which serve as the first and most authoritative commentaries upon the word of God, Islamic sages developed an elaborate doctrine, at once metaphysical, cosmological, and anthropological—in the traditional sense of these terms—concerning the heart. They also continued and elaborated operative methods received from the Prophet and his earliest inheritors involving various modes of prayer and the means of reaching and penetrating the heart.

The answer to the question of what is the heart is almost inexhaustible, but at least some of the major features of it can be mentioned here. The heart is first of all the center of our being on all the different levels of our existence, not only the corporeal and emotive, but also the intellectual and spiritual. It is what connects the individual to the supra-individual realms of being. In fact, if in modern society heart-knowledge is rejected, it is because modernism refuses to see man beyond his individual level of existence. The heart is not a center of our being; it is the supreme center, its uniqueness resulting from the metaphysical principle that for any specific realm of manifestation there must exist a principle of unity.

The heart is the *barzakh* or isthmus between this world and the next, between the visible and invisible worlds, between the human realm and the realm of the Spirit, between the horizontal and vertical dimensions of existence. In the same way that the vertical and horizontal lines of the cross, itself the symbol not only of Christ in Christianity but also of the Universal Man (*al-insân al-kâmil*) in Islam, meet at only one point, there can be only one heart for each human being, although this single reality partakes of gradations and levels of being. The heart, then, is our unique center, the place where the supreme axis penetrates our microcosmic existence, the place where the All-Merciful resides, and also the locus for the Breath of God. Hence the profound relation that exists between invocatory prayer carried out with the breath and the heart.

The heart is also a mirror, which must be polished by invocation (*adh-dhikr*), according to the well known *hadîth*: "For everything there is a polish. The polish for the heart is invocation." Once this act of polishing has been carried out, the heart becomes the locus for the direct manifestations of God's Names and Qualities. The heart in fact is the locus *par excellence* for the theophanies (*tajalliyât*) which descend one after another upon it. This constant change in reflection of ever-new Divine manifestations is related to the root meaning of *qalb*, to which allusion has already been made.

It might of course be asked, if the nature of the *qalb* is to be in constant transformation, what is permanent in the heart and how can the heart be at peace and rest? The answer lies in the quality itself of being a mirror. What is permanent is our nothingness (*al-fanâ'*) before God; one is to become a perfect mirror which, in being nothing in itself, is able to reflect forms emanating from above. The peace of the heart is precisely our total surrender to God, not only on the level of the will, but also on the level of existence. To become "nothing" before God is to be at once "nothing" and "everything"—nothing as the surface of a mirror, and everything in reflecting the never-ending theophanies issuing from the Hidden Treasure of God, which according to the Quran is inexhaustible.

Once the heart has been softened and is polished, it may be described not only as a mirror but also as an eye which has opened and which can now see the Invisible Realm, just as the physical eyes are able to see the external world. The symbol of the "eye of the heart" (*'ayn al-qalb* in Arabic or *chishm-i dil* in Persian) is not confined to Islam but is universal, as we see in Plato's expression "eye of soul", St Augustine's *oculus cordis*, or the "third eye" of Hindu and Buddhist doctrines. But it is especially emphasized in Sufism. The reason that the symbol of vision is used rather than one of the other senses is that vision has an objective character and therefore better symbolizes the function of the heart-intellect. Nevertheless, the heart also has other inner faculties. With the ear of the heart man can hear the silent music of which Plato spoke, and with the olfactory faculty of the heart man can smell the perfumes of Paradise. But it is the "eye of the heart" that is of central importance. The eye of the heart, which is none other than the immanent intellect, is the faculty with which we are able to see the Invisible World and ultimately God, but it is also the eye with which God sees us. When we are *cordial* with God, then God is *cordial* with us, although principially the relation is reversed. Only when God loves us can we love God. The heart also has a face turned toward each world (*wajh al-qalb*), and the face that it turns to God is none other than the Face that God turns to man. That is why to seek to "efface" the Divine

Reality from man's consciousness, as modern agnosticism and secularism attempt to do, leads ultimately to the "effacing" of man himself and his reduction to the sub-human.

In the depths of the heart resides *al-fu'âd* or the heart-center, in which two eyes, one meant to see God and the other the world, are unified. In contrast to the external eyes, which are also two in number and see multiplicity, the inner eye of the heart is essentially one, but is able to perceive both worlds. It therefore has the integrating power of unifying multiplicity in unity. When the eye of the heart has opened, man is able not only to see the One, but also to contemplate the One in the many and the many in the One, thereby achieving unity or *tawhîd* in its highest sense.

Lest one forget the importance of the heart for faith and Divine Love, it must also be mentioned that first of all, according to the Quran and *ahadîth,* real faith (*al-îmân*) is associated with the heart, and not with the mind or the tongue alone. To really believe we must believe in and with our heart where faith resides. Secondly, the heart is not only the seat of human love but also of Divine Love. The fire of love burns in the heart, and it is there that one is to find the Beloved. The heart of the saint is the source of a light resulting from his inner illumination and of a warmth issuing from the fire of the love of God. Knowledge and love at this level are united in a single reality, like the light and heat of a fire, the locus of this sacred fire being the heart.

Although the heart is a single reality, it partakes of many levels, as do the knowledge and love of God. Many Sufi masters, such as Rumi, Attar, and al-Nuri, have referred to the seven levels of the heart, for which various technical terms are used. Hakim Tirmidhi goes a step further to identify these levels with concentric castles of the soul, each with its own covering that defends the innermost heart and provides inner protection for the interior fortified castles which can be penetrated only after great spiritual effort. As has been shown, this schema is very similar to that of St Teresa of Avila in her description of her interior castles, and we find the idea of concentric hearts made of fortified dwellings protected by walls in both Sufi and Christian sources.[3] These correspondences reveal

3. Luce López-Baralt, *San Juan de la Cruz y el Islam* (Madrid: Hipérion, 1985); and "Saint John of the Cross and Ibn 'Arabi", *Journal of the Muhyiddin Ibn 'Arabi Society,* Vol. XXVIII (2000), pp. 57-90.

both historical influences and morphological resemblance. But above all they point to the universal teachings of the *philosophia perennis* concerning the heart and the levels of its existence corresponding to the levels of microcosmic reality.

Returning to the word *qalb*, it is possible to point to another aspect of the reality of the heart by analyzing an Arabic term closely related to *qalb*, namely *qalîb*, which means a well. The heart is a well from which gushes forth the fountain of life and also of the knowledge and love which save. In Islam water is the most direct symbol of God's Mercy and Compassion. It might be said that since the All-Merciful resides in the heart of the faithful, once the veil of the heart is lifted, the water from the well of the heart gushes forth in correspondence to the outward flow of the Divine Compassion and Mercy, one of the most direct symbols of which in this world is water. That is why in the language of *hadîth* the heart is sometimes referred to as *yanbû' al-hikmah*, that is, "the source [or spring] of wisdom". According to a very famous *hadîth*, which is found in many versions and which is foundational to the operative aspect of Sufism, "One who purifies himself for God for forty days, God makes the spring of wisdom (*al-hikmah*) to gush forth from his heart to his tongue." This *hadîth* also links spiritual practice directly to the means of access to the heart and indicates the way to remove the rust or crust from the heart so as to allow what one could call the water of wisdom to flow from the heart to the tongue.

If the heart is the reality described here, then all one would need to do in order to have spiritual realization would be to penetrate into the heart. The problem is that for the human being marked by the fall, the heart is no longer easily accessible, even though it remains the center of our being. For the men of the Golden Age or in the Edenic state, those who lived in the primordial condition (*al-fitrah*), the heart was directly accessible. They lived in the heart, that is, with God and in God. But through a series of falls the heart has become ever more inaccessible, covered by a hardened shell, which symbolizes powerful psychological forces. Long before modern times the heart had already become a crypt and a cave, to be found only with heroic effort and only after an arduous struggle to gain "knowledge of the mysteries" which reside in that cave. The symbolism of the heart as a cave hidden within the breast of man is in fact universal. In the context of Islam, the Prophet taking refuge with Abu Bakr in a cave on their way from

Mecca to Medina, in that journey which is called the *hijrah* or migration, is understood by Sufis not only to signify an external historical event but also to point to the trans-historical and meta-individual reality of the heart where the Friend resides. It is in direct allusion to this truth that Rumi sings in one of his *ghazals*:

> Consider this breast as the cave, the spiritual retreat of the Friend.
> If thou art the companion of the cave, enter the cave, enter the cave.[4]

But how does one enter the cave made inaccessible to fallen man? The answer resides in the reality of the All-Merciful (*ar-Rahmân*), whose Throne is the heart. Through His Qualities of Compassion and Mercy, God has sent revelations which provide the means of access to the heart. To accept a revelation means first of all to possess faith (*al-îmân*), which resides in the heart. Faith is the necessary element for participation in the revelation and the essential condition for the efficacy of the means provided by it to save man and to open the door to the inner kingdom. But in order to penetrate into the heart as the center of our being, we must also undertake the spiritual practices sanctioned and made efficacious by tradition. At the heart of those practices, as far as Islam is concerned, stands quintessential prayer or invocation (*adh-dhikr*), which is ultimately the prayer of the heart. Invocation, sanctified by God Himself and combined with the meditation (*al-fikr*) needed to concentrate the mind and overcome its dispersing effects, is like an arrow which directly penetrates the heart. On a more operative level one could say that the soul of the invoker (*adh-dhâkir*), enwrapped as it is in the *dhikr*, is itself the arrow released by the hands of the master archer or the spiritual teacher toward the target of the heart. As for the energy or force which allows the arrow to travel toward the target and finally to penetrate it, it is the initiatic power (*al-walâyah* or *al-wilâyah* in Islam) without which the arrow would not be able to travel. That is why the practice of spiritual techniques made available by revelation is invalid unless they are carried out in the matrix of an orthodox religion and through the regularity of spiritual and initiatic transmission and guidance. Without orthodoxy and tradition, no one can overcome the obstacles which

4. *Kulliyât-i Shams*, Vol. 5, *ghazal* 2133, p. 12.

at once hide the heart and protect it from demonic forces, for there would be no force to propel the arrow toward its target.

The practice of spiritual techniques made available to those who are qualified, according to criteria established by the tradition, requires ample preparation of both a doctrinal and a practical nature. More specifically it requires the attainment of spiritual virtues, without which man has no right to penetrate the heart-center, and this attainment implies not only thinking about the virtues and speaking about them, but above all *being* the virtues, for the virtues, which ultimately belong to God, are the manner in which we participate existentially in the Sacred. The question of whether the spiritual practices make us virtuous or whether the virtues are necessary for a spiritual practice is a complicated matter with which we cannot deal here. As far as the heart is concerned, suffice it to say that to enter the heart as the spiritual center of our being, which is pure, one must oneself be pure and worthy of the sacred abode into which one is entering.

One might object that the heart of man is not always pure, as mentioned in so many sacred scriptures. The use of the term "heart" in the ordinary sense certainly warrants such an observation, but this ordinary understanding of the heart, which is available to us all, is not the same as the meaning of the heart in its purely spiritual sense, where the All-Merciful is to be found. Nevertheless the two are not totally unrelated. That is why the Prophet calls *dhikr* the polish of the heart, meaning of course the heart which is covered by rust and not that inner heart or Throne which, having never been rusty, does not need to be polished. In any case, as far as the spiritual life is concerned, it is essential not only to polish or purify the heart, but also to keep it pure, to protect it (*hifz al-qalb*) from all defilement.

In Sufism, where the heart is compared to the *Ka'bah*, it has been said that the heart of fallen man is like the *Ka'bah* before the coming of Islam, when it was full of idols. When the Prophet entered Mecca triumphantly, he first went to the *Ka'bah* and asked Ali ibn Abi Talib and Bilal al-Habashi to break all the idols therein and to purify the House of God built by Adam and rebuilt by Abraham to honor the one God. Through initiation and spiritual practice, the person who aspires to reach God must break all the idols in his heart and sweep away everything in it so that God alone can be present therein. God is one and therefore does not manifest

His Presence where there are idols. Alas, the heart of how many of even believers is like the *Ka'bah* during the Age of Ignorance (*al-jâhiliyyah*), full of all kinds of idols. Those who seek to follow the spiritual path in Sufism are taught at the time of initiation, when first embarking upon the path, that they must reserve their heart for God alone, for He alone is the master of the house of the heart. As the Arabic poem says, in response to someone knocking on the door of a Sufi's heart:

> There is no one in the house except the Master of the House.
> (*Laysa fi'd-dâr ghayrahu' d-dayyâr.*)

The inner heart of man is itself the supreme Name of God (*al-ism al-a'zam*) by virtue of the mystery of the creation of man as a being at whose center resides the All-Merciful. That is why it is said in Islam that the saints are themselves the Names of God, men and women whose hearts are the theater of all of God's Names and Qualities. The invocation is the sacred means for the realization and actualization of this truth. The human microcosm is created in such a way that it can transform sound into light in the sense that the invocation performed by the tongue becomes ultimately transformed into light in the heart. Human speech in the form of prayer becomes the vision of the eye of the heart. He who invokes with sincerity, persistence, fervor, and total faith in God becomes the possessor of an illuminated heart. Thanks to the *dhikr*, he is able to break away the crust that veils the light of the inner heart, which is luminous by its own nature. Once this Inner Light is unveiled, it shines forth throughout the whole being of man since the heart is the center of our being.

Ultimately the *dhikr* is itself the heart spiritually understood. Invocation as practiced in Sufism is at the highest level the prayer of the heart and by the heart. The spiritual itinerary of the Sufi is to penetrate the heart with help of the *dhikr* and finally to realize the identity of the two. It is not only to pray but to become prayer, to live at the heart-center, and to experience and to know all things from that center.

To know from the center is also to be able to go beyond the world of forms to the formless, for the heart is not only the center but also the abode of spiritual meaning (*ma'nâ* in the terminology of Rumi), which transcends external form (*sûrat*). The person who has reached the heart in its spiritual sense is also able to see the heart of things, especially sacred forms, and to realize their inner unity. He is able to attest to what Frithjof Schuon, who spoke so eloquently from the heart-center, has called the "transcendent unity of religions", which—from the point of view of the heart—could also be called the "immanent unity of religions", but an immanence which is also transcendent. Sufis have often spoken of the religion of the heart, which Schuon calls the *religio cordis.* Far from being a separate religion, the religion of the heart is that essential and supra-formal reality which lies at the heart of all orthodox religions and which can be reached only through the orthodox and traditional religions. It was to this *religio cordis* that Rumi referred in the following lines:

> The creed of love is separated from all religions;
> The creed and the religion of the lovers of God is God himself.[5]

Furthermore, being open to the reception of theophanies and residing at the same time on the level of the formless, the heart once cleansed becomes the theater for the manifestation of different sacred forms, and the gnostic is able to discern, through his heart-knowledge, the inner unity of religions, while at the same time being aware of their outward differences and the inviolability of their sacred forms. The famous poem of Ibn Arabi, to which allusion was made above, recapitulates these truths in verses of haunting beauty:

> Wonder,
> A garden among the flames!
>
> My heart can take on any form:
> A meadow for gazelles,
> A cloister for monks,
> For the idols, sacred ground,
> Ka'ba for the circling pilgrim,
> The tables of Torah,
> The scrolls of the Quran.
>
> My creed is love;
> Wherever its caravan turns along the way,
> That is my belief,
> My faith.[6]

5. *Mathnawi,* ed. R. Nicholson (Tehran: Sipihr Press, 1981), v. 1770, p. 87.
6. Michael Sells, *Mystical Languages of Unsaying* (Chicago: University of Chicago Press, 1994), p. 90.

Through quintessential prayer, within the framework of an orthodox tradition, one reaches the inner heart, where God as the All-Merciful resides, and by penetration into the heart-center, man moves beyond the realm of outwardness and the domain of individual existence to reach the abode of inwardness and the universal order. In that state his heart becomes the eye with which he sees God and also the eye with which God sees him. In that presence he is nothing in himself, as separate existence. He is but a mirror whose surface is nothing, and yet reflects everything. In the heart, the spiritual man lives in intimacy with God, with the Origin of all those theophanies whose outward manifestations constitute all the beauty that is reflected in the world around us. He lives in that inner garden, that inner paradise, constantly aware of the ubiquitous Gardener. On the highest level of realization, man becomes aware that all theophanies are nothing but the Source of those theophanies, that the house itself is nothing but the reflection of the Master of the house, that there is in fact but one Reality which, through its infinite manifestations and reflections upon the mirrors of cosmic existence, has brought about all that appears to us as multiplicity and otherness, and all the apparent distinctions between I and thou, he and they, we and you. At the center of the heart, there resides but one Reality above and beyond all forms. It was to this Reality, far beyond all individual manifestations, that Mansur al-Hallaj was referring when he sang:

> I saw my Lord with the eyes of my heart;
> I asked Him, Who art Thou? He said, Thou.[7]

Happy is the man who can open the eyes of his heart with the aid of Heaven before his earthly eyes become shut at the moment of death, and who is able to see the countenance of the Beloved while still possessing the precious gift of human life.

7. *Le Dîwân d'al-Hallâj*, ed. L. Massignon (Paris: Paul Geuthner, 1955), p. 46.

The Path of Remembrance

Chapter 4

On the Cosmology of *Dhikr*

William C. Chittick

Let me begin with a prophetic saying that expresses succinctly the basic Islamic understanding of man and the world: *al-Dunyâ mal`ûnatun, mal`ûnun mâ fîhâ illâ dhikr Allâh.* "This world is accursed; accursed is everything within it, save *dhikr Allâh.*" In order to suggest a few of the implications of this saying for the theory and practice of *dhikr Allâh,* "the remembrance of God", I shall review the basic concept of *dhikr* as it appears in the Koran and then look at a few of the teachings of Ibn Arabi (d. 1240 A.D.), one of the greatest Muslim metaphysicians and cosmologists.[1]

The Islamic tradition is rooted in knowledge. This rooting is most evident in the first testimony of faith, "There is no god but God." This statement is taken as epitomizing the first principle of Islamic faith, which is *tawhîd,* the assertion of God's unity. However, even those familiar with Islamic teachings sometimes forget that *tawhîd* has nothing to do with history, because it is simply a statement of the way things are. The more sophisticated of Muslim thinkers have always maintained that *tawhîd* is a universal and atemporal truth. To be human is to have an intuition of this truth, and every one of the "124,000 prophets" that God has sent, from Adam down to Muhammad, came with this truth as the core of his message.

Tawhîd expresses the nature of reality, irrespective of the existence of the universe, man, or any other beings. However, since we do have a world and human beings, the Islamic tradition takes into account a second fact, that of the human situation. It encapsulates this situation in the words "forgetfulness" (*nisyân*) and "heedless-

1. For more on *dhikr* in the Islamic tradition, see Chittick, *Sufism: A Short Introduction* (Oxford: Oneworld, 2000), Chapter 5. On the life and significance of Ibn Arabi, see Claude Addas, *Ibn 'Arabî: The Voyage of No Return* (Cambridge: Islamic Texts Society, 2001). For Ibn Arabi's metaphysical and cosmological teachings, see Chittick, *The Sufi Path of Knowledge* (Albany: SUNY Press, 1989) and Chittick, *The Self-Disclosure of God* (Albany: SUNY Press, 1998).

ness" (*ghafla*). Although people do have an innate intuition of *tawhîd,* they do not necessarily find it ready to mind. It may not be easy for them to bring it from latency to actuality or to voice it in language and put it into practice. They need the help of the prophets. With "prophecy", the second principle of Islamic faith, the perspective shifts from the atemporal to the temporal, from the eternal to the contingent, from God to history.

The first function of the prophets is to "remind" people of their own divinely given reality. In speaking of this "reminder", the Quran employs the word *dhikr* and several of its derivatives (*e.g., dhikrâ, tadhkîr, tadhkira*). Moreover, it calls the human response to this reminder by the same word *dhikr.* The "reminder" that comes from the side of God by means of the prophets calls forth "remembrance" from the side of man. The use of the one word for a movement with two directions—from the Divine to the human and from the human to the Divine—is typical of the Quran's unitary perspective. Here in fact there is only one motivating force, and that is the Divine activity that makes manifest the good, the true, and the beautiful, even if it appears to us as two different movements. Moreover, the Quran also makes it eminently clear that "remembrance"—the human response to reminder—does not mean simply to acknowledge the truth of *tawhîd.* The word itself also means "to mention". On the human side, *dhikr* is both the awareness of God and the expression of this awareness through language, whether vocal or silent.

If reminder is the first function of the prophets, their second function is to provide the instructions that allow people to live a life that is pleasing to God. The Quran calls these instructions "guidance" (*hudâ*). To follow the guidance of the prophets is to remember God in thought, word, and deed. So, *dhikr* is to keep God in view at all times, places, and activities. Ibn Arabi defines it as *al-hudûr ma`a'l-madhkûr,* "presence with the One Remembered" (IV 36.8).[2] If we remain absent from God in thought, word, or deed, we have not remembered Him as He should be remembered.

The Quran and the tradition sum up the practical implications of remembrance with the word *`ibâda,* which means worship, service, and being a servant. This is the most important human task.

2. References are to Ibn Arabi, *al-Futûhât al-makkiyya,* 4 volumes (Cairo, 1911). I indicate volume number, page number, and line number.

In the Quran God says, "I created *jinn* and mankind only to worship Me" or "to serve Me" (51:56). In other words, God created human beings so that they would remember Him and bring themselves into conformity with His Reality. They can do so only by means of right understanding, right faith, right speech, and right activity. The criterion for "rightness" is the degree to which one understands, acts, and exists in the presence of God. Being present with God is precisely *dhikr Allâh*, "the remembrance of God".

Islamic faith has three principles, not just two.[3] After Divine unity and prophecy comes *ma`âd*, the "return" to God, commonly discussed in terms of death and resurrection. Since everyone must die and be brought forth in the presence of God, the afterlife is often called the "compulsory return". But the more sophisticated theologians, philosophers, and spiritual teachers place greater stress on the "voluntary return", that is, the fact that our existential situation demands that we choose freely to return to God here and now. This existential situation is defined by reality itself, which is primarily God, and secondarily the world and the human self as they actually are, which is to say, as they disclose the Reality of God. For those who have eyes to see, the cosmos and the human configuration, by their very nature and their very modality of being, point to God. And the fact of the repeated prophetic reminders leaves no excuse for not seeing and not remembering.

To sum up, the general Islamic understanding of the human situation is that correct knowledge of the world and the human soul demands that we freely and actively undertake the return to God. We return to God by remembering Him on every level of our being. To remember Him is to make the fact of His unity, the fact of His absolute and infinite Reality, the axis of our thought, speech, and activity. We do so by "worship", which is the appropriate response to *tawhîd* and prophecy. Thus the Quran speaks of *tawhîd* and worship as the two basic dimensions of every authentic tradition. God says in the Quran, "We never sent a Messenger before thee without revealing to him, 'There is no god but I, so worship Me'" (21:25).

3. For a detailed review of the three principles of faith and their role in formulating the Islamic worldview, see Sachiko Murata and William C. Chittick, *The Vision of Islam* (St Paul: Paragon House, 1994), pp. 35-264.

The Book of the Soul

A great deal could be said about the various forms that the practice of *dhikr* has taken, not only among those commonly known as "Sufis", but also among Muslims in general.[4] However, my purpose here is to review basic Islamic teachings about the universe and the self in order to suggest not only why *dhikr* is an efficacious contemplative practice, but also why, in actual fact, there is nothing else that we can do. On close analysis, we see that *dhikr* is the practice of God Himself and, along with Him, that of all of creation. Unless we understand this, we will not be able to grasp our human condition or to take advantage of it while we have it. Having failed to do so, "this world" will be "accursed" for us. At our inevitable return to God—when we shall finally recognize with utter certainty that we can do nothing but remember God—we shall taste the fruit of that accursedness.

Anyone familiar with the Quran knows that it speaks of God by detailing His names and activities. In the process, it goes to extraordinary lengths to emphasize that it is God's book, revelation, speech, and words. It maintains that all revelation to the prophets is nothing but God's speech, and that God speaks to the prophets so as to clarify the nature of things and to explain the appropriate human response. Moreover, it tells us repeatedly that God creates the world by speaking to it. Just as the Quran and other scriptures are collections of God's "signs" or "verses" (*âyât*), so also the whole universe is a vast collection of God's signs and verses. In effect, God creates the universe by revealing three books—the universe, the human self, and scripture. In each, He reveals His signs and writes out His words.

Once we understand that reality is configured by speech, we shall also see that the human task is to read and understand what has been written. Then we can follow the instructions laid out in the text of scripture, the world, and the soul. The interpretation of the Quran—which is the foundation and fruit of all the Islamic sciences—has always entailed the simultaneous interpretation of the universe and the soul. Every Muslim, by accepting the Quran as

4. The writings of many of the early Orientalists give the impression that the practice of *dhikr* was invented by the Sufis, probably under the influence of Christian monasticism or *japa yoga*. Although this view has largely been debunked by more careful scholarship, it can still be found in the secondary literature.

God's Word, has accepted the responsibility of understanding what this Word means. The fruit of this understanding redounds on the soul. Every soul will answer for its own reading, not only of the Quran, but also of the other two books, the universe and the soul. And, given the fact that it is the soul itself that reads and understands, the book of the soul is the all-important determinant of our destiny. This helps explain why, in recounting the events that will take place on the Day of Resurrection, the Quran tells us that every human being will be addressed by the words, "Read your book! Your soul suffices you today as a reckoner against you!" (17:14).

The crux of knowledge, then, is to read and know one's own soul. The whole trajectory of the voluntary return to God is to learn how to interpret oneself through understanding the wisdom present in both revelation and the cosmos. The return reaches its fruition on the Day of Resurrection. What we as human beings *should* want to learn is who we are now and who we will be when we arrive back at the meeting with God. All knowledge should serve the goal of this knowledge. As Rumi puts it,

> The spirit of all the sciences is this, only this:
> that you know who you will be on the Day of Resurrection.[5]

In order to know who one is and who one will be, one must know one's relation with God, who created man in His own image. It is clear that the Divine speech creates the world and reveals the scriptures. It is this same speech that appears as the distinguishing feature of man, created in God's image. The same speech reveals the words of reminder, guidance, and prayer whereby man is able to remember his Source and undertake the return journey. And it is also this same speech that will be written plainly in the book of the soul on the Day of Resurrection. The human condition, then, demands knowing that everything we understand, speak, do, and embody is being written and recorded in our own selves.

The Breath of the All-Merciful

Ibn Arabi, who is not known for his reticence, explicates the Divine and cosmic speech in enormous detail and in respect to practically every human possibility. In discussing the implications of

5. Rumi, *Mathnawî* (Nicholson edition), Book 3, verse 2654.

God's creation of the universe by speaking to it, he frequently elaborates on the expression "the Breath of the All-Merciful", which he takes from a prophetic saying. According to the Quran, it is God as the All-Merciful who sits on the Throne. The Throne is typically understood as the outermost sphere, which embraces the whole universe in its infinite spatial and temporal expanse. The King "sits on the Throne" because He is the King and the universe is His kingdom. He sits on it as the "All-Merciful" because the Divine mercy—which is the bestowal of the good, the beautiful, and the true—determines the fundamental nature of the universe. The Prophet tells us that the inscription on the Throne of God reads, "My mercy takes precedence over My wrath." Moreover, within the human microcosm, God's Throne is the heart. It follows that, just as nothing lies beyond the Throne in the macrocosm but God, so also nothing is found within the Throne of the microcosm but God.

When the All-Merciful speaks, He articulates His words in His Breath, just as we speak by articulating our words in our breath. It follows that the All-Merciful's "Breath" is the underlying substance of the universe. It is the page upon which God writes out the book of the cosmos.

The nature of the Divine words that appear in the Breath is suggested already in the derivation of the word *kalâm*, "speech". It comes from *kalm*, a word that the Arabic dictionaries define as *jarh*, which means to cut or wound with a weapon. *Jarh* in turn is explained more generally as meaning *ta'thîr*, which means to leave effects and traces (*athar*). Basing himself on these standard definitions, Ibn Arabi explains that the Divine speech leaves traces in the undifferentiated and unarticulated divine Breath. Each of these traces is then a "word" (*kalima*), that is, a "cut" or an "articulation" in undifferentiated existence. The Breath itself remains forever untouched and unarticulated by the words that it pronounces, just as our breath is unaffected by the words that we speak.

In the eternal now, God speaks one word, and that is the command "Be!" This word gives rise to the beginningless and endless succession of words and worlds that unfolds in the spiritual and corporeal realms. It is this one word "Be!" that bestows being, so all things are implicitly contained within it. God directs this one word toward everything which He wants to bring into existence. As the Quran puts it, "Our only word to a thing, when We desire it, is to say to it 'Be!', so it comes to be" (16:40). The "things" (*ashyâ'*) to whom

God speaks abide in what Ibn Arabi calls "nonexistence" (*`adam*), which is to say that they are nonexistent in themselves, though not unknown to God. In other terms, "nonexistence" is the realm of the Divine omniscience. God knows all things and all "entities" (*a`yân*) for all eternity, but they have no existence of their own before He tells them to come to be. At that point, they become articulated within His Breath. Their "being" belongs not to them, but to the Divine Breath within which they are pronounced. Ibn Arabi writes,

> Nothing becomes manifest in the cosmos except from the attribute of speech. Thus, the All-Merciful turns His face towards one of the entities, and then the individuality that He intends opens up within the Breath. (II 181.12)

Given that creatures are nothing but words uttered by God, our knowledge of things is our knowledge of the Divine words. As Ibn Arabi puts it, "The existence of created being has no root other than the Divine attribute of speech, for created being knows nothing of God but His speech, and that is what it hears" (II 352.14). If creatures know nothing but speech, this is because there is nothing else to be known. The speech that they know is the speech that says to themselves and to others "Be!" It never ceases belonging exclusively to God. This is why Ibn Arabi can write that the true attribute of creation is silence, just as the true attribute of God is speech. When "speech" is attributed to creation, it is done so only inasmuch as God has bestowed it, just as, when "being" is attributed to creation, it is done so only inasmuch as God has said "Be!" to it. Ibn Arabi writes,

> God says, "There is nothing that does not glorify Him in praise" [17:44]. . . . We maintain that there is nothing whatsoever in existence that is silent. On the contrary, all things are speaking in laudation of God. In the same way, we maintain that there is nothing whatsoever in existence that speaks in respect of its own entity. On the contrary, every entity other than God is silent and without speech. Since all things are loci of manifestation [for God's Being], speech belongs to [God, who is] the Manifest (II 77.13).

Elsewhere, Ibn Arabi makes the point in somewhat more detail:

> The servant is silent and listening perpetually, in all of his states, whether moving or still, standing or sitting. For the servant has been granted the hearing of the Real's speech. He never ceases hearing the Real's command to come to be, whatever may be the states and guises in which he is coming to be. Neither the servant

> nor the cosmos is empty for one moment of the inward existence of bringing to be. Hence he never ceases listening, so he never ceases being silent. It is not possible for him to enter along with Him in His speech. So, when you hear the servant speaking, that is the Real's bringing to be within Him. The servant remains in his root, silent, standing before Him—high indeed is He! So, nothing is ever heard but the Real's acts of bringing to be. Understand this, for it pertains to the core of true knowledge (III 218.30).

In short, God speaks through all things. As speakers, the things are "signs" or "verses" that give voice to the names and attributes of God. They are words pronounced in the All-Merciful Breath. They appear in three books—the book of the universe, the book of the soul, and the book of revelation.

Knowledge of the Names

Islamic theology commonly calls creatures the "acts" (*af`âl*) of God. Ibn Arabi explains that these acts are nothing but the "traces" (*athar*) of God's names, the *vestigia Dei.* But what about the Divine names themselves? What exactly are they? Ibn Arabi writes that when we speak of names (*ism*)—whether we are talking about God or creatures—we are speaking about "something that occurs from a trace, or something from which a trace comes to be" (II 120.13). So again, a name, like other words, is a "cut" or an "articulation" in the plain fabric of universal Being.

The ultimate source of all names and all realities is of course the very Selfhood of God, called the "Essence" (*dhât*). In Himself, God knows everything that will appear in the universe for all eternity, because all things are simply the traces of His knowledge of His Essence, which is Infinite and Absolute Being. So, God knows not only His own names, but also the names of all things. If He calls Himself by many names both in the Quran and in other scriptures, it is because the traces of the names are infinitely diverse. As Ibn Arabi puts it, "God made the Divine names many only because of the diversity of the traces that are manifest in created being" (IV 36.19).

So, from a certain standpoint, the Divine names are the traces of all the Divine attributes and qualities that become manifest in creation. God names Himself in terms of the creatures, which are, after all, simply the words that He pronounces. Within the creatures, certain qualities can be discerned, and these can only be the qualities of their Creator, the one who pronounces the words. The words express nothing but the Speaker. The Divine Speaker is revealing Himself through His speech as Merciful, Alive, Knowing, Powerful, Speaking, and so on down the list of the so-called "ninety-nine names" of God.

All names, whether of God or of creation, are in the last analysis traces of the Divine Essence, which is the Absolute and Infinite Selfhood of the Real. In Itself, the Essence is without trace and unknowable to any but Itself. Nonetheless, man has been given the capacity to know all the names—all the traces displayed by the Essence, traces that are nothing but all things that can enter into existence. It is this potential omniscience that sets man apart from all other creatures. When the Prophet reiterated the Biblical statement, "God created Adam in His own image", he certainly had in mind the fact that God had given Adam knowledge of all things. The Quran is explicit on this point: "He taught Adam the names, all of them" (2:31).

Ibn Arabi points out that it is precisely names that make *dhikr* possible. This is true not only for man, but also for God. The Quran often attributes *dhikr* to God, as in the verse, "Remember Me, and I will remember you" (2:152). God, after all, knows things through their "names", which are nothing but their traces in His own omniscience, traces that are commonly called "essences" or "entities". Ibn Arabi writes:

> Adam was preferred over the angels only because he encompassed the knowledge of the names. For, were it not for the names, God would remember nothing, and nothing would remember God. So, God remembers only through the names, and He is remembered and praised only through the names (II 489.21).

In sum, the distinguishing feature of man is knowledge of all the names, which are the traces of the Divine qualities, or the traces of the Divine Essence Itself. In the creative act of the eternal now, God voices the names, and these names appear as the creatures in the All-Merciful Breath. The endless array of creatures other than man are specific words of God. Every creature has a certain "understanding" of God, but only in respect of the name or names that differentiate it from all other named things. Only man was taught all the names, making him somehow equivalent to all the creatures.

In the universe as a whole, the names are infinitely differentiated, but in the Divine image that is man, they are brought together in an all-comprehensive epitome. Adam received the all-inclusive knowledge of the names when God taught it to him, and he was able to know all the names precisely because he was made in the image of God, who knows and utters all things. In actual fact, Adam came to know and understand the names by knowing his own self, made in God's image. This sort of knowledge does not come by the intermediacy of discursive thought, but rather directly from the nature of things. Thus, in the following passage, Ibn Arabi refers to it by a standard Sufi expression for unmediated knowledge, "tasting" (or "sapience" in the etymological sense: *dhawq*). He writes:

> God taught Adam all the names from Adam's own essence through tasting, for He disclosed Himself to him in His entirety. No name remained in the Divine Presence that did not become manifest to Adam from himself. From his own essence he came to know all the names of his Creator (II 120.24).

Achieving the Status of Adam

Quranic theology, rooted in words, names, and remembrance, allows Muslim sages to understand the human role in the cosmos largely in terms of the achievement of true knowledge of God. This is a role that belongs exclusively to human beings, because they alone were created in God's image, and they alone were given the potential to know all the names. Ibn Arabi explains this human uniqueness in many passages. In one of these, he begins by referring to the Quranic verse (2:30) that describes the protest of the angels when God told them that He was going to create Adam as His "vicegerent" (*khalîfa*) in the earth:

> The angels judged that Adam would bring about corruption because of what was manifest in his configuration. They saw that it would stand through the diverse, conflicting, and mutually averse natures. They knew that the traces of these roots must become manifest in him who possessed this configuration. However, if they had known Adam's nonmanifest dimension, which is the reality of the image in which God created him, they would have seen themselves as a part of Adam's creation.
>
> The angels were ignorant of the Divine names that Adam obtained when his all-comprehensiveness was unveiled to him.

> When Adam saw his own essence, he came to know his ground in all things and from all things. For the whole cosmos is the differentiation of Adam, and Adam is the all-comprehensive book. In relation to the cosmos he is like the spirit in relation to the body.
>
> Thus, man is the spirit of the cosmos, and the cosmos is the body. Through both together the cosmos is the macro-anthropos [*al-insân al-kabîr*], so long as man is within it. But, if you look at the cosmos alone, without man, you will find that it is like a body, proportioned and made ready, but without a spirit. The perfection of the cosmos through man is like the perfection of the body through the spirit (II 67.25).[6]

Although man was created as the perfection of the cosmos, or as the active spirit that governs the world's receptive body, any given individual does not necessarily live up to the human role. Clearly, the whole point of the prophetic messages is to remind people that they need to exert their own efforts in order to achieve the perfection of the Divine image that is their birthright. Moreover, given that they cannot see things as they are without Divine help, they need prophetic instructions in order to exert themselves correctly.

Ibn Arabi calls those who do achieve the fullness of human stature "perfect man" (*al-insân al-kâmil*). The historical examples of those who reached this status are provided by the prophets and some of the saints. However this may be, the fact remains that most people remain at the level of what he calls "animal man" (*al-insân al-hayawân*). He reserves the attribute "perfect" precisely for the greatest of all human beings. He tells us, for example, that in every other sort of creature in the universe, some are "complete" (*tâmm*), but none are perfect. "Nothing is perfect save through this perfect, human configuration. When he is not perfect, he is the animal human, named by the definition 'rational animal' [*hayawân nâtiq*]" (IV 75.7).

Perfect human beings actualize God's goal in creating the universe. That goal is explained mythically in the famous *hadîth*, "I was a hidden treasure, and I desired to be known, so I created the creatures that I might be known." Only human beings can know God in the fullness of His divinity, because only they were created in His total image. Indeed, this knowledge of God is demanded by the

6. Ibn Arabi makes the same basic points, though in rather convoluted and obscure language, at the beginning of the chapter on Adam in his famous book, *Fusûs al-hikam*, "The Bezels of Wisdom".

Quranic verse that states God's purpose in creating man: "I created *jinn* and mankind only to worship Me." As the Prophet's companion Ibn Abbas already explained, "to worship Me" (*ya 'budûni*) means "to know Me" (*ya 'rifûnî*).

Especially significant here is this word "know", which also means "to re-cognize". The Arabic word implies that this knowledge is the recovery of a misplaced, innate knowledge. In other words, we come to remember what we have forgotten. It is this same knowledge that is mentioned in the famous saying attributed to the Prophet, constantly quoted in Sufi texts, "He who knows himself knows his Lord"; or "He who recognizes himself recognizes his Lord". In other words, he who recognizes himself for the creature of God that he actually is will recognize His Lord for the God that He actually is. The two verbal nouns deriving from this verb—*ma'rifah* and *`irfân*—are frequently translated as "gnosis". Both are used to designate unmediated knowledge of God.

In one passage, Ibn Arabi explains the purpose of creation as the "worship" that is "recognition" or "gnosis". He points out that human beings are the means whereby this purpose is achieved:

> Human beings are intended by the existence of the world by the second intention, not the first intention. As for the first intention, what was intended by the creation of the world was the worship of God, I mean, worship through recognition [*`irfân*] of the perfection of existence that is achieved by contingent things (IV 75.6).

In short, the only creature—the only contingent thing—that can recognize God in the fullness of His reality and that can know Him in all His names is man. In one of the many passages in which he sums up the significance of human existence, Ibn Arabi writes as follows:

> Since creation has many levels, and since the most perfect level is occupied by man, each kind within the cosmos is a part with regard to the perfection of man. Even animal man is a part of perfect man. So, every knowledge of God belonging to a part of the cosmos is a partial knowledge, except in the case of man, for his knowledge of God is the knowledge of God possessed by all the cosmos. This knowledge of God is a universal knowledge [*`ilm kullî*], though not a knowledge of all [*`ilm kull*]. Were it a knowledge of all, he would not have been commanded to say, "My Lord, increase me in knowledge!" [20:114]. Do you think that [the knowledge he is commanded to seek] is knowledge through other than God? No, by God, it is knowledge through God!

> So, He created perfect man in His image, and through the image He gave him the ability to have all of His names ascribed to him, one by one, or in groups, though all the names together are not ascribed to him in a single word—thereby the Lord is distinguished from the perfect servant. Hence there is none of the most beautiful names—and all of God's names are most beautiful—by which the perfect servant is not called, just as he calls his Master by them (III 409.16).

The House of God

In the diverse creatures of the cosmos other than man—on whatever level they may dwell, from spiritual and angelic to corporeal and sensory—the traces of God's names and attributes are externalized as the specific and unique characteristics of each thing. Every creature in the universe "knows" God in a specific, differentiated, and determined way, defined by the attributes that the thing displays, or by the "word" that it embodies; each thing gives news of God and displays His signs through occupying its specific niche in the never-repeated speech of God that is the universe.

In contrast, in the multileveled reality that is the human self, the traces of God's names and attributes are relatively internalized. The traces extend from the corporeal to the spiritual realm, and they circle around their *Ka'bah,* which is the heart, the luminous center of the being, the spirit that God blew into Adam at his creation. Man alone is given the potential to know God in a global, synthetic manner, because man alone is created in the image not of one or of several specific names, but in the image of the all-comprehensive name Allah, which designates God as such, in both His absoluteness and His infinity, His Essence and His attributes, His incomparability and His similarity, His transcendence and His immanence.

If the fullness of *`ibâda*—"worship" and "service"—is to remember God in a manner appropriate to His total reality, it is obvious that only man, made in God's image, can be a "servant" (*`abd*) of God. Nonetheless, in a narrower sense, *`ibâda* simply means serving God's purposes, and in this sense everything worships God, because a contingent being can do nothing but serve the Absolute Being from which it draws its entire self. As the Quran puts it, "None is there in the heavens and the earth that comes not to the All-merciful as a servant" (19:93). Each thing worships and serves

God in its own specific mode of being. Each creature has a status determined by the manner in which God has articulated it as a word in His Breath. However, man has no specific mode of being, because his awareness and consciousness have no inner limits. Only he is a global image of the All-Knowing and the All-Aware. In effect, man has the potential to be the outward image of the All-Merciful Breath itself, the manifestation of all of Being and of all of the Divine names and attributes.

Man's distinctive status means that only he can fulfill the final purpose of creation, which is for God to be worshiped and served not simply in the passive way that all creatures serve Him, but also in the active way achieved by full consciousness of the Hidden Treasure and the free acceptance of everything that this demands. This is why, according to Ibn Arabi, man's function as vicegerent of God fulfills the creative process and achieves its purpose. So central is the human role that, if it were not fulfilled, the world would simply disintegrate.

> God made this earth a place for the vicegerency. Hence it is the abode of His kingdom and the site of His deputy, who becomes manifest through the properties of His names. So, from the earth He created us. Within it He gave us residence, whether alive or dead. And from it He will bring us forth through the Uprising in the last configuration. Thus, worship never leaves us wherever we may be, in this world and the afterworld, for, even though the afterworld is not an abode of [religious] prescription [*taklîf*], it is an abode of worship.
>
> Among us, whoever ceaselessly witnesses that for which he was created in this world and the next is the perfect servant, the intended goal of the cosmos, and the deputy of the whole cosmos. Were all the cosmos—the high of it and the low of it—to be heedless of God's remembrance for a single moment, and were this servant to remember Him, he would take the place of the whole cosmos through that remembrance, and the existence of the cosmos would be preserved through him. However, if the human servant were to be heedless of remembrance, the cosmos could not take his place in that. That of it which is empty of the human being who remembers would go to ruin. The Prophet said, "The Hour will not come as long as there remains in the earth someone who is saying 'Allah, Allah'" (III 248.12).

To review my main points, the worldview of Islam depicts God, the universe, man, and prophecy in terms of words and speech. The three principles of faith—unity, prophecy, and the Return—are all understood in terms of God's names and naming. Man's task is to respond to his situation by remembering the names of things—that is, the real and actual names of things, which are the things inasmuch as they designate the Divine Reality, or inasmuch as they are articulations of the Divine Speech.

This human task can be accomplished only in the "heart", a word that designates the unlimited realm of human awareness and consciousness. The heart alone, among all created things, is given the capacity to encompass God. As the famous extra-Quranic Divine saying puts it, "My heavens and My earth embrace Me not, but the heart of My believing servant does embrace Me." To remember God fully and actually is to find Him sitting within the heart, which is His Throne in the microcosm. As Ibn Arabi writes,

> God took the heart of His servant as a house, for He made it the locus of knowledge of Him—the knowledge that is gnosis [*`irfân*], not theory [*nazar*]. He defended the house with zeal and jealousy, lest it be a locus for others.
>
> The servant is all-comprehensive. Inescapably, the Real becomes manifest to the servant in sundry forms, or in the form of everything, for the servant is the locus for the knowledge of all things. And there is no locus of knowledge except the heart. But the Real is jealous of His servant's heart, lest anything other than his Lord be within it. Therefore He showed the heart that He is the form of everything and identical with everything, for the servant's heart embraces everything. The reason for this is that everything is Real, because nothing embraces things but the Real. Whoever knows the Real in respect of His Realness has known everything.
>
> However, someone who knows a thing does not thereby know the Real, nor [does he know it] in reality. The servant who supposes that he knows a *thing* does not in fact know it, for if he did know it, he would know that it is the Real. Thus, as long as he does not know that it is the Real, we say concerning him that he does not know it (IV 7.7).

Knowledge of things as they actually are can only come through knowing them as disclosures of the Real, as signs and traces displaying God's names and attributes. This is not a theoretical sort of knowledge, but a knowledge of recognition and gnosis. It is to gain a true vision of the Divine omnipresence, the fact that, as the Quran puts it, "Wherever you turn, there is the face of God" (2:115). Such knowledge comes by way of *dhikr*, which is *al-hudûr ma`a'l-madhkûr*, "presence with the One Remembered".

It is only this sort of knowledge that allows man to see that everything in this world is accursed if he does not see it as displaying the Real, and that he himself is accursed to the extent that he does not know that things do in fact display the Real. Once we see the world for what it is, we see that it is nothing but *dhikr Allâh*—a reminder of God, a mention of God, a remembrance of God. Our response to the world can only be to follow its lead—to mention and to remember God. "Everything is accursed," says the *hadîth*, "except *dhikr Allâh*." But *everything* is *dhikr Allâh*, so *nothing* is accursed. The alchemy of *dhikr* transmutes the accursed into the blessed. The place of that *dhikr*, where God becomes truly present and man becomes truly blessed, is the heart.

Let me leave you with this bit of advice from Ibn Arabi:

> The greatest sin is what brings about the death of the heart. It dies only by not knowing God. This is what is named "ignorance". For the heart is the house that God has chosen for Himself in this human configuration. But such a person has misappropriated the house, coming between it and its Owner.
>
> A person like that is the one who most wrongs himself, for he has deprived himself of the good that would have come to him from the Owner of the house—had he left the house to Him. This is the deprivation of ignorance (III 179.6).

Chapter 5

Presence, Participation, Performance: The Remembrance of God in the Early Hesychast Fathers

Vincent Rossi

> To say "Look to God" is not helpful without some instruction as to what this looking imports: it might very well be said that one can "look" and still sacrifice no pleasure, still be the slave of impulse, repeating the word "God" but held in the grip of every passion and making no effort to master any. . . . "God" on the lips, without a good conduct of life, is but a word.
>
> Plotinus[1]

Professor Andrew Louth, as I am sure you all know by now, was unable to attend this conference, and I am his last-minute replacement. There is actually no replacing a scholar and theologian of his accomplishments. Having spent the greater part of the past ten years studying and working in Oxford and London, I had the privilege of coming to know Dr Louth and hearing him speak on a number of occasions, and I can attest to his extraordinary command of the themes of Patristic theology as well as his commitment to understanding and realizing these themes in a higher spiritual sense that transcends mere academic expertise. Several of his books are familiar companions of mine, including his early *Discerning the Mystery*, with its groundbreaking chapter on the recovery of allegory and *allegoresis* in the Patristic exegesis of Scripture, his study of Dionysios the Areopagite from the Outstanding Christian Thinkers series,[2] and, of course, his more recent translation of some of the most important texts of St Maximos the Confessor,[3] with an exten-

1. *Enneads,* II, ix. 15, trans. S. MacKenna, rev. edn. (London: 1989), pp. 147-8; quoted in Andrew Louth, *Discerning the Mystery* (Oxford: Clarendon Press, Clarendon Paperbacks, 1989), p. 76.
2. *Denys the Areopagite* (London: Geoffrey, Chapman; Wilton, CT: Morehouse-Barlow, 1989).
3. *Maximus the Confessor* (London & New York: Routledge, 1996).

sive introduction that is in my opinion the best short introduction to the thought of St Maximos in English. As the substitute for such a speaker, I must rely heavily on your good will and generosity. I pray your kindly forbearance will be an incentive for me to reach for that grace of God that will carry these moments we share, God willing, beyond whatever intellectual energy I can bring to it by my own unaided efforts. Let us begin with a prayer found in the writings of St Mark the Ascetic, one of the greatest of the early hesychasts: "May He who inaugurates every good thing inaugurate all that we undertake, so that it may be done with His blessing."[4]

The subject of my talk is "Presence, Participation, Performance: The Remembrance of God in the Early Hesychast Fathers". Since Dr Louth's subject was to be "Evagrios on Prayer", you will find as we proceed that Evagrios will also have something to say about our subject, and must be counted as an early Hesychast Father, despite his adherence to a speculative, Origenistic cosmology which the Orthodox Tradition later rejected. Himself a disciple of one of the greatest of the Desert Fathers, St Macarios of Alexandria, and an acquaintance of another towering spiritual master, St Macarios of Egypt, and possessed to an exceptional degree of the gifts of psychological insight and penetrating analysis, Evagrios was steeped in the spirituality of the Desert, and almost single-handedly set the standard and devised the theory and technical vocabulary of hesychasm. Many of the greatest hesychasts, including in particular those from whom we will be hearing, such as St Diadochos of Photiki, St Maximos the Confessor, St Isaac the Syrian, and St John Klimakos, follow this practical side of Evagrios, while avoiding his dicier speculations, and develop even further the profound spiritual psychology to which he first gave definite, even definitive, expression.

This conference seeks to open a dialogue between two "Paths to the Heart", Sufism and the Hesychasm of the Christian East. The two religions from which these paths spring, Islam and Christianity, as has often been pointed out, have much in common, but are sharply divided as regards a single core belief of fundamental importance, namely the unity and unicity of the Divine nature, upon which hangs the acceptance or rejection of the Trinity, Jesus

4. "On the Spiritual Law: Two Hundred Texts", 5. Palmer, Sherrard, Ware in *The Philokalia*, Vol. 1 (London: Faber & Faber, 1979), p. 110.

Christ as the incarnate Logos or as merely one of the prophets, and Muhammad as the greatest of the prophets—the very seal of prophecy—or as a deluded heretic, or even the forerunner of Antichrist.[5] These are stumbling-blocks of the most serious nature, which cannot be wished away with any kind of verbal sleight of hand or sentimental ecumenism. It is important in a conference such as this to bear in mind that nothing we say or do here will change the nature of either Christianity or Islam. The best we can hope for is to deepen our own understanding, not only of the "other" religion, but, even more importantly, of our own faith; and that is not an insignificant achievement. The paradox of religious pluralism can only be resolved by a deeper penetration into the unchanging spiritual realities that lie at the heart of one's own religious path. The affirmation of a universal principle that purports to be "above" all religious differences, and yet requires one to alter fundamental aspects of one's own religious tradition in order to attain it, is firmly to be rejected as delusory.

One of the clearest understandings of the difficulties that lie behind any dialogue between Christianity and Islam may be found in the writings of Frithjof Schuon, a Sufi shaykh who wrote with deep sympathy and insight into both faiths. I refer in particular to his book *Christianity/Islam*,[6] and to a long article entitled "The Human Margin", although pertinent, even arresting, observations on the nature of the two traditions are scattered throughout his many books. I quote now from "The Human Margin", a rather lengthy passage that I feel expresses the full gravity of the difficulties we face in this dialogue. One need not accept Schuon's characteristic solution of an intellectual alchemy transforming the lead of a rigidly exclusive volitive theology into the metaphysical gold of a transcendently unitive truth at the heart of all religion[7] to appreciate the clarity and precision of the following:

> One of the great difficulties of Sufism is that in it the highest metaphysics finds itself inextricably bound up with theology, which tar-

5. See St John of Damascus, in the Second Part of his *Fount of Knowledge*, "On Heresies". Trans. Frederic Chase in *The Fathers of the Church*, Vol. 37 (Washington, D.C.: The Catholic University of America Press, 1970), pp. 153-160.
6. Frithjof Schuon, *Christianity/Islam: Essays on Esoteric Ecumenicism* (Bloomington, IN: World Wisdom Books, 1985).
7. See Frithjof Schuon, *The Transcendent Unity of Religions* (London: The Theosophical Publishing House, 1993).

> nishes it by its habitual confusions with regard to "omnipotence", unless we admit that in this case it is the metaphysical penetration that deepens the theology by eventually inculcating into it some liberating gleams of light. The theologies, by taking upon themselves the contradiction of being sentimental metaphysics, are condemned to the squaring of the circle. They are ignorant of the differentiation of things into aspects and standpoints, and they work in consequence on the basis of arbitrarily rigid data, the antinomies of which can be solved only beyond this artificial rigidity. . . . In Christianity there is the will to admit a differentiation in the Divine Oneness, and the equally imperious will not to admit, practically speaking, that there is any differentiation at all—the Hypostases being "merely relationships"—as if the three dimensions of space were to be willed into one dimension only. In Islam, an obstinate unitarism comes into collision with the existence of the world, whereas there would be no conflict if the unitarism were metaphysical and therefore transparent and supple as its nature demands. On the one side there is a certain dispersion in the object of worship: God, the Persons, Christ, the Eucharist . . .; on the other side there is on the contrary an excess of centralization, on a plane where it cannot possibly be imposed, namely a refusal to admit any cause except God or to be dependent on anything but on Him alone, thus flying in the face of immediate evidence, when in reality such evidence in no sense prevents everything from depending upon God and when one only needs to be conscious of this to be on the side of truth. . . . From the standpoint of an extreme trinitarianism God is certainly One, but He is so only while being Three, and there is no One God except in and by the Trinity; the God who is One without Trinity, or independently of all hypostatic deployment, is not the true God, for without this deployment unity is meaningless.[8]

This text is rich in its content and implications, and to comment on it in the depth it deserves would take up all my allotted time. Let us briefly note what will be important for our purpose in this conference. Schuon outlines above several dichotomies that will undoubtedly underlie all our discussions: metaphysics-theology, intellectual-sentimental, esoterism-exoterism, unitarism-trinitarism, metaphysical transparency of forms-opaque doctrinal formalism, and above all, Divine Center-human margin. All these dichotomies, or rather, hierarchical dualities, for that is what they are in fact, are

8. Frithjof Schuon, "The Human Margin" in *The Sword of Gnosis*, ed. Jacob Needleman (London: Routledge & Kegan Paul—Arkana edition, 1986), pp. 415-417.

rooted in the fundamental epistemic duality: *gnosis* (knowledge)-*pistis* (faith), with the former standing higher on the epistemic ladder than the latter. Knowledge-faith, according to Schuon, is the basic duality of all religious expression. Merely noting these dualities, and mechanically putting each thinker or tradition we encounter into one or the other, does not automatically lead us to perfect clarity. For example, what Schuon calls "theology" or "sentimental metaphysics" is clearly not what the early Hesychast Fathers know as *theologia*, which as an expression indicating union with God transcends even what Schuon calls the "highest metaphysics". Again, what Schuon calls "extreme trinitarianism" is characteristic of each and every one of the early Hesychast Fathers with whom we will be exploring the practice of the remembrance of God.

Sufi metaphysics, as represented by a thinker like Schuon, is grounded in a logically hierarchical and essentialist conception of reality: Beyond-Being, Being, Existence. Only the Absolute, the totally unqualified, non-manifest Essence, is Beyond-Being. This is That which is "the One". The Trinity in this conception cannot represent the totally unqualified Essence. The Trinity necessarily stands at the level of Being, the equally non-manifest but proto-determined principle of Existence. Being is thus the "realm" of the "personal" God, which is the first determination of the Absolute, called by Schuon the relative Absolute. Since the hypostases of the Trinity in this view are determinations of the One, and relative to one another, they necessarily cannot be at the level of the absolutely Absolute, but must be relative to it, that is, to the Essence, yet still absolute with respect to the created world; hence Schuon's notion of Being as the relative Absolute. Such an approach is highly congenial to and perhaps even entirely representative of the "highest metaphysics" of the Sufis, but it is unacceptable to the Hesychasts of the Christian East, whose own understanding of the highest metaphysics is paradoxically Trinitarian, personalist rather than essentialist. This explains Schuon's implied criticism of Christians who are "extreme" trinitarians. He is critical, not of their trinitarianism *per se*, but of their paradoxical insistence that the Trinity is the most appropriate way to speak of the Absolute ("as if the three dimensions of space were to be willed into one dimension only"), and of their insistence that Person in God transcends essence, a concept equally inexplicable to the logically hierarchical metaphysics of the Sufi traditionalists, in which the intellectual principle of logical non-contradiction is primary, whereas among the Hesychasts, the revelational principle of paradox and antinomy is primary. The Hesychasts were not ignorant of the paradoxical nature of their Trinitarian expressions, as even a cursory reading of the *Corpus Areopagiticum* or the works of St Maximos the Confessor must show. Hence their trinitarianism cannot justly be characterized as "devoid of metaphysical penetration" or as a form of "sentimental" or "bhaktic" theology, impervious to the subtle gleams of metaphysical light. Furthermore, in my reading of the greatest of the Hesychast masters, saints such as Dionysios the Areopagite, Maximos the Confessor, or John of Damaskos, their insistence upon and expression of Divine unity in their trinitarianism seems in no way inferior to the most radical of the unitarists of Islam. Nor does one see in their writings (and it would be easy to supply dozens of texts showing this) the slightest indication that in their "trinitarism" they are guilty of that greatest of Islamic sins against Divine Unity, association or *shirk*.

The remembrance of God is central to the practice of both Sufism and Hesychasm. If the God we are seeking to remember is the Divinity Who Alone Is, and if human nature is a unity as both traditions assert, then human beings who are Muslims do not have a different God and cannot have a different kind of heart from those who are Christian. How then does the way Hesychasts seek to remember God differ from that of Sufis, and how different is the path to the heart in the two traditions? Is it possible, given the unity of human nature, that in spite of doctrinal differences, the spiritual pioneers in the two traditions broke out of the human margin to find the same way home to the Divine Center? Do the unitarist dogma of Islam and the Trinitarian dogma of Christianity have some kind of hidden effect upon the hearts and spirits of believers in the two traditions, making them so different that they can no longer share in the universal brotherhood of humanity under God? Is there a place—or, better, a level—of consciousness where the Christian insistence upon the tri-hypostatic Godhead and the Islamic insistence on the absolute unicity and "unshirkability" of the Deity meet? It is not my purpose to explore these matters in any depth dialogically. I shall stay firmly on the Orthodox Christian side of the line. It is important to recognize with utter clarity, however, that these difficulties exist. The "human margin" where such divisions exist must in the nature of things be our inevitable starting point. It is also the starting point of every person, Christian or Muslim, who turns to God in prayer, and true prayer, as the saints bear witness, will always lift us on noetic wings up and in ("further up and further in") from the human margin to the Divine Center. Having thus acknowledged the context of our exploration, it is time to approach the texts of the early Hesychast Fathers themselves.

Hesychia, Hesychasm, and the Early Hesychast Fathers

As the first presenter from the Orthodox Christian tradition, it falls to me to begin with a definition of *hesychia* and Hesychasm. For a working definition, we can do no better than to use the definition found in Volume One of the English translation of the Greek *Philokalia,* the work of G. E. H. Palmer, Philip Sherrard, and my own beloved teacher and one of this conference's keynote speakers, Bishop Kallistos Ware. *Hesychia* is

> stillness: a state of inner tranquillity or mental quietude and concentration which arises in conjunction with, and is deepened by, the practice of pure prayer and the guarding of heart and intellect. Not simply silence, but an attitude of listening to God and of openness towards Him . . . from *hesychia* are derived the words hesychasm and hesychast, used to denote the whole spiritual tradition represented in the *Philokalia* as well as the person who pursues the spiritual path it delineates.[9]

Hesychia, usually translated as "stillness", sometimes as "silence", is much more than either word implies in English. Far beyond the conventional understanding of "inner peace" or "tranquillity", transcending any notion of quietism, *hesychia* denotes a state of intense watchfulness, prayer, and listening to God, which is in itself a transforming energy that curbs passions, unifies the spiritual divisions in the inner man *(eso anthropos)*, and raises the mind to Divine vision.

Hesychasm, according to Bishop Ware's definition I just quoted above, is the whole spiritual tradition represented in the *Philokalia.* The *Philokalia,* as you doubtless know, is a collection of texts written between the fourth and the fifteenth centuries by the spiritual masters of the Orthodox Christian tradition.[10] It was first compiled in its present form in the eighteenth century by two Greek monks, St

9. *The Philokalia,* Vol. 1, p. 364.
10. *The Philokalia,* Vol. 1, p. 11.

Nikodimos the Hagiorite (that is, of the Holy Mountain of Athos—1749-1809) and St Makarios of Corinth (1731-1805). Also in the eighteenth century, by what seems to be a remarkable kind of spiritual synchronicity, a Russian monk, Paisios Velichkovsky (1721-1794), who had visited Mount Athos and later settled in the Karpathian Mountains of Romania, translated a selection of these texts into Slavonic. These translations were later translated into Russian. I must point out here that neither St Nikodimos of the Holy Mountain nor St Paisios Velichkovsky were merely translators and academicians. They were first of all monks and ascetics, entirely devoted to following the traditional way of life of Hesychasm. Both of them were profound spiritual masters and Hesychasts. The genius of St Nikodimos is not fully appreciated in the West because most of his writings have not yet been translated into modern European languages. St Paisios trained an entire generation of monastics in both Russia and Romania in the principles and practices of Hesychasm as found in the texts of the *Philokalia* that he translated—under conditions, I might add, the difficulty of which is almost impossible to imagine, much less appreciate, for people living in a time of computers, fax machines, and "smart" copiers. During his lifetime and after his death, the disciples of Paisios traveled throughout Russia and Romania like a spiritual wildfire, founding new monasteries and renewing those that were moribund. Indeed, the impact of St Paisios's pioneering work on Russian spirituality and culture, and throughout the Slavic lands, is comparable perhaps only to the impact of St Gregory of Sinai (1265-1346), who is credited with inaugurating a spiritual renewal in the monasteries of Mount Athos and, through his travels in the region from Sinai to Bulgaria, among the ascetics and monasteries of the entire Byzantine world.

Who then are the early Hesychast Fathers? Volume One of the Greek *Philokalia* in English lists the following: St Isaiah the Solitary (d. 489 or 491), Evagrios (d. 399), St John Cassian (d. 435), St Mark the Ascetic, also known as Mark the Monk, or the Hermit (d. 420s), St Hesychios the Priest (8th or 9th century), Neilos the Ascetic of Ankyra (d. 430), St Diadochos of Photiki (d. 486), and John of Karpathos (c. 7th century). To this list may be added the names appearing in Volume Two, including St Theodoros the Great Ascetic (c. 9th century), St Maximos the Confessor (580-662), St Thalassios the Libyan (7th century), St John of Damaskos (8th century), Abba Philimon (whose dates are uncertain), and St Theognostos (as early as the 8th century, but perhaps as late as the 14th century). In the *Early Fathers of the Philokalia*,[11] which is a compilation from the Russian *Philokalia* of Theophan the Recluse, besides some of the names listed above, we find also writings from Abba Dorotheos of Gaza (6th century) and St Isaac the Syrian (7th century), two of the most eminent of the early Hesychasts, to which we should add Sts Barsanuphios and John the Prophet (6th century), whose "Letters of Spiritual Direction" are a complete compendium of the spiritual psychology of hesychastic ascesis, and the great St John Klimakos (7th century). Perhaps somewhat arbitrarily, we might draw the dividing line between early and later Hesychasts at the time of St Symeon the New Theologian (949-1022) and his biographer and fellow Hesychast, Nikitas Stithatos (11th century), who together represent a summit and culmination of lines begun in the 4th and 5th centuries and more fully developed in the 6th, 7th, and 8th centuries.

I mentioned earlier the great renewer of Hesychasm in the 14th century, St Gregory of Sinai. There was of course another Gregory, almost the exact contemporary of the Hesychast of Sinai, also associated with the Holy Mountain of Athos, having spent twenty years there in ascetic reclusion, who provided the Orthodox East with the definitive theological, epistemological, and ascetical-methodological justification of Hesychasm. I refer, of course, to St Gregory Palamas (1296-1359). Both of these saints flourished at the high point of the 14th century Hesychast revival, and must therefore be counted among the greatest of the later Hesychast fathers.

The famous Hesychast controversy that took place during the 1330s and 1340s, and in which St Gregory Palamas, but not St Gregory of Sinai, took such a decisive part, produced among its many spiritual fruits a brilliant summary of the principles of Hesychasm in an extraordinarily condensed text that sheds much light on the continuity of the Hesychast tradition. In particular it tells us whom the later Hesychasts called upon as leading authorities in a time of severe crisis. Before the Councils of 1341, 1346, and 1351 affirmed the ontological and existential reality of God's uncreated energies, light, and grace, confirmed the experiential reality of the spiritual methods developed—or, better, discovered—by generations of

11. *Early Fathers of the Philokalia* (London: Faber & Faber, 1969).

Hesychasts to be effective toward the acquisition of the grace of deification, and produced the definitive victory of Hesychasm as a way of life, St Gregory in 1340 drafted a lapidary statement of Hesychast principles known popularly as the "Hagioritic Tome" and officially as "The Declaration of the Holy Mountain in Defense of Those Who Devoutly Practice a Life of Stillness".[12] The document was signed by twenty of the chief elders and spiritual fathers of Mount Athos, and also by the local hierarch, the Bishop of Hierissos in Chalkidiki. Written in the heat of Hesychasm's battle for its very life, the Hagioritic Tome takes a strong polemical stand for all of the themes that are presupposed in the Hesychast practice of the remembrance of God, namely: 1) that salvation consists in participation in the complete reality of the uncreated, ungenerated, deifying grace of God; 2) that perfect union with God is possible in this life, equally in the body as well as the soul and spirit; 3) that the grace of deification is infinitely above nature, virtue, and knowledge; 4) that the intellect or *nous*[13] seated in the heart is the very organ of revelation for the human microcosm; 5) that the light of the Transfiguration of Christ revealed on Mount Tabor and the light experienced by the Hesychasts are one and the same, and that this light is "ineffable, uncreated, eternal, timeless, unapproachable, boundless, infinite, limitless, archetypal, and unchanging beauty, the glory of God, the glory of Christ, and the glory of the Spirit"; 6) that just as the essence of God is uncreated, so are the eternal Divine energies; 7) that spiritual dispositions are stamped upon the body as a result of the gifts of the Spirit, and that dispassion or *apatheia* is thus the key to deification, and, therefore, as a result, the possibility of enjoying an embodied life of incorruption in the age to come requires equally the possibility of the body's participation in the gifts of deification in this life as well. These principles the Tome calls the "doctrine of the saints", which is "taught by the Scriptures" and "received from our fathers", and which "we have come to know . . . from our own small experience".[14]

Who are the saints whose teaching most authoritatively grounds the practice of Hesychasm, according to the Hagioritic Tome? Only eight names appear in the text of the Tome. In order of appear-

12. *The Philokalia*, Vol. 4, (London: Faber & Faber, 1995), pp. 410-424.
13. See footnotes 17 and 26 below.
14. *The Philokalia*, Vol 4, p. 424.

ance, though not necessarily in order of importance, they are: Dionysios the Areopagite, Maximos the Confessor, Macarios of the Macarian Homilies, Athanasios the Great, Gregory of Nyssa, John of Damaskos, Diadochos of Photiki, and Gregory of Nazianzos, the Theologian. None of them is later than the eighth century, three are great doctrinal masters of Nicene Orthodoxy, all are undisputed doctrinal and spiritual Fathers, and all are understood by the later Hesychast tradition to be entirely grounded in the experiential realization of the mysteries of the Spirit, and entirely reliable sources of the way of Hesychasm.

Let us now approach these early Hesychast fathers with reverence and interrogate them on the proper approach to the remembrance of God according to the way of *hesychia*. One of the points made by the early Hesychasts over and over is that the remembrance of God cannot be achieved without the practice of *hesychia* or stillness. *Hesychia* itself is linked with self-mastery and control of all the negative energies and temptations that stand in the way of mindfulness of God. Evagrios says, "Do everything possible to attain stillness and freedom from distraction, and struggle to live according to God's will, battling against invisible enemies."[15] He advises the one who wishes to practice stillness to be ruthless with himself. If one becomes attached to his cell, leave it; if one cannot attain stillness where one presently lives, go elsewhere, even into exile. Alluding to the Gospel text that says that the children of this world are often more astute than the children of the kingdom, he suggests that one should "be like an astute businessman: make stillness your criterion for testing the value of everything, and choose always what contributes to it".[16]

The writings of St Thalassios the Libyan, a Hesychast elder from the 7th century and a personal friend of St Maximos the Confessor, provide an especially good example of the way the early Hesychasts understood the centrality of stillness in the "practice of the presence" of God. Notice that he sometimes sees stillness as a virtue, sometimes as a method of the control of the senses and the acquisition of the virtues, and sometimes as the fruit or end result of ascetic practice and self-mastery:

15. "On Asceticism and Stillness", *The Philokalia*, Vol. 1, p. 33.
16. *Ibid.*

> Seal your senses with *hesychia* and sit in judgment upon the thoughts that attack your heart. . . . Self-control and strenuous effort curb desire; *hesychia* and intense longing (*eros*) for God wither it. . . . *Hesychia*, prayer, love and self-control are a four-horsed chariot bearing the intellect[17] to heaven. . . .[18] Stillness and prayer are the greatest weapons of virtue, for they purify the intellect and confer on it spiritual insight. . . .[19] Enclose your senses in the citadel of stillness so that they do not involve the intellect in their desires. The greatest weapons for someone striving to lead a life of inward stillness are self-control, love, prayer, and spiritual reading. . . .[20] The forceful practice of self-control, and love, patience, and stillness, will destroy the passions hidden within us. . . .[21] Blessed stillness gives birth to blessed children: self-control, love, and pure prayer.[22]

The saint makes no effort at systematic expression, but the centrality of *hesychia* in all spiritual effort is all the more obvious.

St Hesychios the Priest, one of the greatest of the early Hesychast Fathers, identifies *hesychia* or stillness with *prosoche* or inner attentiveness, *nepsis* or watchfulness, and *phylaki kardias* or the guarding of the heart, and links all as closely as possible to the invocation of the Name of Jesus. In his work "On Watchfulness and Holiness", found in Volume One of the *Philokalia*, he writes:

> Attentiveness is the heart's stillness, unbroken by any thought. In this stillness the heart breathes and invokes, endlessly and without ceasing, only Jesus Christ who is the Son of God and Himself God.[23]

A little later in the same work, he adverts even more clearly to the relationship of watchfulness and the Jesus prayer when he writes:

> Watchfulness and the Jesus Prayer, as I have said, mutually reinforce one another; for close attentiveness goes with constant

17. The Greek word is *nous*. "Intellect" here is not the discursive rationality, but the spiritual organ of immediate, direct perception or intuition. See footnote 23 for a more extensive explanation. "Intellect" in this paper always means *nous* in its Patristic, Hesychastic sense, as found in the *Philokalia*.
18. "On Love, Self-control, and Life in accordance with the Intellect", 1: 22, 24; 2: 21. *The Philokalia*, Vol. 2 (London: Faber & Faber, 1981), pp. 308, 314.
19. *Ibid.*, 1: 67, p. 311.
20. *Ibid.*, 2: 10, 11, p. 313.
21. *Ibid.*, 3: 8, p. 319.
22. *Ibid.*, 2: 83, p. 318.
23. "On Watchfulness and Holiness", *The Philokalia*, Vol 1, p. 163.

> prayer, while prayer goes with close watchfulness and attentiveness of the intellect.[24]

Hesychios calls the strength of the heart's stillness "the mother of all virtues", and again links stillness with invocation of the Lord, even quoting the famous phrase of St John Klimakos about using the name of Jesus as a whip to defend oneself from demonic attack:

> That great spiritual master David said to the Lord: "I shall preserve my strength through Thee" (cf. Ps 59:9, LXX). So the strength of the heart's stillness, mother of all the virtues, is preserved in us through our being helped by the Lord. For He has given us the commandments, and when we call upon Him constantly He expels from us that foul forgetfulness which destroys the heart's stillness as water destroys fire. Therefore, monk, do not "sleep unto death" because of your negligence but lash the enemy with the name of Jesus and, as a certain wise man has said, let the name of Jesus adhere to your breath, and then you will know the blessings of stillness.[25]

Summing up the value of stillness coupled with the Prayer of Jesus, St Hesychios adds that the way of *hesychia* with the invocation of the Jesus Prayer preserves all the precious gifts that keep all evil at bay:

> We should strive to preserve the precious gifts which preserve us from all evil, whether on the plane of the senses or on that of the intellect.[26] These gifts are the guarding of the intellect with the invocation of Jesus Christ, continuous insight into the heart's

24. *Ibid.*, p. 178.
25. *Ibid.*, p. 179.
26. Intellect—reason—mind: these three words have similar and overlapping meanings in contemporary English that tend to coincide in the direction of discursive rationality grounded in sense data. Patristic Greek, however, makes a clear distinction between the discursive reason (*dianoia*) and the faculty of direct apprehension or spiritual perception (*nous*). This distinction was also known in the West, as we can see from Latin, which distinguishes between *intellegere*, to perceive, from which English gets "intellect", and *ratio*, from *reri*, to think, from which comes English "reason". Western theology in the Middle Ages, generally speaking, understood the distinction between "intellect" and "reason" in a similar manner to the Greek. Unfortunately this very useful distinction was gradually lost during the centuries following the Renaissance and the so-called Enlightenment. The translators of the *Philokalia*, faced with its absolutely consistent witness of the crucial importance for spiritual discernment of the distinction between immediate apprehension (*nous*) and discursive rationality (*dianoia*), chose—rightly, in my view—to recover this vital distinction and to restore to "intellect" its original meaning as the faculty of direct, immediate perception.

> depths, stillness of mind unbroken even by thoughts which appear to be good, and the capacity to be empty of all thought.[27]

We can see the indispensable relationship of *hesychia* to the remembrance of God in the work of Nikitas Stithatos, the biographer of the great Saint Symeon the New Theologian and a Hesychast in his own right. In his "One Hundred Chapters on the Inner Nature of Things and on the Purification of the *Nous*", he gives the most complete definition of *hesychia* to be found in the *Philokalia*. Nikitas writes:

> Stillness is an undisturbed state of the intellect (*nous*),[28] the calm of a free and joyful soul, the tranquil unwavering stability of the heart in God, the contemplation of light, the knowledge of the mysteries of God, consciousness of wisdom by virtue of a pure mind, the abyss of divine intellections, the rapture of the (*nous*) intellect, intercourse with God, an unsleeping watchfulness, spiritual prayer, untroubled repose in the midst of great hardship, and, finally, solidarity and union with God.[29]

We note that the whole spiritual/ascetic tradition of the *Philokalia* is summed up in this definition of *hesychia*. In studying this passage, my first impression is that Nikitas is simply throwing all the good aspects of stillness together willy-nilly, and my first inclination is to "tidy" up the passage by reordering his qualities, beginning logically with an "unsleeping watchfulness", moving through the attainment of undisturbed repose and tranquility to pure prayer, rapture, and union with God. But if we restrain the impulse to clean up Nikitas's intellectual house, we notice that there is indeed an order to his listing of the qualities of *hesychia*. It is a three-fold order or grouping of qualities according to the progression of faculties, experiences, methods. The first three describe the condition of the various faculties of the human being in the state of *hesychia*: the intellect or *nous*, the soul, and the heart; the next six qualities point to what the Hesychast will experience when his *nous*, soul, and heart are in a state of stillness, dispassion, and peace: contemplation of light, the knowledge of the mysteries of God, consciousness of wisdom when the *nous* is functioning as it should, the abyss of divine intellections, the rapture of the intellect, intercourse with God; the final three,

27. *The Philokalia,* Vol. 1, p. 180.
28. See footnote 17.
29. *The Philokalia,* Vol. 4, p. 124.

especially unsleeping watchfulness and pure prayer, seem to relate to the method and practice of *hesychia*, all leading ultimately to "solidarity and union with God". This progression that we see in Nikitas, from the faculties of the soul, through experiences, to methods that educate and orient the faculties to receive the experiences, is representative of the whole of the *Philokalia*.

Interrogating the Early Hesychasts: What is the Remembrance of God?

In order to approach how the early Hesychast Fathers understood the remembrance of God, we need to address to them the following three simple questions so that we might begin to approximate their own attitude toward the remembrance of God. How do the Hesychasts understand: 1) What or Who is being remembered? 2) Who is doing the remembering? 3) What is the nature of the act of remembering itself? Another way of formulating these three questions is: 1) What or Who is present? 2) Who participates in this presence? 3) How is this participation accomplished or performed?

1) What or Who is being remembered? God, of course, and specifically the Divine Presence, which brings to the fore our previously discussed question of essence versus person. Do we experience the Essence of God or the Person of God in the experience of the Presence of God? How is God understood by the Hesychasts? Let St Dionysios the Areopagite, the first of the traditional authorities mentioned in the Hagioritic Tome, speak for the entire Hesychast tradition. God is

> the inscrutable One [who] is out of reach of every rational process. Nor can any words come up to the inexpressible Good, this One, this unity unifying every unity, this supra-existent Being. Mind beyond mind, word beyond speech, it is gathered up by no discourse, by no intuition, by no name. It is, and It is as no other being is. Cause of all existence, and therefore itself transcending existence, it alone could give an authoritative account of what it really is. . . . We must not dare to apply words and conceptions to this hidden, transcendent God. We can use only what Scripture has disclosed. . . . For the truth is that everything divine and even everything revealed to us is known only by way of whatever share of them is granted. Their actual nature, what they are ultimately in their own source and ground, is beyond all intellect and all being

> and all knowledge. When, for instance, we give the name of "God" to that transcendent hiddenness, when we call it "life or "being" or "light" or "Word", what our minds lay hold of is nothing other than certain activities apparent to us, activities which deify, cause being, bear life, and give wisdom. For our part, as we consider that hiddenness and struggle to break free of all the working of our minds, we find ourselves witnessing no divinization, no life, no being which bears any real likeness to the absolutely transcendent Cause of all things. Or, again we learn from the sacred scriptures that the Father is the originating source of the Godhead, and that the Son and the Spirit are, so to speak, divine offshoots, the flowering and transcendent lights of the divinity. But we can neither say nor understand how this could be so.[30]

The meaning of this passage pivots on the insight that for the Hesychast, God is forever beyond human knowledge, and yet He somehow reveals Himself to those who seek Him with fervency and constancy. Further, though forever beyond human knowledge, to the Hesychasts of the Christian East, God is forever present, not as transpersonal Essence, as traditionalist/Sufi metaphysics would have it, but as trans-essential Person. This is the true meaning of the Hesychasts' "extreme trinitarianism", which insists that the absolute Divine Essence, although totally beyond-being, is not an impersonal or non-personalized principle that transcends everything sequent to it, but subsists only as it is "enhypostasized" in the three Persons of the Trinity. For the Hesychasts, the Divine Personhood enhypostasizing the Divine Essence is the absolutely transcendent principle, not the Divine Essence as an unhypostasized principle standing alone. The Trinity expresses the primacy of the Person of God over the Divine Essence in the experience of His Presence. Person, not Essence, is the ultimate mystery. For the Hesychasts, then, the Absolute is not transpersonal, but trans-essential.

2) The certainty of the Hesychast that God is supremely present as Person leads us to the second question: Who is doing the remembering? The answer given by the Hesychasts is that the created person who is made in the image and likeness of God is capable of remembering God precisely because, like God, he is a *person*. A person is a mystery, never totally circumscribed by a definition, that

30. *The Divine Names,* 1:1; 2:7. Trans. Colm Luibheid in *Pseudo-Dionysius: The Complete Works* (Mahwah, NJ: Paulist Press, 1987), pp. 50, 63-64.

is, as an essence or a "what". A person is not a "what" but a "who", and "who" you are, just as Who God is, is ultimately indefinable, undetermined, and of infinite depth. To say "what" something is, is to circumscribe that something in terms of essence or essential definition; to say "who" is to speak, not of some "thing" which can be defined in terms of its essence, but of some "one", an ultimately uncircumscribable and indefinable "who". To say "one" in this sense is to say "who" not "what". In this same sense, then, the Absolute One is the ultimately uncircumscribable, undetermined, indefinable Who, who is "infinitely beyond all being, potentiality, and actualization".[31] Person transcends essence: this is the heart of the highest metaphysics of Christian *theologia*, not to be confused with the "sentimental metaphysics" that some Sufi traditionalists call theology. Yet the one made in God's image may only approach God's Presence when his personhood becomes like God's Presence, that is, when his "who" becomes like God's "Who". Put in terms of Hesychastic methodology, the human presence may be able to stand in the Divine Presence when the potentiality of the likeness to God inherent in the nature of the created person has been activated by acts of purification, asceticism, and prayer. As St Gregory of Nazianzos, called the Theologian[32] by the Orthodox tradition, also one of the authorities cited by the Hagioritic Tome, declares in one of his fiery sermons:

> It seems to me that, through what is perceived, he attracts me to him (for the one who is totally unperceived gives no hope and no help): and through what is unperceived, he stirs up my admiration; and being admired, he is longed for again; and being longed for, he cleanses us; and cleansing us, he gives us his divine image; and so becoming, he speaks with us like with his household; the word (Scripture) even dares say something bolder; God unites himself with gods and is known by them, namely as much as he

31. St Maximos the Confessor, "First Century of Theology", 2, *The Philokalia*, Vol. 2, p. 114.
32. To be called "theologian" in the Orthodox tradition is a term of the highest respect, and has been given by the tradition to only three saints: St John the Divine, the author of the Fourth Gospel, St Gregory of Nazianzos, and St Symeon the New Theologian. Evagrios in the 4th century gave the key definition: "If you are a theologian, you will pray truly; and if you pray truly you are a theologian" (*On Prayer*, 61). A theologian in the Orthodox sense thus does not designate an academic or clerical professional, but refers to a master of prayer.

> knows those who know him. Therefore God is infinite and difficult to be contemplated. And only this is perceived of him: infinity.[33]

The presence of God as transcendent and uncreated Person, then, is not the conclusion of a rational judgment, but is experienced by a created person in a state of heightened or purified spiritual sensibility, and this cannot come about so long as the soul is dominated by passions of any kind. Transcendent Person gives itself to created person through an uncreated grace in which the created person participates according to the degree of his or her purification and illumination. This participation occurs through the synergy of the benevolence of the Transcendent Person and the efforts of the created person. The ultimate meaning and purpose of the human person created by God is the capacity to participate in the reality of the Divine Transcendent Person through the uncreated energies and attributes of Divine grace. Plato says that time is the moving image of eternity; Blake says that eternity is in love with the productions of time. The Hesychasts embrace both Plato and Blake by saying that time participates in eternity through the love of Divine Person and human person. As St Maximos the Confessor teaches, in a passage from his "Centuries on Theology", which was also quoted in the Hagioritic Tome:

> All immortal things and immortality itself, all living things and life itself, all holy things and holiness itself, all good things and goodness itself, all blessings and blessedness itself, all beings and being itself are manifestly works of God. Some things began to be in time, for they have not always existed. Others did not begin to be in time, for goodness, blessedness, holiness, and immortality have always existed. Those things which began to be in time exist and are said to exist by participation in the things which did not begin in time.[34]

3) Finally we come to the third question we need to ask the Hesychast fathers. What is the nature of the act of remembering as it relates to God? Given the presuppositions of Divine unknowability and yet the human requirement to remember God, what does the remembrance of God mean in the Hesychast tradition? Does it

33. St Gregory the Theologian, *Oration* 38:7, PG 36—317 CD; quoted from Dumitru Staniloae, *The Experience of God* (Brookline, MA: Holy Cross Orthodox Press, 1994), p. 101.

34. "First Century on Theology", 50, *The Philokalia*, Vol. 2, p. 124.

mean merely keeping the thought of God in the mind as much as one can? Does remembering God mean simply an act of praying to God? If you say the name of God repeatedly with your voice or in your mind, is that what remembering God means? When you are saying the word "God", are you then in the act of remembering God, and when you are not saying the word "God" vocally or mentally, are you no longer in the Presence of God because you have forgotten God? Above all, God being God, that is, the Divine Nature being what it is, infinite, ineffable, unknowable, does the word "remember" in the Hesychast's vocabulary have the ordinary meaning of calling back into the memory what has been forgotten, in the everyday manner of recalling a feeling one used to feel or, better, a person one used to know, or does it have a special, technical or mystical meaning? Or both?

St Mark the Monk, called in the *Philokalia* the Ascetic, in his work "On Those who Think that They are Made Righteous by Works: Two Hundred and Twenty-six Texts", provides a definition of the remembrance of God that is so simple, supple, and perfect that it is well-nigh inexhaustible. I have been reflecting on this passage for many years, and I have found simply no end to its depth:

> The remembrance of God is suffering of heart endured in a spirit of devotion. But he who forgets God becomes self-indulgent and insensitive.[35]

When we look closely at this passage, we notice that it is divided into two sections, in a manner similar to the Book of Proverbs. There is a thesis, a positive statement of what the remembrance of God consists in, followed by its antithesis, a statement about the opposite of the remembrance of God. The focus of the thesis is on the optimum attitude that will lead to experience of the remembrance of God. It also gives some indication of the qualities by which the remembrance of God may be known, what the remembrance of God will feel like from within. The statement of antithesis is also focused on experience, the experience of forgetting God. It tells us that forgetfulness of God inevitably and unfailingly produces in the soul a state of self-indulgence and insensitivity.

The thesis contains five elements: remembrance, God, the heart, suffering of heart, and endurance in a spirit of devotion.

35. "No Righteousness by Works", 131, *The Philokalia*, Vol. 1, p. 137.

1) As for remembrance, we are beginning to get a sense that Hesychasts mean something far deeper, more active and all-embracing, than a simple act of calling something to mind in an ordinary sense. This is what we might expect since the remembrance is to be of God, and whatever is applied to God by the Hesychasts is to be understood and realized in a God-befitting way, that is, with a meaning that transcends all human analogies. Since all the other elements of St Mark's definition are included in the nature of such remembrance, we will not attempt a final summing up of remembrance until we have explored those elements in greater detail.

2) As for God, we have seen that the Hesychasts mean the tri-hypostatic Absolute, who is more perfectly understood to be the supreme trans-essential Person instead of the transpersonal Essence. As supreme and transcendent Person, God is "everywhere present and fills all things", and yet is not perceived by the soul when its powers are sullied and atrophied by the passions and sins of our fallen state.

3) As for the heart, the Hesychasts understand it to be the metaphysical center of our being. The heart is the deep, supra-natural center in each person where God sends forth the Spirit of his Son, who cries out, "Abba, Father" (Gal 4:6). "Truly," says St Macarios, "the heart is an immeasurable abyss",[36] with inner chambers and depths beyond the capacity of a consciousness untransmuted by spiritual struggle and God's grace. The heart is God's throne, and if, through the remembrance of God, we allow God to take his seat upon it, then, as St Macarios says:

> If you become God's throne and He Himself takes His seat on it; if your whole soul is a spiritual eye, all light; if you nourish yourself on the sustenance of the Spirit and drink living water and the spiritual wine that rejoices the heart; if you clothe your soul in ineffable light—if inwardly you attain full assurance of all these things, then you will live the truly eternal life, reposing in Christ while still in this present world.[37]

In other words, the heart is, as St Philotheos of Sinai states, the "place of God" in the human microcosm, which, when God dwells

36. St Symeon Metaphrastis, "Paraphrase of the Homilies of St. Macarios of Egypt", *Philokalia*, Vol. 3, p. 321.
37. *Ibid.*, Vol 3, p. 317.

within it as He desires, is "the heaven of the heart",[38] but when the gate to the heart is left unguarded and it is surrounded with the dark and fetid clouds of sin, the heart becomes a tomb where, as St Macarios says, our thoughts and our intellect are buried, imprisoned in heavy darkness.[39] But with the invocation of the Name of Jesus, the heart, once a hellish tomb and a prison for the soul and the *nous*, now becomes the blessed prison and tomb into which the risen Christ descends to free the captives, our soul and spirit.

4) As for the "suffering of heart" in St Mark's definition of the remembrance of God, the emphasis upon suffering in the thesis statement is surprising to our modern mentality, even counterintuitive. In our ordinary understanding of things, or even in a religious attitude of piety in the best sense, we would expect to be told that the remembrance of God will make us happy, reconciled with God, secure in His love, comforted by His presence. Instead we are told that the remembrance of God is "suffering of heart" which must be "endured", even "endured in a spirit of devotion". Not only must we suffer, but we also must be thankful for it! We come to God expecting to be comforted and consoled and justified; but the Hesychast tells us that there is no remembrance of God without suffering of heart, and, furthermore, strongly implies that our desire to come to God without suffering is actually self-indulgence and even insensitivity, because we are not remembering God at all. We will attempt to penetrate the meaning of this seeming paradox further.

5) As for "endured in a spirit of devotion", would not the spirit of devotion be more fully revealed by approaching God through remembering His blessings, His promises to the righteous, His great mercy and goodness? Is this emphasis upon suffering not an example of that self-flagellating, anti-life attitude that Christianity is often accused of promoting, a kind of moral sickness of religion based upon a notion of a vengeful, judging Deity whom we must placate by our willingness to suffer? In answer St Mark might say: Please observe that I did not say physical sufferings are necessary to remember God. I said the remembrance of God is suffering of *heart*, and not merely the heart's suffering—suffering of heart endured

38. "Forty Texts on Watchfulness", *The Philokalia*, Vol. 3, p. 17.
39. *The Philokalia*, Vol. 3, p. 337.

with a spirit of devotion.[40] The focus of the remembrance of God is upon the heart as the center of man's being, and "the spirit of devotion" refers to that combination of compunction, compassion, concentration, and contemplation that transforms the heart into a temple of God.

In the ascetico-spiritual psychology of the *Philokalia*, then, the difference between Godly or conscious suffering and worldly or passionate suffering, unconscious of its true purpose, is identical to the difference between light and darkness. As revealed in the writings in the *Philokalia*, the suffering of heart that the Hesychasts know to be the basis of the remembrance of God has three dimensions: 1) Godly sorrow or inner pain in the soul that is based on true recognition of one's sinfulness when seen in the pure light of the Divine beauty; 2) the suffering that comes from the remembrance of death that is so closely associated with mindfulness of God; and 3) the "suffering" of the Divine, in the sense of the passive reception of the indwellingness of Christ that creates a state of ecstasy. With the help of selected passages from the early Hesychast Fathers, we shall touch briefly on each of these dimensions of the suffering of heart.

Suffering of Heart: The Godly Sorrow that Leads to Spiritual Knowledge (*Gnosis*) of God

Why is a suffering heart necessary for the remembrance of God? The answer of Hesychasm is practical, not theoretical in an abstract sense. The way of the Hesychasts is based entirely on the acquisition of authentic knowledge of and participation in the experience of God. The spirituality of the Hesychasts thus has a two-fold dimension, consisting of an exact discernment between That which alone is reality and that which is illusory, and an unceasing concentration

40. St John Klimakos, with his characteristic dash, says the thought that God is tenderhearted, for the person seeking freedom from slavery to sin and the passions, is a temptation that leads to self-indulgence: "Never, when mourning for your sins, accept that cur which suggests to you that God is tenderhearted (this thought is useful only when you see yourself being dragged down to deep despair). For the aim of the enemy is to thrust from you your mourning and fearless fear" (*The Ladder of Divine Ascent* [Brookline, MA: Holy Transfiguration Monastery, 1979], pp. 66-70.) This is not a denial of the Divine Mercy, but an application of a basic principle of unseen warfare: be suspicious of any thought that suggests to you that you may relax your vigilance in this life.

upon the Reality (that is, the Presence of God). The remembrance of God requires both exact discernment and unceasing concentration. St Mark writes:

> Without remembrance of God, there can be no true knowledge but only that which is false.[41]

This is discernment. In another work, St Mark writes, as a corollary to the above:

> Even though knowledge is true, it is still not firmly established if unaccompanied by works. For everything is established by being put into practice.[42]

This is praxis, the methodic and unceasing concentration upon the real Presence of God through the three-fold method of purification or praxis, illumination or *theoria* (contemplative vision), and deification or perfection or union with God. Throughout the whole of the *Philokalia*, from the Desert Fathers to Palamas, this spirituality of knowledge (*gnosis*) and experience (*peira*) is the very quintessence of the path to the heart of the Hesychasts. From this perspective of discernment and concentration, the early Hesychast Fathers developed a precise and penetrating spiritual psychology, involving an exact method of psycho-therapy (using this word in its literal sense of the healing of the soul) through which the pathology of the spiritual sickness of the fallen human state could be transformed into the transfigured state of the deified saint. The core of the pathology of our fallen state is ignorance and forgetfulness of God, the primary "symptoms" of which are slothful self-indulgence and a hardened insensitivity to spiritual reality. The cure for this pathology of ignorance and forgetfulness and slothfulness is the remembrance of God, and the method of cure is the invocation of the Name of Jesus.

The insensitivity of a heart that has forgotten God must, on the one hand, be pierced, shocked, blown open, broken apart. "The sacrifices of God are a broken spirit: a broken and contrite heart, O God, thou wilt not despise" (Ps 50:17). "The kingdom of heaven suffereth violence, and the violent take it by force" (Mt 11:12). On the other hand, although the invocation of the Divine Name tends to blow away the fog of forgetfulness with the Spirit's mighty wind, we

41. "On the Spiritual Law", 147, *The Philokalia*, Vol. 1, p. 120.
42. "No Righteousness by Works", 12, *The Philokalia*, Vol. 1, p. 126.

must not overemphasize the violence of this experience, for the Hesychasts distinguish between the healing power of Godly suffering which fills the soul with the gentle warmth of compunction, kindling a holy fire in the heart that burns up the passions and illuminates the soul, and the violent, destructive quality of the passionate suffering of a soul bound in the darkness of ignorance, forgetfulness, sloth, and self-love. St Mark shows the traditional Hesychast concern for balance and sobriety in the healing of the heart:

> There is a breaking of the heart which is gentle and makes it deeply penitent, and there is a breaking which is violent and harmful, shattering it completely. Vigils, prayer, and patient acceptance of what comes constitute a breaking that does not harm but benefits the heart, provided we do not destroy the balance between them through excess. He who perseveres in them will be helped in other ways as well; but he who is slack and negligent will suffer intolerably on leaving this life. A self-indulgent heart becomes a prison and chain for the soul when it leaves this life; whereas an assiduous heart is an open door.[43]

Suffering in the spiritual or metaphysical heart is an inner pain or sorrow that is grounded in the searing consciousness of direct perception of the Divine Presence. It is not a worldly sorrow or depression, which is a negative state that leads to despair and psychological paralysis. Quite the contrary, it is a "joy-making mourning" that produces great strength, energy, and inspiration in the soul.

In regard to Godly sorrow, a later passage of St Mark in the same work gives some indication of what he means by linking the remembrance of God with suffering of heart, and is itself characteristic of the ascetical ethos of the Hesychasts:

> If you wish to remember God unceasingly, do not reject as undeserved what happens to you, but patiently accept it as your due. For patient acceptance of whatever happens kindles the remembrance of God, whereas refusal to accept weakens the spiritual purpose of the heart and so makes it forgetful.[44]

Like all true ascetics and spiritual masters, St Mark is highly attuned to discerning the effect upon the "tone" of the soul of various thoughts, practices, and activities. If there is no remembering of

43. "On the Spiritual Law", 18-20, *op.cit.*, p. 111.
44. *Ibid.*, 134, p. 136.

God without suffering of heart, then the otherwise natural human tendency of the avoidance of suffering or resisting or refusing to accept the will of God in what happens to one sets a tone of self-indulgence, weakens the spiritual purpose of the heart, makes the soul forgetful of God and concerned with itself, creating a condition of self-love as the dominant force in the soul, which produces the insensitivity referred to in the antithesis portion of St Mark's definition. St John Klimakos calls this state, produced by self-love, "stony insensibility": and St Maximos the Confessor calls the self-love (*philautia*) that produces this insensitivity the mother of all passions and vices.[45]

In support of the suffering of heart endured with a spirit of devotion that is the doorway to the remembrance of God, we turn now to one of most profound of the early Hesychast Fathers, St Diadochos of Photiki, who lived in the 5th century. His work entitled "On Spiritual Knowledge and Discrimination" possesses a subtitle in Greek that reads: "Explaining what kind of spiritual knowledge we need in order to reach, under the Lord's guidance, the perfection which He has revealed, so that each of us may apply to himself the parable of deliverance and bring to fruition the seed which is the Logos".[46] St Diadochos writes:

> Those who wish to live virtuously should not hanker after praise, be involved with too many people, keep going out, or abuse others (however much they deserve it), or talk excessively, even if they can speak well on every subject. Too much talk radically dissipates the intellect (*nous*), not only making it lazy in spiritual work but also handing it over to the demon of listlessness (*acedia*), who first enervates it completely and then passes it on to the demons of dejection and anger. The intellect should therefore devote itself continually to keeping the holy commandments and to deep mindfulness of the Lord of Glory. . . . When the heart feels the arrows of the demons with such burning pain that the man under attack suffers as if they were real arrows, then the soul hates the passions violently, for it is just beginning to be purified. If it does not suffer greatly at the shamelessness of sin, it will not be able to rejoice fully in the blessings of righteousness. He who wishes to cleanse his heart should keep it continually aflame through prac-

45. St Maximos the Confessor, "Four Hundred Texts on Love", 2:8, 2:59, 3:56-57, *The Philokalia*, Vol. 2, pp. 66, 75, 92.
46. St. Diadochos of Photiki, "On Spiritual Knowledge and Discrimination: One Hundred Texts", *The Philokalia*, Vol. 1, p. 253.

> ticing the remembrance of the Lord Jesus, making this his only study and ceaseless task. Those who desire to free themselves from their corruption ought to pray not merely from time to time but at all times; they should give themselves always to prayer, keeping watch over their intellect even when outside places of prayer. When someone is trying to purify gold, and allows the fire of the furnace to die down even for a moment, the material which he is purifying will harden again. So, too, a man who merely practices the remembrance of God from time to time loses through lack of continuity what he hopes to gain through his prayer. It is a mark of one who truly loves holiness that he continually burns up what is worldly in his heart through practicing the remembrance of God, so that little by little evil is consumed in the fire of this remembrance and his soul completely recovers its natural brilliance with still greater glory.[47]

St Diadochos points out that too much talk, and by implication too much discursive conceptualizing about God, leads to the complete enervation of the *nous*/intellect. But deep mindfulness, by which we should understand the total concentration of the soul's powers of attention upon the remembrance of God, coupled with a total effort to keep the commandments, will lead the soul to feel such deep compunction that it will experience temptations and demonic attacks as burning pain, and as violent hatred for its bondage to the contra-natural passions. Then the heart, practicing *nepsis,* that is, intensely attentive to every psychic and spiritual movement within, will suffer greatly because of the presence within itself of the shamelessness of sin. The suffering described here by St Diadochos in such dynamic, almost vehement, terms is actually an increased awareness and sensitivity to the spiritual world. Suffering of heart is the result of an elevated consciousness.

Sensitivity to the Spirit has, as we have seen, something to do with purification. Both St Mark and St Diadochos tell us that there is something "fiery" about the effect of the remembrance of God upon the soul. The remembrance of God is a burning flame that purifies the dross of the passions like a refiner's fire. Diadochos's metaphorical language of the refiner's fire leaves us with the impression that the suffering endured by the heart may have a real aspect of pain. In order to remember God the soul must be willing to see itself as it really is, to experience sorrow for its sins, and,

47. *Ibid.,* pp. 294-295.

above all, to be willing to endure an unprecedented intensification of its life of feeling, even if that intensification brings with it real pain. Indeed, without the suffering of heart that comes from the deepest compunction upon the recognition of the effect of sin in the soul, the soul will not be able to experience the transfiguration of grace that leads to righteousness and brings joy. We recall here once again that St John Klimakos calls this kind of sorrow for sin "joy-making mourning".

Suffering or pain in the ascetic sense *is* consciousness. Consciousness of sin for the Hesychasts is not a furtive guiltiness that diminishes one's wholeness of being, but a genuine higher level of awareness caused by Divine grace that is the indispensable first step toward true wholeness and healing. The transition from the pain of heart that comes from such a heightened consciousness of sin to "suffering" the Divine ingress in the heart in a state of transfigured joy comes through the portal of that suffering called the remembrance of death. On the path to the heart, mindfulness of death is the means by which the tongues of flame of true compunction are transformed into the rose petals of spiritual compassion.[48]

The Remembrance of Death: The Boundary between the Divine and the Human

The second dimension of the suffering of heart according to the Hesychasts is linked to the remembrance of death. The teaching of the Hesychast Fathers on the importance of the remembrance of death in the practice of the remembrance of God is striking in its unanimity and force. For the entire Philokalic tradition, the remembrance of death is indispensable. Here I must offer a cautionary note. The interest of the Hesychasts in remembering death is neither morbid nor merely pietistic. Its purpose is not to manipulate believers into moral conformity, as does the incessant dwelling on hellfire and punishment for sin of contemporary fundamentalist preachers. Admittedly, the early Hesychasts do insist that ascetics should contemplate the "dread judgment seat of Christ" and face resolutely the certainty of the four last things: "death, judgment, heaven, and hell"; but these injunctions are ascetical in nature, the

48. The lovely image of flames turning into rose petals is taken from George MacDonald's story "The Wise Woman".

purpose of which is to awaken the fear of the Lord, which is the beginning of wisdom and the foundation of all spiritual practice.

For the Hesychasts, the chief purpose of the contemplation of death is the awakening to knowledge and the transformation of consciousness that comes with the breaking of the power of forgetfulness in the soul. And there is something beyond even this. The more one reads these writings, the more one gets the sense that the great Hesychast elders are not merely presenting a "technique" for the acquisition of Godly fear, but are above all describing what they actually experience when they approach the Divine, or better, when God approaches them. For example, St John Klimakos writes in *The Ladder of Divine Ascent*:

> And I cannot be silent about the story of Hesychios the Horebite. He passed his life in complete negligence, without paying the least attention to his soul. Then he became extremely ill, and for an hour he expired. And when he came to himself, he begged us all to leave him immediately. And he built up the door of his cell, and he stayed in it for twelve years without ever uttering a word to anyone, and without eating anything but bread and water. And, always remaining motionless, he was so rapt in spirit at what he had seen in his ecstasy that he never changed this manner of life but was always as if out of his mind, and silently shed hot tears. But when he was about to die, we broke open the door and went in, and after many questions, this alone was all we heard from him: "Forgive me! No one who has acquired the remembrance of death will ever be able to sin." We were amazed to see that one who had before been so negligent was so suddenly transfigured by this blessed change and transformation.[49]

Here we have an account of a negligent monk from the Sinai desert who endured what today would be called a "near death" experience. We are not told the nature of that experience. We are told that it transformed his life, opened the door to *hesychia*, freed him completely from slavery to the passions, rapt him away from total forgetfulness into a state of ceaseless remembrance, and gave him the power to remain without sin until his own death. Is it only a strong dose of fear that could change a man so completely? Fear alone, that is, a worldly fear based on a selfish interest in one's own well-being, could hardly account for his behavior over so long a time, for

49. St John Klimakos, *The Ladder of Divine Ascent*, Step 6: "On Remembrance of Death".

self-centered fear dissipates quickly when the immediate occasion for fear is removed. To live for twelve years in total seclusion and silence, that is, in complete *hesychia*, demands a level of consciousness, a power of will, and a spiritual sensibility of an entirely different order. St John alludes to this when he speaks of Hesychios being "rapt in spirit", "as if out of his mind", in an "ecstasy" in which he shed "hot tears". All of these terms have specific technical meaning in the "psycho-therapeutic" vocabulary of Hesychasm.

In particular, what the Hesychasts call the "gift of tears" is a sign of the grace of God that awakens in the soul heart-transforming compunction and true prayer through the remembrance of death that closely accompanies the remembrance of God. We could cite many texts from the early Hesychasts on this point. Let St Hesychios the Priest and St Isaac the Syrian speak for all of them. St Hesychios in the following passage links purity of heart, Godly sorrow, tears, and mindfulness of death:

> If we preserve, as we should, that purity of heart or watch and guard of the intellect whose image is the New Testament, this will not only uproot all passions and evils from our hearts; it will also introduce joy, hopefulness, compunction, sorrow, tears, an understanding of ourselves and of our sins, mindfulness of death, true humility, unlimited love of God and man, and an intense and heartfelt longing for the divine.[50]

The remembrance of death is not just a "mind-control" technique to quell the restless antics of the "monkey-mind",[51] but is the actual experience of being at the boundary between time and eternity. Death is a crossing of the boundary between the present life and eternal life. St Isaac the Syrian, in a striking passage, reveals the gift of tears as a sign of the boundary equally between the body and the spirit, between the death of soul in the passions and the purity of heart which is true life, and between this present age and the age to come, which is present in the here and now through the remem-

50. "On Watchfulness and Holiness", 113, *The Philokalia*, Vol 1, p. 181.

51. I refer here to the comparison found in Sufic writings between the ordinary mind and the mind of the Sufi: the former is like the antics of a monkey chained to a post; the latter is like the path of a bird which periodically changes its level of flight. Similar observations may be found in Hesychast writings; this understanding is particularly prominent in the writings of St Symeon the New Theologian.

brance of death. Forgetfulness of death is the spiritual death of the soul buried in the passions:

> Tears are established for the mind as a kind of boundary between what is bodily and what is spiritual and between passionateness and purity. Until a man receive this gift, the activity of his work is still in the outer man and he has not yet at all perceived the activity of the hidden things of the spiritual man. But when a man begins to relinquish the corporeal things of the present age and crosses this boundary to that which lies inside of visible nature, then straightway he will attain to the grace of tears. And for the first hospice of this hidden discipline tears begin to flow and they lead a man to perfection in the love of God.... This therefore is the exact sign that the mind has left this world and perceived that spiritual world. But the more a man draws near in his mind to the present world, the more tears subside. And when his mind is totally enmeshed in the world, a man is totally deprived of these tears. This is a sign that a man is completely buried in the passions.[52]

St Isaac, one of the greatest lights in the Hesychast tradition, follows that tradition in making a precise distinction between the outer man and the inner man (*eso anthropos*).[53] The outer man for the Hesychasts is not the body alone but every thought, feeling, or sensation that is bound to or, better, buried in, the *kosmos aisthetos* or the physical universe, or, speaking in terms of time rather than space, everything connected with "this present age". The inner man cannot be identified with the emotions alone or with what today we might call the "personality" or the "individuality". The inner man is the interior spiritual cosmos, the center of which is the heart.

St John Klimakos underscores the indispensability of the remembrance of death, for those who practice *hesychia,* in the following passage:

52. *The Ascetical Homilies of St Isaac the Syrian* (Brookline, MA: Holy Transfiguration Monastery, 1984), p. 174.
53. The traditional teaching of the *eso-anthropos,* which in Christianity is rooted in the Gospels and the Pauline Epistles and transmitted to us through the Patristic and Hesychastic Fathers, is the authentic basis of the esoteric dimension in Christianity. The esoteric, far from a distortion of the Christian tradition, as sometimes thought, is central to the expression of, and participation in, the fullness of the truth of Christianity, as long as we understand "esoteric" not in terms of a secret teaching arbitrarily limited to a chosen few, but as the inner dimension of the spiritual cosmos, open to all through the heart, the center of the inner man, in which the eschatological realities of the future are ever-present, but which requires a total commitment to the way of the cross.

> As of all foods, bread is the most essential, so the thought of death is the most necessary of all works. The remembrance of death amongst those in the midst of society gives birth to distress and meditation, and even more to despondency. But amongst those who are free from noise, it produces the putting aside of cares and constant prayer and guarding of the mind. But these same virtues both produce the remembrance of death, and are also produced by it.[54]

Note that here again the saint makes a distinction between a remembering of death that is worldly and the remembrance of death of the Hesychasts (those who are free from noise). Just as there is a worldly suffering that produces despondency, depression, and despair, so too the dwelling on the thought of death for those still caught up in self-love and the passions produces morbidity, depression, and suicidal despondency. This is so because their primary motivation is self-love, by which they seek to pursue pleasure and avoid pain. The thought of the inevitability of death produces in all such people a debilitating depression. Depression of soul is always a sign of the absence of God, which makes the God-shaped abyss in the heart that is God's throne seem like an infinite emptiness in the soul, so hard to bear. But for those seeking to remember God through attention and *hesychia*, the remembrance of death is an awakening that produces Godly sorrow, which turns into tears of joy precisely because God, their heart's true desire, is near. The nearness of God inflicts the heart first with sorrow because the spiritual impurities in the soul are thrown into sharp relief in the light of the Divine Presence; followed by the relief of soul that comes with detachment from sinful selfishness and the burning up of the passions; and culminating in joy and peace beyond all telling, which is the "peace that passeth all understanding".[55] St Philotheos of Sinai even describes the remembrance of death in terms of beauty, ecstasy, and being enraptured:

> Having once experienced the beauty of this mindfulness of death, I was so wounded and delighted by it—in spirit, not through the eye—that I wanted to make it my life's companion; for I was enraptured by its loveliness and majesty, its humility and contrite joy, by how full of reflection it is, how apprehensive of the judgment to

54. St John Klimakos, *The Ladder of Divine Ascent*, Step 6: "On Remembrance of Death".
55. Phil 4:7.

> come, and how aware of life's anxieties. It makes life-giving, healing tears flow from our bodily eyes, while from our noetic eyes rises a fount of wisdom that delights the mind.[56]

Remembrance of death for the Hesychasts always corresponds to the teaching of St Paul, who speaks of the fact that when we are present in the body we are absent from the Lord. Being "present in the body" is not merely a way of saying being alive, but of living as though the source of life were the body, the world, and the self, which from the perspective of eternity is actually a living death. When the Lord approaches—when, that is, the Lord becomes present to us—then the opposite takes place, and we become absent from the body and present to the Lord.[57] To know the Lord's Presence, to be present to the Lord, requires dying to the world and all self-centered concerns for survival. This is the dying that leads to true life. This alternation between absence and presence in the body and to the Lord is precisely the spiritual boundary that we approach by the remembrance of death, and why the Hesychasts deem mindfulness of death indispensable to the remembrance of God. Let us listen to St Hesychios the Priest, who writes:

> The unremitting remembrance of death is a powerful trainer for body and soul. Vaulting over all that lies between ourselves and death, we should always visualize it, and even the very bed on which we shall breathe our last, and everything else connected with it.[58]

And again from St Hesychios:

> Whenever possible, we should always remember death, for this displaces all cares and vanities, allowing us to guard our intellect and giving us unceasing prayer, detachment from our body, and hatred of sin. Indeed, it is a source of almost every virtue. We should therefore, if possible, use it as we use our own breathing.[59]

For St Diadochos of Photiki, the remembrance of death is the only sure way to bring us to the remembrance of God:

> We should also think about death when the demons that attack the body try to make our hearts seethe with shameful desires, for only

56. St Philotheos of Sinai, "Texts on Watchfulness", *The Philokalia,* Vol. 3, pp. 17-18.
57. 2 Cor 5:1-11.
58. "On Watchfulness and Holiness", 95, *The Philokalia,* Vol. 1, p. 178.
59. *Ibid.,* pp. 189-190.

> the thought of death can nullify all the various influences of the evil spirits by bringing us back to the remembrance of God.[60]

To remember death, then, is not the cringing of a slave before an implacable and all-powerful lord who has the power to torture and kill him, but an awakening from the sleep of forgetfulness. Godly remembrance of death is like a release from a spell that has put the soul to sleep, a sleep that is a kind of waking death. Indeed, the remembrance of death is the beginning of the supreme Awakening that awaits all human beings as their final destiny. It is, for the Hesychast, that is, for the Christian practitioner of attention and the guarding of the heart, an entirely positive experience (although it may not at first be pleasant). The remembrance of death is above all an awakening to authentic life. True awakening to the reality of death—not merely the reality of the fact of our mortality, but the reality of what lies behind, beyond, and above death as a transition of states—causes the Godly fear known in Scripture as the "fear of the Lord", which fills the soul with power, resolve, nobility, and ultimately the "peace that passeth all understanding".[61] Without awakening, there is no possibility of remembering; without waking up to the remembrance of death, there can be no authentic experience of the remembrance of God, but only the idolization of words and concepts about God. The remembrance of death is thus the experience of the boundary between the Divine and the human.

Remembering as Ecstasy: "Suffering" the Divine

In connection with the meaning and function of "suffering of heart" in the Hesychastic remembrance of God, there is another meaning of the word "suffer" which was well known to the early Hesychasts through personal experience, and which shows the hidden depths or dimensions in the remembrance of God. To suffer is not only to experience disagreeable sensations or feelings; it also carries the meaning of to bear or to endure, to experience in a receptive or passive manner. The Greek *paschein*, which means to suffer and also to be passive, is the root of the word for the passions. In Hesychasm there is both a good passivity and a bad passivity.

60. "On Spiritual Knowledge", p. 282.
61. Phil 4:7.

When the soul is enslaved by sin or, as St Maximos puts it, the law of sin, it is slavishly in the thrall of the passions, which are acting in it contrary to nature. This is the evil passivity of the soul. But when the soul is under the influence of uncreated grace, or when the Divine Presence overwhelms the soul, then it is also passive, that is, receptive to the grace of God, the energies of the Divine acting in the receptive soul. This is the good, deifying passivity of the saints.

St Dionysios the Areopagite, in speaking of his spiritual father, the holy Hierotheos, declared that he "not only learned, but suffered Divine things".[62] In the writings of Dionysios there is an emphasis upon human and creaturely passivity before the Divine action (*energeia*). Maximos also had this understanding. Following Dionysios, and speaking not of an individual person but of the whole of rational creation, and by implication the entire cosmos, he writes, "It is for creatures to be moved to the unoriginate end, to rest their operations in the unquantitative perfect end, and to suffer, but not to be, or to become substantially, the unqualified." It is the nature of the created order to receive (that is, suffer) creation. "Whatever comes to be, suffers, receiving movement, as not being self-motion, self-power," says Maximos.[63] The creation itself suffers the Divine energies at the root of its very existence. Existence itself in its true nature is a kind of ecstasy. No wonder the birds sing the way they do!

Now we come to something really interesting, indeed, one might call it "mind-boggling", and in doing so one would not be outside the vocabulary of Hesychasm! If the very existence of creation is a kind of cosmic ecstasy, the act of creating the cosmos is, according to Dionysios, a kind of ecstasy on the part of God. The relationship between the Uncreated and creation is one of mutual or reciprocal ecstasies.[64] The Divine, says Dionysios, "descends to immanence by means of an ecstatic and supra-essential power while remaining within itself".[65] The notion of the "suffering" of Divinity

62. *Divine Names*, 2:9—648B.

63. *The Earlier Ambigua of St Maximus the Confessor and His Refutation of Origenism*, trans. Polycarp Sherwood (Rome: Herder/Orbis Catholicus, 1955), pp. 128-129. *Ambiguum* 7—1073B7-11.

64. See, for a good discussion of the reciprocal ecstasies of God and creation, Alexander Golitzin, *Et Introibo ad Altare Dei: The Mystagogy of Dionysius Areopagitica* (Thessaloniki: Patriarchikon Idrima Paterikon Meleton, 1994).

65. *Divine Names*, 4:12—712B; see Golitzin, *op. cit.*, p. 48.

here points both ways, both to the ecstasy of the creature in its encounter with God and the "ecstasy" of God in his loving condescension to his creature. God in communion with His creature is no longer God in Himself, but God, as it were, "outside" of Himself, says the Areopagite. God "brings essences into being by means of an out-going from essence".[66] The metaphor of the downward ecstasy of God is balanced by the upward ecstasy of the creature.

This remarkable Hesychast concept of mutual ecstasy in the relationship between God and man, grounded in the ultimate relationship between the Uncreated and the created, also underlies the theory and practice of the early Hesychasts on the remembrance of God. When the created intellect/*nous* encounters God in reality, not in concept, word, or thought—that is, in the Divine darkness or, equally, in the unapproachable light proper to God and in the *agnosia* proper to the created intellect—the creature is no longer creature in itself, but in God, and hence, in the words of the Second Epistle of Peter, a "partaker of the Divine nature".[67] St Maximos the Confessor agrees, in a passage referring to the ecstatic suffering of the Divine by the Hesychast, and in language the meaning of which could refer either to the Divine or the human ecstasy in love:

> But if he acts intelligently, he also loves the object understood; but if he loves, he also surely suffers ecstasy towards it as loved; but if he suffers, it is clear he hastens on; but if he hastens on, he surely intensifies the vehemence of the motion; and if he intensifies the vehemence of motion, he does not stop till he has become entire in the whole loved object and is comprehended by the whole, himself willing by choice and accepting the saving circumscription.[68]

Maximos further explains, speaking clearly of the rational creature suffering God in ecstasy:

> I do not say that is the doing away of the freewill (*to autexousion*); rather it sets it up in accord with nature firm and immutable—that is, there is a voluntary outpassing (*ekoresis gnomiki*) that whence being comes to us; thence also we may desire to receive movement, as the image passes over to the archetype, and like a seal, is well adjusted to the signet, the archetype, and neither has nor can have

66. *Divine Names*, 5:8—824C, see Golitzin, p. 48.
67. 2 Pet 1:4.
68. *Ambiguum* 7—1073 C9-D4.

> anywhere else to be carried or, to speak more expressly and truly, being unable so to wish, as having laid hold of the Divine operation, nay, rather, becoming god by deification and delighted further by the being outside (*ti exstasei*) of those things that naturally belong to it or are thought about it. Because of the grace of the Spirit that conquers it and shows it alone to have God operating in it, so that there is in all only one operation, of God and the worthy ones, rather of God alone, inasmuch as he, after the manner of his goodness, entire, pervades the worthy entirely.[69]

In the last passage above we note how the Confessor employs this metaphysical principle, the radical distinction between the Uncreated and the creation manifesting as the receptivity and passivity of the created order—that is, the creature receiving its being, movement, and energy from God and God alone—as the very principle of deification, at once ontological, cosmological, and epistemological. The purpose, beginning, and end of creation is deification. Man "suffers" the uncreated grace and uncreated energies of God in a passively-active or actively-passive manner. Yet deification, Maximos insists, is not a natural power of human nature, but solely a gift of God, which human beings, those who have been made worthy by repentance and suffering of heart, receive from God by grace (the holy passivity) through the desire of their hearts (the godly activity). God moves human nature toward its divinizing end, as its beginningless beginning and endless end, and human nature, being so moved, is moved in accord with its nature as created by God, that is, intelligently, noetically, and "cardiatically". Human nature in the Divine intention is created to surpass itself, to reach out beyond itself, and in His Divine Providence and Love, God will reach down to lift human nature up to Himself. The energy of our human nature reaches out to the uncreated energy of God's grace. This "synergy" between Divine and human natures is insisted upon by Maximos and is the reason why he emphasizes that suffering the Divine does not entail the doing away of the free will. The whole of man, body, soul, spirit, intellect, and will, is deified without in any way violating the essence and freedom of any aspect of human nature. Maximos continues:

> The whole man is deified by the grace of God-made-man, remaining entirely man in soul and body by reason of his nature

69. *Ambiguum* 7—1076 B10-C13.

> and becoming entirely God in soul and body by reason of the grace and divine brightness of the blessed glory that quite becomes him, than which there is nothing brighter or more exalted to be conceived. For what to those that are worthy is more an object of love than deification, in which God, united to those that become gods, makes the universe his because of his goodness. Therefore such a state they well named pleasure, suffering, joy—(a state characterized) by godly understanding and the consequent fruition of gladness: pleasure indeed as the end of operations in accord with nature—for thus they define pleasure—suffering however as an ecstatic power, bringing over the suffering thing to the active, according to the reason already given in the example of air and light or of fire and iron, and persuading that apart from this, in nature and in truth, there is no other high point for things—upon which suffering dispassionateness necessarily follows, and finally joy, as having no element opposed to it either in the past or in the future.[70]

The "whole man is deified by the grace of God-made-man". In this phrase, St Maximos brings us to the very door to the heart of the invocatory path of Hesychasm. It is through God, as incarnate Person, that deification—the actual participation in the Divine nature—is made possible for humanity. And it is through the remembrance of God that the "process" of deification begins, although the experience of God—crossing of the boundary between created and Uncreated—cannot be adequately described as a process but as an epiphany or irruption of grace. God unites Himself to those made worthy by grace to become gods through this "process" of reciprocal ecstasy, in which the "whole man", body and soul, remains entirely man in soul and body according to his created nature, yet—and here one is struck by the boldness and certainty of the saint's language, holding nothing in reserve—becoming entirely God in soul and body by reason of the grace and the Divine illumination through uncreated energies, which unite with him totally and "become" what he is. In this state, suffering becomes first dispassion then joy, becomes "active" while still remaining "passive", in a state otherwise called by St Maximos the "ever-moving rest" of those living in, participating in, the heaven "around" God.

70. *Ambiguum* 7—1088 C6-89A3.

Invocation of the Divine Name of Jesus as the Very "Heart" of the Remembrance of God

The reciprocity (*perichoresis,* in Greek) of Divine incarnation and human deification is central to the path to the heart of the Hesychasts. *Perichoresis* is the theological ground of the Jesus Prayer. St Maximos states this saving truth in a beautiful, lapidary expression of the very principle that grounds the invocation of the Divine Name of Jesus:

> We are told that God and man are exemplars of each other. Man's ability to deify himself through love for God's sake is correlative with God's becoming man through compassion for man's sake. And man's manifestation through the virtues of the God who is by nature invisible is correlative with the degree to which his intellect is seized by God and imbued with gnosis.[71]

This passage links the incarnation of God in Christ with the deification of humanity in Christ in the closest possible way. It is a restatement of the basic principle of deification as originally found in St Irenaeos and St Athanasios: "God became man so that man might become a god", which is itself grounded in the two basic Scriptural warrants for deification: "I said you are gods and all of you sons of the Most High" (Ps 82:6); and "precious and very great promises have been granted to us, that through these you may become partakers of the divine nature" (2 Pet 1:4). The principle of *perichoresis*—the reciprocity of incarnation/deification—is the basis of the Hesychasts' conviction that the surest means of receiving the deifying energy of the Holy Spirit is ceaseless mindfulness of God through the invocation of the Name of Jesus. The "new theandric energy" brought to us by Jesus who is God incarnate has established for all time the mutual interpenetration without confusion of the Divine and the human. As St Dionysios writes in his fourth letter:

> It was not by virtue of being God that [Jesus} did Divine things, not by virtue of his being a man that he did what was human, but rather, by the fact of being God-made-man, he accomplished a certain new theandric energy in our midst.[72]

This "new theandric energy" is the gift of divinizing participation in the Divine Presence in Jesus, and it is activated by invoking the

71. *Ambiguum* 10—1113B; *The Philokalia,* Vol. 2. p. 278.
72. *Epistle* IV—1072C.

hidden power of the Name of Jesus. To invoke the Divine Name of Jesus in the Jesus Prayer is to pray for the gift of the influx of this deifying energy. In the tradition of the Hesychasts, the practice of the remembrance of God through the Prayer of Jesus is at one and the same time preparation, participation, and performance of the Divine-human synergy of deification.

The Name of Jesus is the pre-eminent Divine Name for the Hesychasts because in it the entire mystery of existence is both hidden and revealed. Through the Name of Jesus flows the fullness of Divine Providence and Justice and Mercy to the whole creation; and through that sacred Name God saves man by becoming human so that the human might become deified. In that Name is hidden and revealed the full transcendence and immanence of God. To invoke the Name of Jesus is to pray "an effectual, fervent prayer" that "availeth much"[73] for the epiphany of God in the heart of a righteous man.

In the Quran there is a phrase much used by Sufis: "Whithersoever ye turn, there is the Face of God". The Hesychasts of the Christian East would agree entirely with the Quran at that point, but then they would add that Jesus is the very Face of God. Thus to invoke the Name of Jesus is ceaselessly to turn to the Face of God, Who in His incomprehensible love for mankind, His "philanthropy" as the Hesychasts say, ceaselessly turns His Face toward us.

I use the word "epiphany" in the context of remembering God through the invocation of the Name of Jesus, because, as suggested above, the remembrance of God is not a process, but an experience. We may rightly consider the method of invocation to be a procedure, but if we are following the lead of the early Hesychasts, it will be evident by now that they distinguish between the *process* of invocation and the *experience* of remembering God. Invocation begins on the "human margin" as a process or method of attention and guarding the heart, but remembering God is a matter of approaching or, better, being approached by the Divine Center, which is ever moving toward us, in the words of C. S. Lewis, "at infinite speed", which is just another way of saying that God is "everywhere present and fills all things". The experience of remembering God is always an epiphany, a sudden realization. The boundary

73. Jam 5:16.

between the Eternal and the temporal cannot be reached by a "gradual" approach. The infinite cannot be experienced by increments, but only all at once. God is not present by degrees.[74] Graduality is a function of time, while "the sudden" is a sign of time-transcendent Eternity. St Dionysios the Areopagite in his letters strikingly links the Name of Jesus with "the sudden":

> "The sudden" means that which is brought out of the hitherto invisible and beyond hope into the manifest. And I think that here the theology [i.e., sacred scripture] is suggesting the philanthropy of Christ. The super-essential has proceeded out of its hiddenness to become manifest to us by becoming a human being. But he is also hidden, both after the manifestation and, to speak more divinely, even within it. For this is the hidden Name of Jesus, and neither by reason nor by intellect can his mystery be brought forth, but instead even when spoken it remains ineffable, and when conceived unknowable.[75]

The Name of Jesus is the Divine Name par excellence because it contains both the super-essential (the "beyond-being") and the Divine manifestation. The Name contains the fullness of both the apophatic and cataphatic theological approaches to God. In the Name of Jesus, transcendence and immanence are simultaneously present, and yet the mystery of the Divine Presence remains ineffable and unknowable, whether spoken or conceived. When the Hesychasts say with St Paul that "at the name of Jesus every knee should bow" and that "every tongue should confess that Jesus Christ is Lord, to the glory of God the Father",[76] they are not speaking the language of "sentimental metaphysics" or "bhaktic" theology, to use Schuon's terms, but the language of *gnosis* or experiential realization. The invocation of the Name of Jesus in the form of the Prayer of Jesus, for the early Hesychasts, is the quintessence of doctrinal

74. "For he whom God hath sent speaketh the words of God: God giveth not the Spirit by measure unto him" (Jn 3:34).
75. *Epistle III,* P.G. 4—1069B. The "sudden", understood as the epiphany of eternity, is well attested both in the Platonic tradition (Plato, *Parmenides,*156de; *Epistle* VII, 341cd; *Symposium,* 210C; Plotinus, *Enneads,* V. 3.17, 5.7, VI. 7.16) and in Scripture (Lk 2:13, Mk 13:36, Acts 9:3, 22:6, and especially Mal 3:1: "And suddenly the Lord whom you seek will come into his temple, and the angel of great counsel whom you desire."). These citations are taken from Golitzen, *Et Introibo Ad Altare Dei,* who provides an illuminating discussion of this theme, pp. 222-229.
76. Phil 2:10-11; cf. Eph 3:14, Rom 14:11, Isa 45:23.

fullness, methodical concentration, and effective realization of the remembrance of God.

St Hesychios the Priest, who as we saw earlier puts much emphasis upon *nepsis*, watchfulness, and spiritual sobriety in the invocation of the Jesus Prayer, describes the methodical dimension of the invocation of the Name:

> We should strive to preserve the precious gifts which preserve us from all evil, whether on the plane of the senses or on that of the intellect. These gifts are the guarding of the intellect with the invocation of Jesus Christ, continuous insight into the heart's depths, stillness of mind unbroken even by thoughts which appear to be good, and the capacity to be empty of all thought. In this way the demons will not steal in undetected; and if we suffer pain through remaining centered in the heart, consolation is at hand.[77]

As the preferred method of invocation for the Hesychasts, the Prayer of Jesus encompasses attention-*prosoche*, watchfuness-*nepsis*, the guarding of the heart, stillness-*hesychia*, dispassion-*apatheia*, suffering of heart and spiritual consolation. Invocation of Jesus Christ (the method) leads to continuous insight into the heart's depths, unbroken stillness, and spiritual consolation (a sign of the experience of the Divine Presence). Just as constant watchfulness and diligence in guarding the heart produce an equilibrium in the *nous* that is God-given, leading to the peace that passes understanding, so the invocation of the Divine Name of Jesus in the Jesus Prayer leads to the true remembrance of God. St Hesychios says that the true task of the Hesychast is always the same and always accomplished in the same way, by the ceaseless invocation of the Lord Jesus Christ with a burning heart:

> A certain God-given equilibrium is produced in our intellect through the constant remembrance and invocation of our Lord Jesus Christ, provided that we do not neglect this constant spiritual entreaty or our close watchfulness and diligence. Indeed, our true task is always the same and is always accomplished in the same way: to call upon our Lord Jesus Christ with a burning heart so that His holy name intercedes for us.[78]

As invocatory method, the prayer of Jesus is the chief weapon of the Hesychast in the spiritual warfare that must be fought in the battle-

77. *The Philokalia,* Vol. 1. p. 180.
78. *Ibid.,* "On Watchfulness and Holiness", p. 178.

ground of the heart. The method is to invoke the name of Jesus over and over again in the heart, as flashes of lightning appear in the sky before the rain. The name of Jesus is the lightning flash which, when repeated in the sky of the heart (the *nous*), induces the healing rain of Divine grace to water the "earth of the heart".[79]

> The name of Jesus should be repeated over and over in the heart as flashes of lightning are repeated over and over in the sky before rain. Those who have experience of the intellect and of inner warfare know this very well. We should wage this spiritual warfare with a precise sequence: first, with attentiveness; then, when we perceive the hostile thought attacking, we should strike at it angrily in the heart, cursing it as we do so; thirdly, we should direct our prayer against it, concentrating the heart through the invocation of Jesus Christ, so that the demonic fantasy may be dispersed at once, the intellect no longer pursuing it like a child deceived by some conjuror.[80]

Effectively waging the unseen warfare with the demons and the passions requires a precise sequence of actions: first, attention or attentiveness (*prosoche*); then a repelling of the hostile thought by a counterattack that St Hesychios calls "rebuttal" (*antilogia, antirrisis*); followed by prayer (*proseuche*), which takes the form of the invocation of the Name of Jesus Christ. This is the essence of the method of invocation in the Hesychast tradition. Summing up the invocatory method of the Hesychasts of the Christian East, by playing on the similarity of the words attentiveness (*prosoche*) and prayer (*proseuche*), St Hesychios writes:

> Watchfulness and the Jesus Prayer . . . reinforce one another; for close attentiveness goes with constant prayer, while prayer goes with close watchfulness and attentiveness of the intellect.[81]

The essence of the path to the heart of Hesychasm is to pass from the practice of invocation to the participation in the Divine Presence. The hesychasts accomplish this by a kind of noetic alchemy in which attention is transmuted into prayer, which is in turn transfigured by uncreated grace into the Presence of God in the heart.

79. A phrase often used in Hesychast writings, particularly in the Macarian homilies.
80. *Ibid.*
81. *Ibid.*, p. 178.

Conclusion

The Path to the Heart through the Remembrance of God—Presence/*Apophasis*, Participation/*Apatheia*, Performance/*Agape*

Let us attempt to summarize what we have discovered so far about the remembrance of God according to the early masters of Hesychasm.

1) The remembrance of God for the early Hesychasts is intimately linked with the practice of *hesychia.*

2) *Hesychia*—the peace and stillness of heart based on the undisturbed return of the *nous* (the intellect or eye of the heart) to the heart caused by the liberation of the powers of the soul from the passions—is the only sure way to attain *theosis.*

3) The aim of the remembrance of God is *theosis* (divinization) or *theopoisis* (deification): participation by man in the uncreated grace of God, grounded in *theoria* or the vision of uncreated light and attained through the energy of grace by the operation of God and the cooperation (synergy) of man.

4) The remembrance of God is both a practice and an experience. The essence of the practice is the method of invocation of the most holy Name of Jesus. The essence of the experience is participation in the Divine Presence, which is signaled by an unprecedented intensification of human energy called "suffering of heart".

5) The remembrance of God as suffering of heart is grounded in the remembrance of death, which is the conscious experience of the ever-present boundary between our sinful mortality and the unbearable limpidity of the immortal Divine Presence. Mindfulness of death is conscious experience of sin, desire for repentance, intense compunction that leads to the concentration of the soul's powers on the contemplation of God.

6) The basic function of the Jesus Prayer in the remembrance of God is to unify human nature fragmented by sin, because God, Whose Presence is perfect Unity, can be realized only in unity. Without the unification of all the powers of the soul, rational, appetitive, and irascible, there can be no true remembrance of God but only ignorance, forgetfulness, and self-indulgent insensitivity.

7) The invocation of the Name of Jesus moves through several stages, of which three are fundamental: first, attentiveness (*prosoche*), which requires vocal recitation of the prayer; then noetic

prayer (*noera proseuche*), in which the attention is first internalized in the *nous*, which then descends into the heart and becomes self-activating; and finally, the incarnation of Jesus in the heart, in which the remembrance of God becomes the ceaseless Presence of Christ in the heart.

The act, that is, the *phenomenon*, of the remembrance of God, if it is genuine, is a paradox walking on the invisible waters of an abyss. On the one hand, the Hesychast tradition insists on the radical unknowability of God. We can know *that* God is, the saints insist, but we cannot know *what* God is. On the other hand, the Hesychasts insist equally strongly, as we have seen in the Hagioritic Tome, on true *gnosis*: the real experience of God in the heart. It is a kind of knowing the unknowable through an unknowing knowledge. St Maximos the Confessor expresses this paradox thus:

> When the intellect (*nous*) is established in God, it at first ardently longs to discover the principles of His essence. But God's inmost nature does not admit of such investigation, which is indeed beyond the capacity of everything created. The qualities that appertain to His nature, however, are accessible to the intellect's longing: I mean the qualities of eternity, infinity, indeterminateness, goodness, wisdom, and the power of creating, preserving, and judging creatures. Yet of these, only infinity may be grasped fully, and the very nature of knowing nothing is knowledge surpassing the intellect, as the theologians Gregory of Nazianzos[82] and Dionysios[83] have said.[84]

Later in the same work, Maximos writes:

> A perfect intellect (*nous*) is one which by true faith and in a manner beyond all unknowing supremely knows the supremely Unknowable, and which, in surveying the entirety of God's creation, has received from God an all-embracing knowledge of the providence and judgment which governs it—in so far, of course, as all this is possible to man.[85]

As we bring to a close our interrogation of the early Hesychast Fathers on the meaning of the remembrance of God, we are hopefully beginning to appreciate that what they understand by remembrance involves something far deeper and more meaningful than

82. See footnote 33.
83. *Epistle* I, PG 4: 1065AB.
84. "Four Hundred Texts on Love", 1:100, *The Philokalia*, Vol. 2, p. 64.
85. "Four Hundred Texts on Love", 3:99, *Ibid.*, p. 99.

the mere thought of God in the mind or even a pious devotional prayer. To them the remembrance of God is an utterly real experience, indeed a transformative experience. If the experience of the remembrance of God does not involve an actual transformative and transfiguring confrontation with the fire of the Divine Presence, a searing awareness of God as a "consuming fire" that actually reveals sin in all its starkness in the soul as it burns it up while healing and transforming the inner man, then it is not really the remembrance of God, but a state of forgetfulness in which the soul indulges itself in the illusion of religious activity while being ignorant of its own radical insensitivity to the Divine Presence.

Is there no place, then, for having a thought of God or for pious spiritual discourse? Are such activities not also in some sense the remembrance of God? The Hesychasts allow that at every stage on the path to the heart, the grace of God may be experienced according to the possibilities of that state. Generally there are three main stages recognized: beginners, the intermediate—those on the way—and the perfect. Evagrios speaks of the three stages in terms of 1) the practical man at the stage of the practice of the virtues, involving ascetic purification and the keeping of the commandments; 2) the contemplative man or "gnostic", involved with *phusiki* or natural contemplation, a kind of spiritual illumination that recognizes the Presence of God in all created beings; and 3) the theological man, the one who experiences *theologia*, which is the realization of spiritual knowledge in union with God, an active and conscious participation in the perceptions and realities of the Divine world. Dionysios speaks in a similar manner of the stages of purification, illumination, and perfection. Maximos in places follows Evagrios in speaking of *praktiki*, natural contemplation (*phusiki*), and *theologia*, and in other places uses more Dionysian language. In the *Mystagogia*, Maximos speaks of "the three classes of the saved as found in the Scriptures", the "slaves, mercenaries, and sons", corresponding to the faithful, the virtuous, and the knowing, or beginners, the proficient, and the perfect.[86] Although the Hesychasts are not overly systematic about these degrees, it is possible to discern that there are levels in the practice of the remembrance of God that conform to these stages. For the beginners or the faithful,

86. Maximos the Confessor, *The Mystagogia*, in *Maximus Confessor: Selected Writings*, trans. George Berthold (New York: Paulist Press, 1985), p. 210.

the practice of the remembrance of God will be to try to hold the thought of God in the mind as much as possible through oral invocation of the Divine Name of Jesus. For the proficient or the virtuous, the practice of the remembrance of Jesus descends into the heart with deep compunction—in Diadochos's words, as sole study and ceaseless task. For the knowing ones, the perfect, the fire of the remembrance of God becomes so entirely wedded to the whole person that the heart itself becomes heaven, the soul becomes an eternal flame of uncreated light, and the body becomes an illuminated temple of the Holy Spirit. For all classes of the saved, beginners, proficient, and perfect, the practice of the Prayer of the Heart or the Jesus Prayer is the basic form of the practice of the remembrance of God.

Presence, participation, performance: these are the three dimensions or "moments" in the experience of the remembrance of God, which are simultaneous and paradoxical, because the true experience of the remembrance of God means that the soul stands at the very boundary of the gulf between the created and the Uncreated. "Presence" refers to approaching or being approached by the Divine Presence. "Participation" is the mystery of the participation of the created order in the uncreated energies of God, to which the invocatory practice of the remembrance of God points. "Performance" is the paradoxical experience at one and the same time of actively performing and passively suffering the synergy between God and man in the remembrance of God in intense longing and love. In other words, in the Hesychast practice of the remembrance of God as invocation, one seeks to approach the unapproachable, know the unknowable, think the unthinkable through controlling and refining the power of attention until it becomes a powerful prayer which descends into the heart and is transformed into a presence beyond itself. The heart of the remembrance of God is the art of the created becoming uncreated.

These three ontological dimensions of remembering God are each governed by its respective epistemological principle: *apophasis* or unknowing, *apatheia* or dispassion, *agape* or self-sacrificing love. In his approach to the presence of God, the Hesychast is safeguarded from delusion and idolatry through the apophatic principle which declares the unknowability of God in His own essence. The mystery of participation in the uncreated energies of the Divine Presence is governed by the principle of *apatheia* or dispassion, because without dispassion, which is the transfiguration of the soul's powers from dispersive dissipation to concentrated unity, there can be no participation in the Divine energies through which God is known in unknowing knowledge. The synergy between the Divine and the human requires a certain performance that the Hesychasts call *agape*, or sometimes even *eros*, a suffering of the Divine in a personal act of love. These three governing principles—*apophasis, apatheia, agape*—are insisted upon by the Hesychast tradition because the "highest metaphysics" of the Fathers of the *Philokalia* is grounded in the inescapable reality of the infinite gulf between the Uncreated and the created, and the paradoxical experience—not abstract doctrinal expression, but practical experience—of simultaneously bridging the unbridgeable gulf in a Person to person relationship, while acknowledging its eternal reality.

Let us end as we began by turning to the words of Frithjof Schuon, who, in his many writings, has often produced passages of extraordinary clarity, beauty, and depth. None is more remarkable and appropriate to our subject than one he called the "chain of quintessences":

> The quintessence of the world is man. The quintessence of man is religion. The quintessence of religion is prayer. The quintessence of prayer is invocation. . . . If man had no more than a few instants to live, he would no longer be able to do anything but invoke God. He would thereby fulfill all the demands of prayer, of religion, of the human state.[87]

"The quintessence of prayer is invocation." This chain of quintessences is entirely in harmony with the teaching of the early Hesychast masters, except they would add that the quintessence of invocation is the Divine Name of Jesus. Let me close by briefly reflecting on Schuon's last two sentences in light of the terrible terrorist attack of September 11, which has been an invisible, inaudible, uninvited, spectral, but very tangible "presence" at this conference. Schuon concludes his chain of quintessences with the following words: "If man had no more than a few instants to live, he would no longer be able to do anything but invoke God. He would thereby fulfill all the demands of prayer, of religion, of the human state." A stewardess on high-jacked American Airlines Flight 11 out

87. Unpublished Text 358.

of Boston, Madeline Amy Sweeney, called her ground manager in the final moments before the terrorists crashed the plane into the World Trade Center in New York. With remarkable presence of mind, she calmly reported the high-jacking, the slaying of a passenger and two flight attendants, the number of the high-jackers, and even gave her ground manager the seat numbers of four of the high-jackers. Then in the final moments of the flight, as the plane rapidly descended and lined up on its target, the World Trade Center, her last words were recorded, which are unforgettable. She said, calmly, "I see water and buildings." There was a pause, then, in an entirely different tone of voice, "Oh, my God!" Again a pause, and again "Oh, my God!" In those final seconds Madeline Amy Sweeney undoubtedly realized what was about to happen. She was thirty-five years old, married, the mother of two children, and had worked for American Airlines for twelve years. It is probably safe to say that she was neither a Sufi nor a Hesychast, and that her last words began as an involuntary exclamation wrung from her shocked heart, not a consciously intended prayer. But instinctively and, I believe, unerringly in the final moments of her life, her soul found its true center, and at the last possible instant, she invoked God. Her last three words were, I am convinced, truly an invocation, and, if Schuon's chain of quintessences reflects the nature of things, then by the mercy of God Madeline Amy Sweeney thus fulfilled "all the demands of prayer, of religion, of the human state". May it be so for each of us.

Chapter 6

Paths of Continuity: Contemporary Witnesses of the Hesychast Experience

John Chryssavgis

When we explore the ways of the heart articulated in the classics of the Christian East, it is critical that we examine them in the context of a living tradition. Scholars may tend to undermine the continuity of this tradition, even as they underline the impact or influence of particular individuals in the earlier or later medieval ages. Whenever, therefore, we study individual writers or their writings, we must remember that, behind these, there stands an entire and uninterrupted path of continuity. We do not do proper justice to authors such as Evagrius of Pontus (d. 399), John Klimakos (d. c. 649), Symeon the New Theologian (d. 1049), or Gregory Palamas (d. 1359) unless we study them in light of numerous other persons, in relation to "a cloud of witnesses" (Heb 12:1)—at once known and unknown, both men and women, early and medieval and modern alike—who paved as well as followed the way to the heart. Alongside the more institutional unbroken "apostolic succession" of the Christian Church, we must also discern a parallel charismatic "spiritual succession" that rejuvenates the Church through the centuries.

In tenth-century Constantinople, Symeon the New Theologian, Abbot of the Monastery of St Mamas, warned his community that to believe the ways of the heart are not a reality experienced in contemporary times but restricted only to the distant past is doctrinally and spiritually dangerous:

> I call heretics those who say that there is no one in our times and in our midst able to keep the commandments and become like the Fathers. . . . Now those who claim that this is impossible have not fallen into one particular heresy but rather into all of them, if I may say so, since this one surpasses all of them in abundance of blasphemy.[1]

1. *Catechetical Discourse,* 39, 3-5. See *Classics of Western Spirituality* (New York: Paulist Press, 1980), pp. 311-313.

In modern-day Greece, the same conviction is affirmed by Archimandrite Vasileios, Abbot of the Monastery of Iveron on Mount Athos or the Holy Mountain, as it is known—a peninsula in northeastern Greece and a key center of Orthodox monasticism since the tenth century. His creative exploration of the liturgy and life of the Orthodox Church, in a book entitled *Hymn of Entry*, describes the experience and role of the contemporary monastic community in relation to the third- and fourth-century situation of early monasticism. After introducing the spiritual life and liturgical prayer of monks on the Holy Mountain, Fr Vasileios endeavors to convey to the reader the indisputable reality of his conclusions, by sketching the portrait of a monk who remains unnamed, yet whom he claims to know. "Such monks," he writes,

> unknown and anonymous, but full of light, exist. I know one. He literally overflows. That is an expression that gives some idea of the truth about him. He has a treasure of inexpressible joy hidden in an earthen vessel, small and fragile. And this joy overflows and spreads all around him, filling his surroundings with its fragrance. Light shines from his being. . . . And whether he speaks or whether he is silent, whether he sleeps or whether he is awake, whether he is present or whether he is absent, it is always the same thing that he says, the same thing that he is, the same grace and the same power. . . . It is something that renews man, calms his nerves, extinguishes his anger, enlightens his mind, gives wings to his hope, and prepares him for a struggle that gives quiet and peace to a whole people. . . . He is free, a man of the age to come. For this reason he alone speaks justly of this present age. . . . He is weak, like a spider's web, and yet all-powerful. He receives such a deluge of grace that his house of clay is overwhelmed. His feeble body can no longer endure; he overflows, is set on fire, and all within him and round him becomes light. . . . In the presence of such a man you understand the theology of St Gregory Palamas. . . . In his presence you feel that the saints of old continue to live amongst us, just as he himself, being dead to the world, lives among us in another way, in the Holy Spirit. . . . You understand too how the Christian doctrine of the immortality of the soul is to be interpreted, how the resurrection of the body will be. Things present and things to come are made clear, not by discursive reasoning, but by appearing, by being made manifest in life. . . . So the presence of the saints of old becomes evident. And the grace of the saints of our own time transcends history, leading us here and now into eternity. . . . They show us that there is no difference between the old and the new in the Church, which is

the body of the risen Christ 'who makes all things new' (Rev. 21:5).[2]

Indeed, the Holy Mountain itself is a powerful symbol of this living continuity in the Christian East of a monastic tradition dating back to the earliest centuries. To visit any of the twenty monastic communities, or to journey to one of hundreds of cells inhabited by hermits, to learn even of the inconspicuous existence of those whose invisible life leaves no mark beyond a shadow of the ineffable divine light—this is to experience a way that has been continued and confirmed without interruption through the ages.

The three figures portrayed in this paper all lived on Mount Athos. I was privileged to know the first and the third, while I had on several occasions encountered the closest companion of the second. All three complement one another: Sophrony analyses the Jesus Prayer and its methodology; all of his life, Joseph made the Jesus Prayer his unceasing activity; and, while Paisios hardly mentions the Jesus Prayer, certainly all that he does stems from the prayer of the heart. Each of them played a critical role in the revival of the monastic ideal in the twentieth century. Their spiritual heritage has proven intangible, reaching far beyond the borders of the Holy Mountain and Greece or Russia, with an especially strong influence in Western Europe and North America. In an effort to provide a conversation with these elders, I have quoted extensively from their own words to describe their perception of the paths to the heart. They are representatives of the diversity of the heart's ways and the breadth of desert spirituality, alive today no less than in the past. "Indeed," to paraphrase Bishop Kallistos of Diokleia, "there are times when they seem to be speaking to us not from the past or the present but from the future, as prophetic witnesses to the Age to Come."[3]

2. Originally appearing in Greek in 1974, *Hymn of Entry* was published in English by St Vladimir's Seminary Press in 1984. The passage quoted above is taken from chapter 6 (pp. 126-131), although the text was delivered as an address to students in France in 1974, printed in *Contacts* 27 (in French: 1975) and in *Sobornost,* series 7, no. 1 (in English: 1975), and not included in the Greek edition of *Hymn.* I shall return below to this passage and the anonymous monk.
3. From the foreword to Elder Joseph's *Elder Joseph the Hesychast: Struggles, Experiences, Teachings* (Mount Athos: Vatopaidi Monastery, 1990), p. 24.

The Wisdom of the Heart: Sophrony of Essex (1896-1993)

Archimandrite Sophrony Sakharov was born Sergei Symeonovich in Tsarist Russia in 1896.[4] It is said that, as a young child, Sophrony possessed an eager desire to penetrate the mystical way of the heart through prayer and contemplation of the visible world. He elected to study fine arts in Moscow, and it was during his student years that he developed a parallel interest in Buddhism and Indian culture that proved formative. With the outbreak of World War I and the subsequent Revolution in Russia, Sophrony came to meditate on the primary cause of suffering and the absolute source of truth, while always retaining his keen awareness of the beauty of nature. In his aesthetic pursuit, he embarked on an ascetic struggle to maintain a balance between body and soul, mind and heart, visible and invisible, finite and eternal.

By 1921, Sophrony had emigrated to Europe, traveling through Italy and Germany to France, where he exhibited his work in the most elite of salons. He was soon to lose interest in matters purely intellectual, including his artistic creations. At this point he remembered Christ's injunction to love God "with all one's heart and with all one's mind" (Lk 10:27). The insight was definitive for the maturing Sophrony, who thereupon enrolled in the then recently opened Orthodox Theological Institute of St Serge in Paris. However, he soon left his formal studies to make his way to St Panteleimon Monastery on Mount Athos. Prayer became second nature to him, unceasing even in his sleep. Four years later, in 1930, Sophrony first encountered Staretz Silouan, whom he acclaimed as the greatest gift from above, a miracle from God's providence. For eight years, Sophrony enjoyed the spiritual direction of this elder, until—on the death of the *starets*—he departed the monastery for the "desert" of the Holy Mountain.

4. See Archimandrite Sophrony, *His Life is Mine* (Crestwood, NY: St. Vladimir's Seminary Press, 1977), especially pp. 7-13. For a personal interpretation of the biography of Fr Sophrony, see Maxime Egger, "Archim. Sophronie: Moine pour le Monde", in *Le Buisson Ardent: Cahiers Saint Silouan l'Athonite* (no date), nos. 1-5, pp. 23-39, 40-53, 17-30, 76-81, 31-47. For a study on the spiritual teaching of Fr Sophrony, see Archim. Zacharias (Zacharou), *Report on the Theology of the Elder Sophrony* (Essex, UK: Monastery of St. John the Baptist, 2000). Other brief testimonies on Fr Sophrony may be found in Kleitos Ioannides, *Contemporary Holy Elders*, in Greek (Lefkosia, 1994), pp. 219-236.

During the years of World War II, Sophrony was called to serve as the confessor and spiritual advisor of St Paul's Monastery as well as for other communities of the Holy Mountain, a ministry that he considered to be an act of compassion. Four years later, he moved to a more remote region of the Athonite "desert", where he inhabited a small chapel (some 10' x 7') hewn out of the rock-face. There he endured rigorous conditions (no fire, and much dampness) for a life of reading and prayer. After three winters, failing health obliged him to relinquish the cave, and he traveled once again to France, where surgery left him unable to entertain the thought of returning to Athos. He decided to record the biographical details and spiritual teachings of his *starets,* Silouan. In 1952, Sophrony published *The Undistorted Image,*[5] the story of the holy *starets,* whose accuracy was confirmed by other ascetics on the Mountain as being a genuine reflection of the ancient traditions of Eastern monasticism. Thus, the *starets* was recognized as a spiritual heir to the great teachers of the paths to the heart, being "canonized" by the official Church in 1988.

In 1958, Sophrony founded a small community in Essex, England, where for years he served as a spiritual guide, faithful always to the legacy of his beloved *starets.* It is in that community that he died and lies buried since 1993.

*

* *

This section of my paper explores the theology of Fr. Sophrony in one of his earlier works, entitled *His Life is Mine.*[6] In this book, Sophrony reveals certain insights further developed in his later works, such as the themes of divine knowledge, light, and vision, as well as the way that leads to these: struggle, prayer, and repentance. Sophrony is aware that spiritual knowledge is "preserved and handed on . . . from generation to generation".[7] His own foundation and roots clearly lie in the tradition of Mount Athos, which he explicitly acknowledges in speaking of "this great culture of the

5. The book subsequently appeared in two separate parts with the titles *The Monk of Mount Athos* (the biography) and *Wisdom from Mount Athos* (the teachings), published by St. Vladimir's Seminary Press, New York.
6. Published by Mowbray (Oxford, UK) and St. Vladimir's Seminary Press (New York) in 1977.
7. *Ibid.*, p. 90.

heart [that] I met with on the Holy Mountain".[8] And on prayer of the heart, he notes: "It is not my aim here to examine all aspects of so exceptionally complex a matter, but to pass on some of the teachings given to me on the Holy Mountain, first in the monastery, then in the 'desert'."[9]

In the Old Testament, the term heart has an all-embracing sense, signifying the spiritual center of the entire human person, as well as being at once the seat of emotion and reason.[10] The New Testament reflects this Semitic approach: after the incarnation, Mary is said to have kept everything in her heart (Lk 2:19) like a treasure (Mt 6:21); evil thoughts arise in the heart (Mk 7:21; Rom 1:24) as the moral and intellectual center of the human person, the inner person (Eph 3:16-17) or the unifying center of the spiritual life (Gal 4:6). For Sophrony, "The human spirit hungers for knowledge—for entire, integral knowledge. . . . The heart is opened wide to embrace a multitude of lives and *aeons* of time."[11] The reference here to "the human spirit" indicates Sophrony's inconsistent use of terminology relating to the spiritual center of the person, as well as to the Divine source of grace. Among the terms adopted to define the former are "spirit", *persona*, "soul", and "mind"; terms referring to the latter include "Spirit", "Divine breath", and "grace".[12] The inconsistency, however, may be a deliberate emphasis on the diversity of the heart's ways or the intensity of the Divine impact on the heart, which "can only be assimilated by degrees, after long ascetic struggle". Sophrony refers to the never-ending growth of the soul which, "as a matter of course, aspires to ever deeper knowledge".[13] "There is," he says, "no end to this learning"[14]—in this respect, he is part of a long lineage of authors who write of *epektasis*, the inexhaustible nature of the knowledge of God. And, while he desires to

8. *Ibid.*, p. 112. On p. 52: "This [healing of the passions] happened often on the Holy Mountain." On p. 69: "I found that the monks of the Holy Mountain understood this well." On p. 100: "I met with such ideas as these on the Holy Mountain. And naturally I wanted to learn from the fathers how they understood this aspect of the ascetic life."
9. *Ibid.*, p. 99.
10. For a similar understanding in American Indian belief, see C. Jung, *Memories, Dreams, Reflections* (London, 1973) p. 276.
11. *Op.cit.*, pp. 17, 87.
12. *Ibid.*, pp. 41-45 and 106.
13. *Ibid.*, p. 44.
14. *Ibid.*, p. 89.

communicate the beauty of this experience, he confesses that it is "impossible to keep silent; impossible to give voice"[15]—he is again within the succession of spiritual authors who refer to *apophasis*, the ineffable nature of the experience of God.

The human person is a mystery. Sophrony speaks of "man as being indeed an enigma".[16] "[Man] is more than a microcosm—he is a microtheos."[17] The human heart, too, is a mystery in the "image and likeness of God" (Gen 1:26). No one but God knows it (1 Sam 16:17; Lk 16:15). Mark the Monk calls God "knower of hearts", and Abba Isaiah says that only God knows the depth of our heart.[18] "The heart is deep" (Ps 63:7). For Sophrony, this personal and mystical dimension of the heart is both central and critical. The personal character of the Absolute God or Being is precisely the mystical characteristic of the human heart.[19] Without this relationship—or reflection—between the depth of the human heart and the depth of Divine Being, there would be no possibility to repent or even—Sophrony claims—to sin.[20]

As the meeting-point between God and the human person, the heart is considered to be the place where the Divine light is beheld. For the ascetic tradition, darkness spells sin and ignorance; it signifies the absence of God's incandescent grace, rather than the presence of Divine transcendence and mystery.[21] And, similarly, for Sophrony, "God reveals Himself, mainly through the heart, as Love and Light."[22] This Divine light is an existent reality, not merely an imaginary figment or mere figure of speech. Sophrony represents the "mystics of light", a tradition dominant in the Christian East. "There have been," he writes, "not a few witnesses in the past, as there are in the present."[23] Sophrony stands alongside Origen (second-third centuries), Evagrius (fourth century), the Desert Fathers (fourth-fifth centuries), the *Homilies* attributed to Macarius (fourth-fifth centuries), Diadochus (fifth

15. *Ibid.*, p. 76.
16. *Op. cit.*, p. 85.
17. *Ibid.*, p. 77.
18. Mark the Monk, *De his* 15 (PG 65.932D) and Abba Isaiah, *Logos* 4, 7 and 15, 1.
19. *Op. cit.*, pp. 19, 23.
20. *Ibid.*, p. 42.
21. See John Klimakos, *Shepherd* 100.
22. *Op. cit.*, p. 44.
23. *Ibid.*, p. 128. These are the closing words of his book.

century), and John Klimakos (seventh century), a line continued right up to Symeon the New Theologian (eleventh century) and Gregory Palamas (fourteenth century).

Curiously, Sophrony is reserved when it comes to drawing parallels between his tradition or theology of light and other eastern systems or practices of illumination, such as "yoga or transcendental meditation and the like," for "the practice of the [Jesus Prayer] has been distorted into a so-called 'Christian yoga' and mistaken for 'transcendental meditation'." If he is careful to distinguish between Christian and non-Christian methods, I feel that it is for two reasons: first, in order to "stress the danger of such errors [which] look upon prayer as one of the simplest and easiest 'technical' methods leading to immediate unity with God". And, second, in order to emphasize that "outward similarities can be vastly different in inner content". Perhaps a mysticism of love should not lead to a relativism of faith. It is, therefore, to preserve the integrity of every culture, and not only every religious culture, that he avoids simplistic comparisons and sweeping generalizations.[24]

The "depth of illumination" is found in love, which "shines in our hearts", "a light which shines in a dark place" (2 Cor 4:6, 2 Pet 1:19). The notion of "the eyes of [one's] understanding being enlightened" (Eph 1:8) expresses an idea central with Sophrony:

> Sometimes prayer consumes the heart like fire; and when the heart succumbs to the burning flame, unexpectedly there falls the dew of Divine consolation. When we become so conscious of our frailty that our spirit despairs, somehow, in an unknown fashion, a wondrous light appears, proclaiming life incorruptible. When the darkness within us is so appalling that we are paralyzed with dread, the same light will turn black night into bright day. . . . When we are overwhelmed by the feeling of our own utter nothingness, the uncreated light transfigures and brings us like sons into the Father's house.[25]

Sophrony adopts the image of a centuries-old tree whose roots must lie deep in the earth if its branches are to reach up to the clouds.[26] The whole human person, including the body, shines if the heart is illumined (Prov 15:13). The heart beholds this light

24. *Ibid.*, pp. 115 and 119.
25. *Ibid.*, p. 60. See also p. 41 and the title (on p. 77) of Chapter 10: "Through Dark to Light".
26. *Ibid.*, pp. 85-86.

when it is pure: "if your eye is simple, the whole body shall be full of light" (Mt 6:22). Yet it is not a natural light, resembling a personal gift or artistic talent. Sophrony is convinced that it is supernatural: "He who accepts it knows from whence it came—knows whether it was pronounced of man or whether it did verily come down 'from the Father of Lights' (Jas 1:17)."[27] "This light is the Light of Divinity . . . hidden, mysterious by nature."[28] In the end, it is God who "creates a clean heart and renews the right spirit within" (Ps 50:10). According to the *Ladder* of John of Sinai, one is unable to see one's sins and thus confess them in order to be cleansed, unless they are first revealed, just "as a ray of sun, passing through a crack, lights everything in the house and shows up even the finest dust".[29] Without an illumined heart, one is no longer human; one is in fact inhuman. Indeed, for John Klimakos, the true "monk [read: Christian] is unfailing light . . . in the heart."[30] Purity is the heart's natural condition, its fulfillment; pride is the heart's unnatural state, its defilement. In fact, Sophrony identifies darkness with pride, and illumination with humility.[31]

Hence, the intellect must guard the heart against the sin of pride. On the one hand, the heart's function is *ascetical*: it is a struggle to attain to spiritual liberty. For Sophrony, the sign of this freedom of the Spirit is, first, "a disinclination to impose one's will on others" and, second, "an inner release from the hold of others on oneself".[32] Such a liberation, or revelation, will come only "after long years of ascetic striving".[33] On the other hand, the heart's function is *liturgical*: as the unifying organ of the entire person, it offers up the human person to God.[34] Sophrony declares that "the priest's whole being— heart, mind, body—must unite in sorrowful prayer for the world".[35] And liturgy is more than "simply a form of psychological or mental 'remembering'"; it is the preservation and continuation of knowledge through "generations of priests".[36] The place

27. *Ibid.*, pp. 80-81. See also pp. 55-56.
28. *Ibid.*, p. 79.
29. *Step* 26, 111, 29.
30. *Step* 22, 22.
31. *Op. cit.*, p. 78.
32. *Ibid.*, p. 73. On spiritual warfare, see chapter 9 (pp. 71-76).
33. *Ibid.*, p. 125.
34. Cf. *Macarian Homilies*, 15, 20.
35. *Op. cit.*, p. 87.
36. *Ibid.*, pp. 108-109.

where the ascetical and the liturgical coincide lies in prayer, which is described as "infinite creation, a supreme art".[37] "Of all ascetic practices the striving for prayer is the most arduous."[38] Indeed, many of the chapters in this book open with a creative and poetic prayer by the Elder, who also introduced personal prayers into his celebration of the Divine Liturgy.

Two final points should at this point be highlighted. First, while in this book by the Elder Sophrony, unlike the writings of Philo the Jew (first century), Clement of Alexandria (third century), Gregory of Nyssa (fourth century), and Dionysius the Areopagite (c. 500), there are no traces of any "mysticism of darkness", there is a great deal of emphasis on the significance of suffering. It is a suffering of the heart, or "broken-heartedness" (Ps 50:17). For Sophrony, "through suffering we penetrate the mysteries of Being".[39] He devotes the entire thirteenth chapter to "the prayer of Gethsemane". Ultimately, all suffering is contained and comprehended on the Cross:

> This spiritual vision . . . dissolves into contemplation of the crucified Christ. The way to this . . . lies through the depths of hell. . . . The hands of Christ crucified link the far ends of the abyss. . . . Thus the first dread vision of darkness and mortality changes to a vision of light and life indestructible. [Then] the touch of divine love in the heart is our first contact with the heavenly side of the abyss.[40]

Even the physical heart feels this sensation of pain within the arduous act of prayer:

> This concentration within may take the form of a cramp whereby heart, mind, and body are contracted together, like a tightly

37. *Ibid.*, p. 64. Although Fr Sophrony devotes the smaller, second part of his book (pp. 99-128) to the Jesus Prayer, this prayer will not constitute the focus of my attention here. However, Sophrony does in fact refer to the "technical [psycho-somatic] method of bringing the mind down to the heart", which he feels may assist a beginner and which includes the verbal sequence and varied formula(e) that begin with the lips and move to the mind and are "confirmed" and "grafted" in the heart.
38. *Ibid.*, p. 82.
39. *Ibid.*, p. 59.
40. *Ibid.*, pp. 61-62. Prayer, he notes, "eventually enables the mind to see, not the physical heart but that which is happening within it and . . . to feel the heart" (p. 112).

> clenched fist. Prayer becomes a wordless cry, and regret for the distance separating him from God turns to acute grief.[41]

While at the outset of the path "now there is suffering and now rejoicing," at the final destination "there is no more alternating between elation and depression, since all states are gathered into a single whole. Through knowledge of God the soul has acquired profound peace."[42]

Second, Sophrony believes that "when God by the Holy Spirit gives us understanding our prayer assumes cosmic proportions". Although it is not always clear whether these proportions extend beyond "mankind",[43] the implication is that "the intrinsic quality of life is enhanced" and "everything that happens will take on a different character".[44] So, knowledge of God involves contemplation of the world.[45] Darkness and "death engulf all creation, ourselves first and foremost".[46] So too does God's light and life:

> When you feel the touch of the Eternal Spirit in your heart. . . . love streams like a light on all creation. Though the physical heart feels this love, in kind it is spiritual-metaphysical. . . . Yet only those . . . who keep a clear conscience not only before God but toward their neighbor, towards animals—even towards the material things which are the product of men's labor—will care for all creation. . . . [Love] embraces all created beings in joy over their salvation. It is saddened by anyone's downfall. . . . For the Divine Spirit draws the heart to compassion for all creation.[47]

Such is the path that Sophrony learned directly through the inspiration of his elder, *starets* Silouan, who taught him—in his classic exhortation—to "stay his mind in hell and despair not": "We are naturally attracted to the All-Highest, but our pilgrimage must start with a descent into the pit of hell. Then we are nearing the end of our long search to discover the depth of Being."[48]

41. *Ibid.*, p. 74-75.
42. *Ibid.*, pp. 63. For the reference above, see p. 82.
43. *Ibid.*, p. 68. See also p. 87.
44. *Ibid.*, p. 54. Sophrony also observes: "The man of prayer beholds the surrounding scene in another light. Concern is quickened. . . ."
45. *Ibid.*, p. 110.
46. *Ibid.*, p. 79.
47. *Ibid.*, pp. 81 and 115-117.
48. *Ibid.*, pp. 78 and 82. Silouan's words are quoted on p. 126.

The Depth of the Heart: Joseph the Hesychast (1898-1959)

The biographer of Elder Joseph the Hesychast describes him as a "legitimate continuator of the patristic tradition".[49] As in the case of Sophrony, who recorded the life of his own *starets*, the author of this elder's life is Joseph the younger (b. 1921), who lived for twelve years with his spiritual father until the latter's death in 1959. Joseph the Hesychast was born in 1898 on the small island of Paros in Greece. Orphaned as a young child, Joseph (*né* Francis) began to work from a tender age in order to assist his family. At the age of twenty-three, he first encountered the writings of the Church Fathers, deciding early on that he would follow the monastic path. He made his way to Athens where he met with Athonite monks whom he followed to the Holy Mountain. There he sought especially to learn the concepts of *hesychia* (silence) and *nepsis* (attentiveness) from a variety of persons and lifestyles. One day, filled with tears, he prayed to the Mother of God. "At last," he writes,

> I was completely changed, and forgot myself. I was filled with light in my heart and outside and everywhere, not being aware that I even had a body. The 'prayer' [that is, the Jesus Prayer] began to say itself within me, so rhythmically that I was amazed, since I myself was not making any effort.[50]

Thereafter, he tried to spend all of his time in quiet and remote regions of the Great Lavra Monastery.

Joseph was not alone in his struggles. Arsenios (d. 1984), a monk of Stavronikita Monastery, was to become his inseparable companion and ascetic partner. He too was interested in stillness and attentiveness. They met at the peak of the Mountain on the Feast of the Transfiguration (August 6). The well-known hermit, Elder Daniel of Katounakia, advised them to seek out a spiritual

49. *Elder Joseph*, p. 30. This biography resembles more a personal and edifying spiritual treatise than a detailed historical account. Other accounts on the life of the Elder Joseph may be found in Constantine Cavarnos, *Anchored in God: Life, Art, and Thought on the Holy Mountain of Athos* (Belmont MA, 1959), pp. 203-209; and K. Ioannides, *op. cit.*, pp. 131-138. For the writings of the Elder in English, see Elder Joseph, *Elder Joseph the Hesychast and the Patristic Tradition* (Vatopedi Monastery, 1997), which contains thirty-four letters based on the Church Fathers; and *Monastic Wisdom: The Letters of Elder Joseph the Hesychast* (Florence AZ, 1998).

50. *Ibid.*, p. 44.

guide. It was not long before they met up with two other monks, Joseph and Ephrem, the latter of whom became the mentor of the young monks.

Joseph the Hesychast was enthusiastic about the inner way of the heart. He would pray for long hours in silence, sitting in a remote cave on a small wooden stool and keeping his mind in his heart. He fasted intensely (eating only three ounces of food near the time of sunset) and kept extended vigil. He continued wandering the Mountain for eight years after the repose of his elder, finally settling in the Scete of St Basil. He even practiced no handiwork, so as not to become distracted from his concentration on prayer. His ascetic discipline included standing upright for long periods and even inflicting self-beatings. Yet no matter how austere Joseph was to himself, he always remained lenient toward his disciples. His extreme self-denial did not prevent him from relating in humility and even humor to his disciples. He understood well that monastic perfection was to be found not in outward ascetic feats or rigorous deprivations, but in the inward life of the monk, hidden in silence and cultivated in stillness. The inaudible prayer of the heart, he knew, was far louder than many more noticeable, external acts of the outward man. Yet the Hesychast taught his disciples "to stay within [their] own measure, and not extend [themselves] beyond [their] strength".[51]

From St Basil's Scete, Joseph and Arsenios moved to a small cave in Little St Anne. After repairing the cell, the two ascetics lived in three small cells (6' x 5'), one for each of them, and one for the visiting clergyman who celebrated the liturgy. In that cave, Joseph practiced vigil, which he reckoned to be "the most practical method in the spiritual life, essential in all three states of the struggle": purification, illumination, and repose or love.[52]

After attracting a small number of close disciples, and out of concern for their health, even at the cost of his own silence, Joseph encouraged Arsenios to make a last move, this time to New Scete (in 1951). There, after falling ill on New Year's Eve 1958, and following a painful few months, Joseph prepared for his death by fasting from everything except holy communion for almost forty days, the last of his earthly life. On August 15, 1959, on the Feast of his beloved

51. *Ibid.*, p. 125.
52. *Ibid.*, p. 134.

Mother of God, after predicting his own repose on the previous day, Joseph was seated in liturgy when he passed into the heavenly age.

*

* *

The biography of Joseph the Hesychast underlines the dangerous "'fashion' for self-appointed experts speaking about mental prayer, the uncreated light, deification and the like".[53] Tradition is regarded as the only safeguard against this danger, and Joseph is for this reason continually referring to the Church Fathers, virtually on every page quoting from the writings of the *Philokalia.* Joseph believed that "if such people as continue this tradition disappear, then the end of this world will come". And his disciple Joseph, who believes that his elder was one such person, often begins a section with the words: "The Elder used to tell us. . . ."[54] The aim of the spiritual life beside the Elder Joseph is best described as a return to childhood rather than as a development into maturity; it was a way of learning to trust one's elders and one's tradition.[55]

For the Hesychast Joseph, the way of following the path to the heart, the way of appropriating the way of the ascetics, is the way of obedience. "There is no other road to salvation like this," he writes.[56] Yet, while obedience is a mystery, it is not magical; Joseph's teaching is quite radical: "As I have said before, the Divine will with its transcendent character is not magically contained within positions or places or instruments." He is not recommending a slavish adherence to a set of regulations or doctrines. Often Joseph will say: "Do as you think best."[57] The ascetic discipline is closely related to spiritual disciple-ing: disobedience implies disorder; obedience includes a "regime" of prayer and struggle. This is why the Elder insisted on a *typikon* or rule, which actually looked more to the future kingdom than to the past tradition. His way was identified with that of the Fathers: "Testing and experience have convinced me to act in this way. . . . This is the common path of the Fathers." In all things, the question which was on his mind and which he put

53. *Ibid.*, p. 203.
54. *Ibid.*, pp. 206-207.
55. *Ibid.*, p. 166. See also p. 215. Joseph the Hesychast used the work of Isaac the Syrian as a spiritual manual.
56. *Ibid.*, pp. 215, 169-170, and 214
57. *Ibid.*, pp. 170-171 and 216-217.

to his disciples was forward-looking: "Where is God?" The "new creation," as he called it, was always the spiritual focus of the elder.[58] Indeed, this is the context within which Joseph also comprehends and criticizes non-Orthodox practices of prayer and contemplation. In an effort to dispel the concept of prayer as magic or illusion, Joseph is determined to treasure and transmit the wisdom he has received from his own elders.

While reverence to tradition is important for Joseph, the rigor or violence of ascetic struggle is the most striking aspect of his spiritual way. "The right use of conceptual images follows the right use of things."[59] Or, otherwise put, the way that we regard our world is reflected in the way that we treat our world. "The mysteries of the unseen war," as Joseph would refer to them, are real.[60] Joseph learned the "almost indistinguishable" details and trials, the various changes and dispositions, of the spiritual struggle:

> As night follows day, so successes are followed by trials that test us. . . . It is difficult for someone inexperienced to escape from these [nets]. . . . The main path is the martyrdom of our conscience . . . and unceasing self-denial.[61]

This was a struggle he undertook and understood personally: "Since I first put on this [monastic] habit, I have not had my fill of bread or sleep."[62] And he would never for anything exchange this experience:

> If you are going to lose grace and not know how to recall it, I prefer you not to find it, however harsh this may seem. This is why I wish you experience rather than grace. Experience brings many graces and recalls them if they hide themselves, but premature grace brings no experience.[63]

The spiritual struggle, however, is not a way of personal triumph or achievement. Rather, for Joseph, it is a way of sharing through

58. *Ibid.*, pp. 175-178. For remembrance of the Kingdom, see p. 197 and especially p. 215. For Joseph's understanding of non-Orthodox practices, see pp. 203 and 212.
59. *Ibid.*, p. 162.
60. *Ibid.*, pp. 163-166.
61. *Ibid.*, pp. 188-189, 197, 202, and 228. He spoke of changes from the outside and from the inside, from the right and from the left, and even of changes of climate and changes of conscience. See pp. 188-190.
62. *Ibid.*, p. 225. See also p. 198 where it is said "how [Joseph] behaved mercilessly toward himself."
63. *Ibid.*, pp. 226-227.

suffering. The spiritual law of suffering is a reality whereby one assumes responsibility for affliction in the world.[64] Exposure to trials (*peirasmoi*) engenders experience (*peira*) in "bearing one another's burdens" (Gal 6:2). Passion is ultimately a way to com-passion. The aim is to endure patiently the spiritual warfare until the very wounds of the heart and the weaknesses of the world are transformed.[65]

"The dogma of love," then, transcends and exceeds "the law of duty."[66] The ascetic reaches the point where "he neither blames nor condemns anyone for anything, not even Satan himself."[67] The opposite—or enemy—of love is self-love, but in particular it is the vice of negligence, caused by the "complications of indifference".[68] The cure for negligence is remembrance of the kingdom. It must be borne in mind here that the Greek term for memory (*mneme*) is etymologically related to the Greek term for lover (*mnester*). Remembrance is more than purely verbal or primarily mental. Remembrance of the kingdom is another way of learning to love. Beyond the gift of any spiritual visions, the state of love is identified with the grace of Theology.[69] Love is impossible without complete obedience; and prayer is impossible without true love.[70]

Nevertheless, the spiritual struggle is not an end in itself; on the contrary, "the battle against the passions is the beginning of the path to pure prayer. . . . The work of prayer . . . is superior to every virtue and commandment."[71] Prayer of the heart always remained "the chief preoccupation and the chief goal" of the Elder.[72] He too is vague and inconsistent about the terms adopted to describe the heart, an inconsistency that is nevertheless consistent with tradition: he speaks of "heart", of "soul", and even of "character".[73] And Joseph has more to say about the stages of the struggle to regain purity of heart than he has to say about the ideal condition of the heart or the

64. *Ibid.*, pp. 179-180.
65. *Ibid.*, pp. 182-183.
66. *Ibid.*, pp. 165 and 194.
67. *Ibid.*, p. 195.
68. *Ibid.*, pp. 197, 196, and 195.
69. *Ibid.*, pp. 200-203. On visions, see pp. 211, 221, 227.
70. *Ibid.*, pp. 217 and 201.
71. *Ibid.*, pp. 201 and 205.
72. *Ibid.*, pp. 198-199.
73. *Ibid.*, for example, p. 186. This inconsistency, however, is consistent with his tradition.

ultimate results of the struggle. He feels more comfortable admitting the mysteries of the heart—"beyond speech, beyond substance, ungraspable, contained only to the extent that it itself extends the mind".[74] Yet he understands the purpose of prayer as being love, a goal achievable by every person under any conditions and within all circumstances.[75] "Obedience is the principle and means whereby created things are reconnected with their Creator," but

> when grace is operative in the soul of someone who is praying, then that person is flooded with the love of God, so that he can no longer bear what he experiences. Afterwards, this love turns towards the world and man. . . . In general he suffers with every grief and misery, and even for the dumb animals, so that he weeps when he thinks that they are suffering. These are properties of love, but it is prayer that activates them and calls them forth. That is why those who are advanced in prayer do not cease to pray for the world. To them belongs even the continuation of life, however strange and audacious this may seem.[76]

The Breadth of the Heart: Paisios the Elder (1924-1994)

The elder Paisios was born in 1924 in Cappadocia of Asia Minor, a region traditionally renowned for its Byzantine heritage and popular piety. He was baptized by his village priest, Fr Arsenios (d. 1924), receiving the name Arsenios.[77] That priest was recently recognized as a saint in the Orthodox Church (1988). His family fled as refugees from Asia Minor to Greece where they first settled on the island of Corfu and finally in the northeastern town of Konitsa in Epirus.[78] There, Paisios completed his elementary education and military service.

74. *Ibid.*, pp. 220 and 197.
75. *Ibid.*, p. 228.
76. *Ibid.*, pp. 207 and 217.
77. The Elder Paisios authored a very popular book on *Saint Arsenios of Cappadocia* (Convent of St John the Theologian, 1975). Paisios is also the author of two other books published by the same convent: *Elder Hatzi-Georgis the Athonite 1809-1886* (1986) and *Fathers and Stories of the Holy Mountain* (1993). The convent has also posthumously published some of the elder's *Letters* (1994) and *Homilies*, Vols. 1-3 (1998-2001).
78. For biographical and other anecdotal stories about the Elder Paisios, see Fr Christodoulos [Angeloglou], *Elder Paisios of the Holy Mountain* (Mount Athos,

In 1950, a year after being discharged from the army, Paisios set out for Mount Athos, where he submitted to the spiritual guidance of a virtuous monk named Cyril and where he received his monastic tonsure and name, Averkios. His favorite reading included the *Sayings of the Desert Fathers* and Abba Isaac the Syrian, whose *Mystic Treatises* he kept beneath his pillow at all times.[79] He also enjoyed visiting many of the well-known monastic figures of the time. Four years later, under the direction of another spiritual monk, Fr Symeon, Paisios received his monastic habit (or *schema*) and the new name Paisios. In 1962, he traveled to Mount Sinai, where he remained for two years in a mountainous cell opposite the holy mount of the Burning Bush and St Catherine's Monastery. The Bedouins loved Paisios, who used to carve wooden crosses and sell them to pilgrims in order to buy food for the natives.

In 1964, he returned to the Holy Mountain, where he settled in the Scete of Iviron. His spiritual father during this period was a charismatic Russian elder named Tychon (1884-1968), on whose death and at whose advice Paisios moved into his cell until 1979. In 1968, Paisios encouraged one of his closest disciples—Vasileios (Gondikakis)—to serve as Abbot in order to restore Stavronikita Monastery, a step that proved crucial for the revival in recent decades of monasticism on the Holy Mountain. Although Fr Vasileios, arguably the most eloquent and articulate theological voice on Mount Athos today, is conspicuously absent from all published accounts of the life of the Elder Paisios, I am convinced that he was the closest spiritual disciple of the elder and that his words quoted in the introduction to this paper in fact refer anonymously to Paisios.

In 1979, Paisios moved yet again to a cell called "Panagouda" (or "little Virgin Mother"), which was to be the last cell that he inhabited on the Mountain. From this cell, he directed the lives of numerous people who sought his advice through visitations and correspondence alike. I recall the small bottle with paper and

1994; English trans. 1998); *idem, Chosen Vessel* (Mount Athos, 1996); Athanasios Pakovalis, *Father Paisios Told Me . . .* (Thessaloniki, 1997); English translation: *Talks with Father Paisios* (2000); and Athanasios Melissaris, *Paisios: Fragrant Flower of Orthodoxy* (Katerini: Epektasi Publications, 1997). Other brief accounts may be found in Constantine Cavarnos, *New Library*, Vol. 2 (Belmont, MA, 1992), pp. 131 and 192-198.

79. See Christodoulos, *Elder Paisios*, p. 129.

pencil outside the fence that surrounded his cell, where people would leave notes with personal problems, names of those seeking intercession, letters requiring counsel, and gifts for distribution to the poor. Paisios literally became a magnet that drew out and transformed human pain and suffering. Even if he could not possibly meet with everyone who came to his door,[80] yet Paisios had a way of making people feel his presence and comfort.

His own health problems began as early as 1966, when he experienced respiratory difficulties. It was during one of his hospitalizations in Thessalonika that the Elder became acquainted with the Convent of St John the Theologian at Souroti, a small town outside of Thessalonika. When in 1988, Paisios's health deteriorated further—he was diagnosed with liver and lung cancer—it was the nuns of this convent who nursed him. In November of 1993, unwittingly, Paisios departed Mount Athos for the last time. He died on July 12, 1994, being buried in the same convent, where in 1970 he had also transferred the relics of his elder, Fr Arsenios of Cappadocia, who was originally buried on the island of Kerkyra.

*

* *

Paisios knows that he too is part of a long spiritual tradition, not only because of the holy man who baptized him, but also because of the holy mountain on which he dwells. However, for him, tradition is more than a mere historical lineage; it implies an *unbroken sacramental heritage*: "We are in no way inferior to the Apostles," he observes. "The Apostles were physically close to Christ. . . . However, we, too, have Him inside our soul from a very young age, through the grace of Holy Baptism."[81] He does not simply belong to a tradition; he has appropriated the very conviction of that tradition: "I do not care any more if someone tells me that God does not exist!"[82] It is because he knows! He is one of the few ascetics—of the contemporary present and even the classic past—who refers to the sacraments, and especially to Baptism: "The grace of God entered our

80. A key was attached to a ring on a rope, and this would be drawn up or down along a line leading from the window of his cell to the gate at the fence. If Paisios could open his door, he would let down the key—sometimes foreseeing the spiritual need of the visitor.
81. Cf. Christodoulos, *Elder Paisios*, pp. 54-55. On tradition, see p. 104.
82. *Ibid.*, p. 59.

soul through Holy Baptism; it is a gift granted to all of us."[83] This grace constitutes the starting-point and goal of ascetic discipline. The aim of self-purification is to allow more room for Divine grace to function: *ascesis* looks to *kenosis*. Or, put differently, *labora* leads to *ora*: "Do your spiritual work," he recommends, "and say the Jesus Prayer. Your thoughts, will, and desires are where your mind is."[84] The purpose of ascetic renunciation is "to count down from ten to zero before sending off our missile into space!"—"like the Americans do!"[85] He strongly advises people to "live as simply as they can", not allowing their lives to become complicated.[86]

Yet perhaps the most apparent feature of Paisios's life and teaching is his positive and edifying counsel. His spirituality resembles that of the Desert Fathers, with their emphasis on honesty and integrity. Be who you are, is the advice he often gives people who approach him; "do not pretend."[87] For him, the heart is also the seat of authentic being. *Positive spirituality* might aptly describe his path to the heart. In words reminiscent of Mark the Monk, Paisios believed that positive thoughts beget positive thoughts:

> Think positively. . . . Try to develop positive thoughts. . . . It is more important for one to develop good thoughts than to be guided by a spiritual father who is considered a living saint. . . . A single positive thought equals a vigil [*i.e.*, an entire night in prayer] on Mount Athos.[88]

He is at home with the ways of thoughts, and he understands how people think:

> I know from experience that in this life people are divided into two categories. A third category does not exist; people either belong to one or another. The first resembles the fly. The main characteristic

83. *Ibid.*, p. 54. See also p. 88. For the sacrament of the Eucharist, see p. 115.
84. *Ibid.*, p. 53. On the Jesus Prayer, see pp. 26 and 144. On prayer in general, see pp. 79-83.
85. *Ibid.*, p. 54. The heart, he believes, is the battleground for this warfare. See pp. 118 and 159.
86. *Ibid.*, p. 138.
87. *Ibid.*, pp. 26 and 29. This book is the main source for this part of my paper; I have slightly edited the translation. See also p. 25. For a collection of apophthegmatic sayings by the Elder, see especially pp. 127-145.
88. *Ibid.*, p. 29. See also pp. 31-32, 34, and 44. One of his favorite sayings was: "Thoughts are like airplanes flying in the air. If you ignore them, there is no problem. If you pay attention to them, you create an airport inside you and permit them to land" (p. 48).

> of the fly is that it is attracted to dirt. . . . The other category is like the bee, whose main characteristic is always to look for something sweet.[89]

The reality is, of course, that Paisios has a sound knowledge of his own heart and mind:

> It is much better to be aware of our own weakness, than to struggle very hard while neglecting it. . . . I have been a monk for many years and among the virtues I have acquired, I have also developed some weaknesses, which I have not managed to get rid of.[90]

Even when Paisios felt a fatherly obligation to respond to the growing apocalyptic insecurity in his country about "the sign of the times 666", he began his brief pamphlet with the words: "After the devil's cataclysm, God's sunshine will appear." And when he no longer felt that the issue was as relevant, he encouraged people to be silent: "A good dog barks when it sees a thief coming. But when the thief disappears, it stops barking. If it continues, then there is something wrong with the dog!"[91]

However, his is not simply a spirituality of "feeling good" or "self-help". Paisios is careful to underline the importance of guidance in our thoughts: "You can turn the wheel [of thoughts], but your spiritual father will show you the direction."[92] Indeed, Paisios would further qualify his "positive spirituality" by adopting an *apophatic* attitude. He insists that the "soul must be cleansed from positive thoughts as well":[93]

> We must not have any thoughts in our mind or heart [note the same vagueness in terminology here and elsewhere as in Sophrony and Joseph], neither positive ones nor negative ones, for this space inside us belongs to the grace of God. . . . We must ignore both positive and negative thoughts, and always confess them to our spiritual father, and obey whatever he tells us.[94]

Reference here to God's grace leads to another fundamental element in Paisios's teaching, namely, the emphasis on Divine grace and human gratitude. Without this particular element, Paisios says,

89. *Ibid.*, pp. 43-44. For his understanding of human thoughts, see p. 40.
90. *Ibid.*, pp. 130-131, and 45.
91. *Ibid.*, p. 98. For the pamphlet, see pp. 94-97.
92. *Ibid.*, p. 36.
93. *Ibid.*, p. 29.
94. *Ibid.*, p. 30 and 40. For the inconsistent use of terminology, see also p. 54.

"we do not only not seek Divine assistance, but we also misuse our own logic."[95] In fact, lack of gratitude for God's grace leads to grief; the vocation of human beings is to be "filled with responsive gratefulness!" (Greek term: *filotimo*).[96]

Finally, in describing the spiritual teaching of Paisios, positive thinking reflects one aspect; *spiritual practicality* reflects another. He is balanced in his outlook, even in matters of prayer and discipline: "Everything must be done with discretion. We should not indiscreetly hold long services that make most of the monks fall asleep. During vigils, we should take into consideration both the younger monks, who are still weak, and the older ones."[97] Among the "practical" matters broached by the Elder are: taking medication (he says that "pills will not solve the problem, but only temporarily cover it"), problems of the church hierarchy (he advises us to "mind our own humble thoughts"), ecumenism, extraterrestrial creatures (he says not to worry about them!), voting and taxes, questions relating to raising children (he says that children should be scolded in the morning so as to have the entire day to take their minds *off* the discipline, noting also that "while children are young, they are like angels; when they enter their teens . . . they become small beasts!"), getting good grades at school, finding a spiritual father, obedience to spiritual elders and bishops (the latter, he notes, we should obey "with discretion"!), dealing with magic, doctors and obstetricians, cursing, material things, abortion, disability, lying, business, mobile telephones (he feels that they disturb the silence of the Mountain), fear of war, the rule of prayer, the life of the sacraments, and patience:

> Live with patience, because there is no other way to get through life today. Be patient, and do not take everything too seriously. Go to a large supermarket, and buy yourself a good dose of apathy![98]

The practicality, or realism, of his teaching stems from a sense of compassion that allows the Elder to remain connected with society,

95. *Ibid.*, p. 30.
96. *Ibid.*, pp. 45 and 58. See also p. 133: "Lack of gratitude is a very serious sin."
97. *Ibid.*, p. 103. It is interesting that Paisios feels that it is the younger monks who are the weaker ones.
98. *Ibid.*, p. 145. *Apatheia,* of course, signifies not indifference but acceptance in silence and love. For the other references, see pp. 39-41 (also p. 108), 114-115, 117, 122-123, 125 (also p. 135), 128, 135-136, 138, 140-144.

in spite of any monastic isolation.[99] Paisios is anxious to stress personal freedom and responsibility in the struggle against thoughts and passions, which are neither destroyed nor ignored, but rather restrained and redirected:

> Evil does not exist in this world. Everything was created by God and created "good". . . . Evil exists when we make wrong use of the things God granted to us for our benefit. . . . Therefore, we must use everything in the right way, the natural way, and not abuse them or go against nature.[100]

When one contains the passions, one gains a sense of com-passion, which is none other than the experience of Divine justice or the vision of the world through the eyes of God—"an expression of God's sympathy towards humanity", of "God's providence for the whole creation", of "God's joy over the repentance even of the devil". Compassion toward others is another way of giving and, therefore, yet another form of renunciation. Put simply, "God tolerates everybody." So too should we![101] Paisios was convinced that if people "applied to their lives the things they understand" from the Scriptures, then there would be greater affinities between Christians and Muslims: both religions seek to love God, to love the neighbor, and to endure with patience.[102]

Paisios wanted himself—and wanted others too—to participate in people's problems and pain: "When we are awake at night praying, we should ask God to help those who suffer from insomnia and require sleeping pills."[103] The imagery he adopts is preciously simple, reminiscent of the Desert Fathers: "[Divine] justice is like a cork; no matter how hard we press it to the bottom of the sea, it will always come back to the surface."[104]

99. *Ibid.*, pp. 33-34, where Paisios tried to imagine the suffering of the Vietnam war in the midst of city noise. When a person asks Paisios to pray for his eye surgery, Paisios says: "Humanly speaking, I am telling you that if you lose your eyes, I will give you mine so both of us will be able to see with one eye" (pp. 120-121).
100. *Ibid.*, pp. 112-113 (and Paisios goes on to discuss the "good use" of money, drugs, and knives), 50, 46, and 48.
101. *Ibid.*, pp. 63, 133, and 132. See also pp. 61-67.
102. *Ibid.*, p. 119.
103. *Ibid.*, pp. 130-131.
104. *Ibid.*, p. 64. When he once received an overcoat as a gift, he regarded it as a gift for another person who was poor.

It is this lens of "Divine sympathy" or "Divine justice" that further permits Paisios to feel close to the animal world. While there may be stories of visions that he experienced of the Divine light, of the Lord, of the Virgin Mother, of St Euphemia, or even of the "saint of the day", it is stories of his connection to animals that most color the life of the Elder. This connection—the development of, as he calls it, "a different attitude inside the soul"—comes less from a sense of abstract identity than from a profound humility and obedience, ultimately from a keen sense of listening. Silence is yet another function of the heart, and the only fitting response to God's word. A heart listening humbly to God listens also to God in others and in everything: "My mind tells me that even animals are better than I; so, I humble myself before them and obey them. . . . What do you think then? Should I obey the animals or not? My thoughts tell me that I should."[105] Paisios even encourages those of us who write on environmental issues: "Ecological destruction is taking place. Those who can should write and talk about it."[106] Such an attitude, caused by the softening of the heart, results in the "partial experience in this life of heaven or hell". According to one's clean or unclean conscience, the heart becomes either a place of paradise or else of torment.[107]

Conclusion

The three monastic elders referred to in this paper embrace a tradition they both deeply respect and genuinely reflect. Yet the manner in which they embody and extend this very tradition differs greatly. One is an educated man, able to articulate the spiritual nuances of *ascesis* and contemplation; another is an unlettered and austere monk, willing to share with his disciples the fruits of his ascetic discipline; the third is a simple, yet popular spiritual guide, who was able to touch the lives of numerous people in our times.

105. *Ibid.*, p. 86. See also pp. 109-110, 118, 137, 156, and 172. For the various visions, see pp. 150-155, 158, and 170. In keeping with the rest of the ascetic tradition, Paisios stresses obedience; when it comes to obedience to bishops, he shrewdly observes: "We should practice obedience with discretion" (cf. p. 139).
106. *Ibid.*, p. 136.
107. *Ibid.*, pp. 135 and 106. For "our duty to make the pain of others our own", see pp. 134, 136, and 111.

Even the style and content of the works explored in this paper—while clearly adhering to particular principles of the spiritual life and reflecting certain writings in the long heritage of classics on the prayer of the heart—reveal a breadth of insights and represent a variety of paths to the heart. The Elder Sophrony discerns and declares the fundamental truths of the Kingdom in a personal and genuine way. He learned this way from his elder, St Silouan the *Starets,* whose teaching he also bequeathed to later generations. Joseph the Hesychast is interpreted by an elder who lived beside him for eleven years and who conveys and interprets the wisdom of his master in an authentic way. Once again, we are exposed to a charismatic succession, with a disciple recording the life and teachings of his spiritual master. Finally, the Elder Paisios reaches us through another Athonite monk who transmits the counsels of the Elder to issues apparently—and perhaps, on occasion, unfortunately—raised for the most part by himself. Yet this Paisios is also the one who shared with our generation the wisdom and holiness of St Arsenios of Cappadocia.

While in their solitude living apart from the world, each of these elders remained an integral part of the world, comprised the very heart of the world. It is not the great individual fast or the personal ascetic feat, but the heart of what really matters that counted in their lives. They were pursuers of depth in detail: Sophrony took the time to look you in the eyes; Joseph ignored his disability to pick up a lentil from the floor; and Paisios conversed with a lizard on his porch.

There were times in reading these works, I admit, when I felt discomfort with the particular paths adopted or advised by these elders. Yet Sophrony refers to an "eternal Truth transcending all 'scientific truths'".[108] "In the spiritual sphere," writes Joseph, "human rules of ordinary logic do not apply."[109] "The [light and] law of the Spirit" (Rom 8.2)—a phrase used repeatedly in the book on Joseph the Hesychast and sealing the life of Sophrony, Joseph, and Paisios—regulate every movement and detail of life. This further constitutes the lenses through which we must look at the writings of the elders we have examined. Paisios warns that in order to communicate with those who have received this eternal knowledge,

108. *Ibid.*, p. 80.
109. *Op. cit.*, p. 159.

"you need to be tuned in to the same spiritual frequency". And he continues with the positive and non-judgmental counsel that is so characteristic of him:

> Do not try to use your logic. . . . Sometimes, I do not understand what I read. I only sense there is something good in it. But it seems it is not the right time for me to absorb this specific good, so I leave it aside.[110]

Joseph too is encouraging:

> For those who have ears to hear and eyes to see, the grace which indwells in the words and experiences of the[se] Elder[s] will not be hidden, but will make known to them that these are the fruit of many struggles and labors . . . and bear the seal of the full patristic tradition.[111]

110. *Elder Paisios*, pp. 118-120. See also pp. 25-26.
111. Joseph, *op. cit.*, p. 229.

Toward an Esoteric Ecumenism

Chapter 7

The Metaphysics of Interfaith Dialogue: Sufi Perspectives on the Universality of the Quranic Message

Reza Shah-Kazemi

> Truly those who believe, and the Jews, and the Christians, and the Sabeans—whoever believeth in God and the Last Day and performeth virtuous deeds—surely their reward is with their Lord, and no fear shall come upon them, neither shall they grieve.
>
> Quran 2:62

This paper is focused upon the Quran as a source of inspiration for interfaith dialogue. The Quran is indeed unique among the revealed scriptures of the world in the explicit manner in which it refers not only to dialogue between adherents of different faith-communities, but also to the divine ordainment of religious diversity, and, in consequence, to the spiritual validity of these diverse religious paths, which are presented in the Quranic discourse as so many outwardly divergent facets of a single, universal revelation by the unique and indivisible Absolute.

It would be a relatively straightforward task to let the Quran speak for itself, by citing one after the other such verses as that used in our epigraph, verses which relate to these universal themes; the result would be, we believe, a compelling argument in favor of religious dialogue, based on the metaphysical premise that the different revealed religions are truly and effectively paths to salvation. But such a presentation, however immediately intelligible it might be to some, would leave out of account the diverse ways in which the verses in question are, and have been, interpreted.

What follows, therefore, is a presentation of these key verses from a particular point of view, that adopted by those most steeped in the spiritual and mystical tradition of Islam, Sufism. For Sufi expositions of the metaphysical and spiritual dimensions of the Quranic revelation can be of inestimable value to all those engaged in religious dialogue, and to those, in particular, who see the different religions not so much as mutually exclusive and inevitably antagonistic systems of dogmatic belief, but rather as so many "paths to the heart", as the title of the present volume of essays puts it.

The most eloquent and compelling contemporary expression of such a view of the religions of the world is to be found in the corpus of Frithjof Schuon (d.1998).[1] In asserting the validity of Schuon's principle of the "trancendent unity of religions", from the point of view of the Islamic tradition as a whole, Seyyed Hossein Nasr's "Islam and the Encounter of Religions" is an important point of reference.[2] After describing the encounter between Islam and other religions on different planes—historical, legal, theological, philosophical, and scientific—Nasr writes that it is on the level of Sufi esoterism that

> the most profound encounter with other traditions has been made, and where one can find the indispensable ground for the understanding in depth of other religions today. The Sufi is one who seeks to transcend the world of forms, to journey from multiplicity to Unity, and from the particular to the Universal. He leaves the many for the One, and through this very process is granted the vision of the One in the many. For him all forms become transparent, including religious forms, thus revealing to him their unique origin.[3]

This unique origin is described as the "Centre where all the radii meet, the summit which all roads reach. Only such a vision of the Centre," Nasr continues, "can provide a meaningful dialogue between religions, showing both their inner unity and formal diversity."[4]

The present paper takes this affirmation as its point of departure. Specifically, in the first part of the paper, the aim is to show the ways in which key Sufi themes of gnosis or *ma'rifah* arise organically out of meditation and reflection upon particular Quranic verses,

1. See especially his seminal work, *The Transcendent Unity of Religions* (London, 1953). T. S. Eliot wrote of this book that "I have met with no more impressive work on the comparative study of Oriental and Occidental religion" (quoted by Huston Smith in his Introduction to the revised edition of the book [Wheaton, IL, 1993]).
2. Published in his work, *Sufi Essays* (London, 1972), pp. 123-151.
3. *Ibid.*, p. 146.
4. *Ibid.*, p. 150.

and to allude briefly to some of the implications of these themes for interfaith dialogue or simply dialogue as such. In the second part of the paper, the aim is to show how a spiritual appreciation of the essence of Islam, based on Sufi exegesis of particularly direct Quranic verses, opens up a path leading to the heart of religion as such, and how such a conception, in turn, helps to situate particular religious traditions within a spiritual universe defined by "quintessential Islam"—that is, Islam understood as universal submission to God, rather than only as a particular religious denomination. In the process, we hope to stress the importance of those Quranic verses which deal with the universality of the religious phenomenon, to show that it is in the hands of the Sufi commentators that the deeper meanings and implications of these important verses are brought to light, and to relate the principles derived from this encounter between Sufi spirituality and Quranic universality to themes germane to dialogue.

As regards spiritual exegesis of specific verses, we shall be drawing from a small number of eminent representatives of the Sufi tradition, such as Ibn Arabi, Ghazzali, and Rumi, but our principal source of esoteric commentary is that written by Abd al-Razzaq Kashani (d.730/1329), a distinguished representative of the school of Ibn Arabi. This commentary has played a role of great importance in the tradition of esoteric commentary in Islam, its renown having been amplified in recent times as a result of its erroneous attribution to Ibn Arabi.[5] Its value lies principally in the fact that it presents a complete exegesis, chapter by chapter, of the Quran, and it does so from an uncompromisingly esoteric perspective. It thus leads us, according to Pierre Lory, "to the very root of the Sufi endeavour: the encounter with the holy word, and the spiritual force proper to it, not only on the level of meaning, but in the most intimate dimension of the meditating soul."[6]

5. The commentary was published under the name of Ibn Arabi, with the title *Tafsîr al-Shaykh al-Akbar*, in Cairo (1866), and in Cawnpore (1883); and under his name, with the title *Tafsîr al-Qur'ân al-Karîm*, in Beirut (1968). We are using the Cairo 1283/1866 edition.

6. P. Lory, *Les Commentaires ésoteriques du Coran d'après 'Abd ar-Razzâq al-Qâshânî* (Paris, 1980), p. 7. It is also noteworthy that Kashani was a "Shi'i Sufi", and that his work thus constitutes, as Abdurrahman Habil writes, "one of the several points where the Shi'ite and Sufi commentary traditions meet each other". See his very useful essay, "Traditional Esoteric Commentaries on the Quran", in *Islamic Spirituality*, Vol. I: *Foundations*, ed. S. H. Nasr (London, 1987). See also

The Metaphysics of Oneness and Dialogue with the "Other"

What is meant by the phrase "the metaphysics of oneness" is the metaphysical interpretation given by the Sufis to the fundamental message of the Quran, the principle of *tawhîd*, expressed in the creedal formula: *Lâ ilâha illâ'Llâh* —no god but God. Whereas theologically the statement is a relatively straightforward affirmation of the uniqueness of the Divinity, and the negation of other "gods", metaphysically the formula is read as an affirmation of the true nature of being: no reality but the one Reality. Kashani comments as follows on one of the many verses affirming the central principle of *tawhîd*, namely, 20:8: "Allâh, there is no god but Him": "His unique essence does not become multiple, and the reality of His identity derives therefrom, and does not become manifold; so He is He in endless eternity as He was in beginningless eternity. There is no He but Him, and no existent apart from Him."[7] We have here not only an affirmation of the oneness of God to the exclusion of other gods, but also, and more fundamentally, the affirmation of a unique reality, which is exclusive of all otherness, or rather in relation to which all otherness is unreal.

The shift from "theological" *tawhîd* to "ontological" *tawhîd* is one of the hallmarks of another great representative of the school of Ibn Arabi, Sayyid Haydar Amoli (d. 787/1385), in whose works one observes a remarkable synthesis between Shi'ite gnosis and Sufi metaphysics. He refers to the "folk of the exterior" (*ahl al-zâhir*) who pronounce the formula *Lâ ilâha illâ'Llâh* in the sense conveyed by the following Quranic verse, an exclamation by the polytheists of the strangeness of the idea of affirming one deity: "Does he make the gods one God? This is a strange thing" (38:5). This monotheistic affirmation is, for Amoli, the essence of the *tawhîd* professed by the folk of the exterior, and is called "theological" *tawhîd* (*at-tawhîd al-ulûhiyy*). In contrast, the "folk of the interior" (*ahl al-bâtin*) negate the multiplicity of existences, and affirm the sole reality of Divine being; their formula is: "There is nothing in existence apart from God (*laysa fi'l-wujûd siwa'Llâh*)", and they cite the verse "Everything

the excellent work by Abu Bakr Siraj ad-Din, *The Book of Certainty* (Cambridge, 1992), which offers a concise and profound exposition of Sufi gnosis based principally on Kashani's commentary on certain Quranic verses.

7. Kashani, *Tafsîr*, Vol. II, p. 17.

is perishing save His Face" (28:88) in support. This, Amoli maintains, is "ontological" *tawhîd* (*at-tawhîd al-wujûdiyy*).[8]

Despite appearing to be the concern only of mystics with an otherworldly and introspective orientation, such metaphysical perspectives on the central Quranic message of *tawhîd* are in fact highly pertinent to the theme of dialogue. In particular, the implications of *tawhîd* with respect to notions of "self" and "other" are potentially of considerable value in helping to overcome one of the key obstacles to authentic and fruitful dialogue in today's multi-religious world. This obstacle consists in a notion of "identity" or "selfhood" that has become opaque, congealed, or reified. When the self is regarded as the absolute criterion for engaging with the other, there arises a suffocating notion of identity which feeds directly into chauvinism, bigotry, and fanaticism—qualities that are expressed by the Arabic word *ta'assub.* In its root meaning, this word graphically conveys the self-indulgence that constitutes the life-blood of all forms of fanaticism; the verb *ta'assaba* primarily signifies binding a cloth around one's head.[9] One becomes literally self-enwrapped, each fold of the cloth compounding the initial preoccupation with one's own congealed frame of identity; one becomes imprisoned within a mental "fabric" woven by one's own prejudices, and as the head swells, the mind narrows.

If the "I" be identified in a quasi-absolute manner with the ego, the family, the nation, or even the religion to which one belongs, then the "other"—at whatever level—will likewise be given a quasi-absolute character. It is precisely such exclusivist notions of "self" and "other" that contribute to the dynamics of suspicion and fear, fanaticism, and conflict. The metaphysics, or science, of oneness, on the other hand, does not so much abolish as attenuate, not equalize but situate, all limited conceptions of identity. It serves to relativize every conceivable degree of identity in the face of the Absolute; in other words, it ensures that no determinate, formal conception of the self is absolutized, or "worshipped", however unconsciously, as an "idol". The metaphysics of integral *tawhîd* can

8. Sayyed Haydar Amoli, *Jâmi' al-asrâr wa manba' al-anwâr,* ed. H. Corbin, O. Yahia (Tehran and Paris, 1969), p. 72.

9. Lane, *Arabic-English Lexicon,* Vol.2, p. 2058. Needless to say, in the Islamic tradition, the turban is also, and pre-eminently, endowed with a positive value, indicating nobility, dignity, and grace, as attested by numerous sayings of the Prophet.

be regarded as the most complete and effective antidote to fanaticism insofar as it undermines this idolatry of selfhood, a type of idolatry tersely summed up in the Quranic question: "Hast thou seen him who maketh his desire his god?" (25:43; almost identical at 45:23).

In the Quran, God says to Moses at the theophany of the burning bush, *Innî ana'Llâh*—"Truly I, I am God" (20:12). The following extremely important comment is made on this by Jafar al-Sadiq (d. 148/765), Shi'ite Imam, regarded also in the Sufi tradition as one of the "poles" (*aqtâb*) or supreme authorities of the early generations. This comment comes in a *tafsîr* that was to have a profound influence both on the unfolding of the genre of esoteric exegesis, and on the articulation and diffusion of Sufi metaphysical doctrines:

> It is not proper for anyone but God to speak of Himself by using these words *innî anâ*. I [that is, Moses, according to al-Sâdiq's commentary] was seized by a stupor and annihilation (*fanâ'*) took place. I said then: "You! You are He who is and who will be eternally, and Moses has no place with You nor the audacity to speak, unless You let him subsist by your subsistence".[10]

This expresses a theme of fundamental importance in Sufi metaphysics, or in that dimension of the Sufi tradition that pertains directly to gnosis, *ma'rifah*. The primary focus of *ma'rifah* is God conceived of as *al-Haqq*, the True or the Real,[11] in the face of which the individual "I", on its own account, is reduced to naught. Human subjectivity is strictly speaking nothing when confronted by the divine "I". Another important early Sufi, al-Kharraz, defines *ma'rifah* in relation to this principle of the one-and-only "I-ness" of God: "Only God has the right to say 'I'. For whoever says 'I' will not reach the level of gnosis."[12]

10. Quoted in C.W. Ernst, *Words of Ecstasy in Sufism* (Albany, 1985), p. 10.
11. As regards the increasing use by Sufis of the name *al-Haqq* for God, which is of profound significance for the shift from "theological" to "ontological" oneness, Massignon argues, in his essay on the lexicography of Islamic mysticism, that "it was from the *tafsîr* of Jafar and the mystic circles of Kufah that the term *al-Haqq* spread, through Dhul-Nun al-Misri and others, to become the classic name for God in *tasawwuf*" (cited in John Taylor, "Jafar al-Sadiq: Forebear of the Sufis", *Islamic Culture* [Vol. XL, No. 2, 1966], p. 110).
12. Cited in A. Schimmel, *Mystical Dimensions of Islam* (University of North Carolina, 1975), p. 55. Also Abu Nasr al-Sarraj makes the statement that none can say "I" but God, because "I-ness" (*al-anniyya*) pertains only to God. See the chapter on

It is difficult to over-emphasize the importance of this perspective in both the speculative metaphysics and the spiritual realization proper to Sufism. If the Quranic presentation of the principle of *tawhîd* predominantly stresses the objective truth of the message, Sufi spirituality finds its apotheosis in the realization of the subjective concomitant of this message, this subjective element being, paradoxically, the very extinction of individual subjectivity, expressed by the term *fanâ'*.[13] One might almost say that the truth of *tawhîd* is realized in direct proportion to the realization of *fanâ'*, or to the realization of the realities that flow from the attainment of this state;[14] on the other hand, to the extent that one falls short of the realization of one's nothingness, one cannot escape the "sin" of idolatry (*shirk*): the setting up of "another" as a "partner" or "associate" of the one-and-only Reality, the "other" being one's own self.

The truth which *tawhîd* declares is thus, from this perspective, radically different from the truth of dogmatic theology, of proposi-

tawhîd in his *Kitâb al-Luma'*, ed. R. A. Nicholson (E. J. Gibb Memorial Series XXII, London, 1963), p. 32 (of the Arabic text).

13. It ought to be said that in fact the ultimate "apotheosis" of Sufism is not *fanâ'*, but *baqâ'*, or subsistence, which follows the state of extinction, as is indicated in the sentence quoted above from al-Sadiq's commentary. The "return" to the world of phenomena, and to the individual condition, after having realized one's nothingness in the state of *fanâ'*, is deemed a "higher" or more complete attainment than the state of absorption, extinction, or annihilation. Ibn Arabi distinguishes between those "sent back" (*mardûdûn*) and those "absorbed" or effaced (*mustahlikûn*); the former are deemed "more perfect" and are in turn sub-divided into those who return only to themselves, and those who return with the mandate to guide others to the Truth, these latter being the highest of all. See his *Journey to the Lord of Power: A Sufi Manual on Retreat*—this being a translation of his treatise entitled *Risâlat al-anwâr fimâ yumnah sâhib al-khalwa min al-asrâr*, which is literally a "treatise on the lights in the secrets granted to the one who enters the spiritual retreat". Trans. R. T. Harris (New York, 1981), p. 51. See also our forthcoming publication, *Paths to Transcendence: Spiritual Realization according to Shankara, Ibn Arabi, and Meister Eckhart* (State University of New York Press), where the theme of the "existential return" is discussed in comparative context.
14. Ghazzali mentions various gnostic sciences (*ma'ârif*, pl. of *ma'rifah*) that are revealed only in the state of *fanâ'*, the reason for which is given as follows: the operations of the individual faculties act as obstacles to this mode of inspired disclosure, being tied to the sensible world which is "a world of error and illusion". See No. 56 of his treatise *al-Arba'în*, quoted in F. Jabre, *La Notion de la Ma'rifa chez Ghazali* (Paris, 1958), p. 124. He also speaks of the ultimate degree of *ma'rifah*, the revelation of the sole reality of God, which comes about only through the state of *fanâ'*. See *ibid.*, p. 65.

Place
Stamp
Here

World Wisdom
P. O. Box 2682
Bloomington, IN 47402-2682
U.S.A.

tional logic, or of empirical fact: this truth is the intelligible face of an infinite Reality, a Reality which cannot be exhaustively defined or confined by any words, a Reality before which the individuality as such is extinguished.[15] Thus the greatest of all sins is identified by the Sufis not in moral but ontological terms: it is the sin of one's own separative existence. Commenting on the words of the Quran which describe the qualities of the believers, those who avoid the worst of sins (42:37), Kashani writes, "Those sins are constituted by their existence (*wujûdâtihim*), and this is the most despicable of the qualities of their souls, which manifest through actions in the station of effacement."[16] In relation to the plea for forgiveness at 2:286, Kashani comments, "Forgive us the sin of our very existence, for truly it is the gravest of the grave sins (*akbar al-kabâ'ir*)." He then offers the following couplet, referring to a statement by the famous woman saint of Basra, Rabiah:

> When I said I have not sinned, she said by way of response, "Thine own existence is a sin to which none can be compared."[17]

The relationship between the "truth" of *tawhîd* and the soul of the individual is thus elevated beyond the spheres of morality, theology, and all formal thought as such. The soul does not "acquire" some cognitive content that is called "knowledge of divine unity"; rather, its very manifestation as soul precludes or contradicts the full, mystical realization of that unity. Ibn Arabi quotes Junayd: "When He is there, thou art not, and if thou art there, He is not."[18]

15. The Arabic root *ha'-qâf-qâf* represents very clearly this relationship between truth and reality: *haqq* means both "true" and "real" as well as "right", "due", "worth", *etc.*, with the emphasis on true; while *haqîqah* means both "reality" and "truth", with the emphasis on reality.
16. Kashani, *Tafsîr*, Vol. II, p. 213.
17. *Ibid.*, Vol. I, p. 100. For a discussion of this theme in the context of the doctrine of *wahdat al-wujûd*, see the chapter "Oneness of Being" (pp. 121-130) in M. Lings, *A Sufi Saint of the Twentieth Century* (London, 1971). The statement attributed to Rabi'ah is found on p. 125, n.2. See also the discussion of Kashani's treatment of evil by Pierre Lory in Chapter 8, "La Nature du Mal" (pp. 88-97) of his *Les Commentaires ésoteriques*. He cites the reference to Rabi'ah at p. 90, but translates the words *mâ adhnabtu* as a question, *quelle faute ai-je commise?* ("what sin have I committed?") instead of as an affirmation, "I have not sinned". Both are possible readings, but the context favors the latter, to which Rabi'ah's words are a fitting riposte: you have indeed sinned, inasmuch as your very existence is a sin.
18. *The* Tarjuman al-Ashwaq: *A Collection of Mystical Odes by Muhyiddin Ibn al-Arabi*, trans. R. Nicholson (London, 1978), p. 90.

The exoteric notion of a conceptual truth which, *qua* notion, is appropriated by the individual is here inverted: according to Sufi gnosis, it is the reality alluded to by conceptual truth that assimilates the individual to it.[19] On the one hand, there is the effacement of the individual before a truth whose fulgurating reality infinitely transcends all conceptually posited notions, principles, and dogmas; and on the other, there is the entrenchment of the individuality by the appropriation of a truth whose very conceptual form can become a veil over the reality it is supposed to reveal, and which is its *raison d'être.* In relation to the words of the verse describing the hypocrites as those who are wandering blind in their rebellion (2:15), Kashani refers to one of the characteristic properties of hypocrisy as being "the acquisition of *gnoses* (*ma'ârif*) and sciences (*'ulûm*) and realities (*haqâ'iq*) and words of wisdom (*hikam*) and Divine laws (*sharâ'i'*), only in order to adorn the breast with them, so that the soul might be embellished thereby".[20] All knowledge and wisdom, even if Divine in origin, can be so many veils if they contribute not to the effacement but to the glorification of the individual soul.

We have here the definition of hidden, as opposed to overt, *shirk*, polytheism, or "associationism": this is the *shirk* that, even while affirming theological *tawhîd*, violates ontological *tawhîd.* Overt, evident, or legalistically defined *shirk* means simply associating other gods with God, attributing "partners" to Him in Divinity; while hidden, subtle, and spiritually defined *shirk* means implicitly attributing to God a "partner" in being, namely, oneself. The only remedy for this subtle form of polytheism is *fanâ'.* It is *fanâ'*, ultimately, which enables one to see through the artificial walls—individual and collective—that surround the ego, and which allows one to perceive in all its plenitude the truth that there is nothing real but God. It is not difficult to appreciate what the implications of this principle are in relation to the requirements for effective dialogue with the "other"; in the light of these absolute values, it becomes dif-

19. It is difficult to refrain from mentioning here the words of a Christian mystic whom most Sufis would have no difficulty whatsoever in recognizing as an *'ârif bi'Llâh*, a "knower of God", namely, Meister Eckhart. He said in one his sermons: "The bodily food we take is changed into us, but the spiritual food we receive changes us into itself" (*Meister Eckhart: Sermons and Treatises*, trans. M. O'C. Walshe [Dorset, 1979], Vol. I, p. 50).
20. Kashani, *Tafsîr*, Vol. I, 17.

ficult to shut oneself up within the blindingly evident relativity of one's ego, this diminution of egocentricity being essential for really engaging with, and opening oneself up to, the "other", defined both in terms of the human and the divine.

It might however be objected here that such sublime metaphysical ideals and the spiritual states they call forth can be the concern only of a small number of mystics, and highly accomplished ones at that. Can ordinary people concerned with dialogue and coexistence in the modern world really benefit from such perspectives? We would readily answer in the affirmative. For not only do the principles in question—even on the discursive plane—help dissolve the fixations on selfhood that give rise to pride and arrogance, on the individual and collective levels, but also, more directly, the key Quranic verses from which these principles and perspectives flow can bring about, in the heart of the receptive reader, a penetrating sense of the ephemerality of all things, including, crucially, the ego and its manifold extensions.

Two of the most important of these verses are the following:

> Everything is perishing except His Face [or Essence] (28:88).

> Everything that is thereon is passing away; and there subsisteth but the Face of thy Lord, possessor of Glory and Bounty (55:26-27).

It should be noticed here that the words indicating the ephemeral nature of all things—*hâlik,* perishing", and *fân,* "passing away" or "evanescing"—are both in the present tense: it is not that things will come to naught or perish at some later point in time; they are in fact, here and now, "extinguishing" before our very eyes. In the treatise entitled *Kitâb al-fanâ' fi'l-mushâhadah* ("The Book of Extinction in Contemplation") Ibn Arabi writes that the elimination of "that which never was" is tantamount to realization of "that which never ceased to be".[21] That which will not be is already "not", in a certain sense, and one grasps this not only in the ineffable moments of mystical experience, but also in the very measure that one understands

21. This pinnacle of contemplation, which is predicated on extinction, is discussed in relation to the prophetic definition of *ihsân,* or spiritual excellence: "that you should worship God as if you could see Him, and if you see Him not, He sees you". By effecting a stop in the phrase "if you see Him not" (*in lam takun: tarâhu*), the phrase is changed into: "if you are not, see Him". See pp. 48-49 of the French translation of M.Valson, *Le Livre de l'Extinction dans la Contemplation* (Paris, 1984).

the following principle: Reality is not subject to finality, cancellation, extinction, non-being. That which is absolutely real is That which is eternal: it is the Face of thy Lord that, alone, subsisteth. Conversely, all that which is impermanent is, by that very fact, unreal in the final analysis.

Reflection on the verses above, then, can heighten the sense of the relativity of all things—and, pre-eminently, of the ego, with all its pretensions and extensions—in the face of the one, sole, exclusive Reality. Instead of allowing an egocentric conception of selfhood to be superimposed onto religion and even onto God—both of which are then "appropriated" by the ego[22]—such a perspective helps to engender the opposite tendency: to see the ego itself *sub specie aeternitatis*. What results from this perspective on the ego is a more concrete apprehension of its essential limitations: the contours that delimit and define the ego are more vividly perceived against an infinite background. Thus, what is in question here is not so much a vaguely mystical notion of universal illusion, but a concrete, realistic and effective sense of spiritual proportions. The existential limitations and the psychological pretensions of the ego are cut down to size, and a consciously theocentric focus replaces the all too often unconsciously egocentric one: nothing is absolute but the Absolute. Herein lies the first major lesson given by Sufi gnosis to those engaged in dialogue, a negative one, that is, the negation of egocentricity as a source of pride, exclusivity, and fanaticism.

As for the second lesson, this is the positivity which flows from the complementary aspect of gnosis. For the verses quoted above not only assert the exclusive reality of God; they also contain a subtle allusion to the inclusive reality of God. The Face of God, which alone subsists, is not only the transcendent, Divine Essence, in relation to which all things are nothing; it is also the immanent presence which pervades and encompasses all things, constituting in fact their true being. Before focusing on the verse "Everything

22. This is one meaning of Ibn Arabi's daring phrase "God created in beliefs" (*al-haqq al-makhlûq fi'l-i'tiqâdât*); see his *Fusûs al-hikam* (Cairo, 1306 AH), p. 225; and p. 224 of the English translation, *Bezels of Wisdom*, by R. Austin (New York, 1980). What is in question here are conceptions of God that are pre-determined by the contours of an inherited confessional faith; as such they are more indicative of the believer's own mind than of the Reality of God. See the chapter entitled "Transcending the Gods of Belief" in W. C. Chittick's *The Sufi Path of Knowledge* (Albany, 1989), pp. 335-356.

perisheth except His Face", and in particular on the important and illuminating interpretation of it given by Ghazzali, one should take careful note of the following verses, which refer to this complementary, inclusive dimension of the Divine reality.

> And unto God belong the East and the West; and wherever ye turn, there is the Face of God (2:115).
>
> He is with you, wherever you are (57:4).
>
> We are nearer to him [man] than the neck artery (50:16).
>
> God cometh in between a man and his own heart (8:24).
>
> Is He not encompassing all things? (41:54).
>
> He is the First and the Last, and the Outward and the Inward (57:3).

Each of these verses contains the seeds of the most profound spiritual doctrines;[23] and each has given rise to the most fecund meditation upon that most mysterious of all realities, the immanence of the Absolute in all that exists—the inalienable presence of the transcendent, one-and-only Reality within the entire sphere of relativity, of all that which is, from another point of view "other than God". Ali ibn Abi Talib, the first Shi'ite Imam and one of the primary sources of what later crystallized as Sufism, sums up the mystery in these terms: God is "with every thing, but not through association; and other than every thing, but not through separation".[24] Nothing that exists can be altogether separate from the all-encompassing reality of God; and yet this reality has no common measure with anything that exists. His Oneness both includes and excludes all things; hence the affirmation of God's immanence within the world—His

23. See the article "The Qur'ân as the Foundation of Islamic Spirituality", by S. H. Nasr in *Islamic Spirituality, op. cit.*, pp. 3-10. Frithjof Schuon cites the following relevant verses: "The Hereafter is better for thee than this lower world" (94:4); "The life of this world is but sport and play" (29:64); "In your wives and your children ye have an enemy" (44:14); "Say: Allah! Then leave them to their vain talk" (6:91); "Whoso feareth the station of his Lord and restraineth his soul from desire" (79:40). Then he adds, "When the Quran speaks thus, there emerges for the Moslem a whole ascetic and mystical doctrine, as penetrating and complete as any other form of spirituality worthy of the name" (*Understanding Islam* [Bloomington, 1994], p. 60).
24. *Ma'a kulli shay' lâ bi muqârana; ghayr kulli shay' lâ bi muzâyala.* This sentence is found in the first sermon of the *Nahj al-Balâgha.* See the English translation of the sermon in *Peak of Eloquence*, by Sayed Ali Reza (New York, 1996), pp. 91-97.

being "with every thing"—does not imply any diminution of His transcendence; and conversely, the affirmation of God's transcendence above the world—His being "other than every thing"—does not imply His absence from the world.

Returning to the last of the verses cited in the group above, "He is the First and the Last, and the Outward and the Inward", the Sufi shaykh Mawlay al-Arabi al-Darqawi relates the following incident, which we can take as an indirect commentary on the verse. He writes that he was "in a state of remembrance" when he heard a voice recite the words of the verse. "I remained silent, and the voice repeated it a second time, and then a third, whereupon I said: 'As to the First, I understand, and as to the Last, I understand, and as to the Inwardly Hidden,[25] I understand; but as to the Outwardly Manifest, I see nothing but created things.' Then the voice said: 'If there were any outwardly manifest other than Himself, I should have told thee.' In that moment I realized the whole hierarchy of Absolute Being."[26]

The voice declaring that there is nothing outwardly manifest in the world of "created things" other than the being of God can be seen here as providing a commentary on the meaning of God as *az-Zâhir*, "the Outward", or "the Evident". Likewise, the following remarkable affirmations by Ibn Ata'illah al-Iskandari, an earlier Sufi master in the same *tarîqah* as Mulay al-Arabi, the Shadhiliyya, can also be read as an exegesis on the meaning of God's name, *az-Zâhir*:

> The Cosmos (*al-kawn*) is all darkness. It is illumined only by the manifestation of God (*zuhûr al-Haqq*) in it. He who sees the Cosmos and does not contemplate Him in it or by it or before it or after it is in need of light and is veiled from the sun of gnosis by the clouds of created things (*al-âthâr*). That which shows you the existence of His Omnipotence is that He veiled you from Himself by what has no existence alongside of Him.[27]

If, in one respect, God veils Himself from His creatures by Himself, in another, more fundamental respect, He reveals Himself to Himself through His creatures. The central idea here is that of the manifestation (*zuhûr, tajallî*) of Divine reality in, through, and as the

25. This is the translation of *al-Bâtin* in the text in which this report is translated by Lings; likewise, *az-Zâhir* is rendered as "the Outwardly Manifest".
26. Cited in M. Lings, *A Sufi Saint of the Twentieth Century: Shaikh Ahmad al-'Alawi* (London, 1971), p. 131.
27. Ibn Ata'illâh's *Sufi Aphorisms* (*Kitâb al-Hikam*), trans. V. Danner (Leiden, 1973), p. 25.

forms of created things, the cosmos in its entirety. Every phenomenon in creation thus constitutes a locus of manifestation, a *mazhar* for the *zuhûr* or *tajallî* of the Real, the means by which the Real discloses itself to itself through an apparent "other". Herein, one might venture to say, lies the ultimate metaphysical archetype of all dialogue. What we have here is a kind of "dialogue" or communication between different aspects of the Absolute, a dialogue mediated through relativity.

The idea of the self-disclosure of the Absolute to itself by means of the relativity of "the other" lies at the very heart of Ibn Arabi's metaphysics.[28] The whole doctrine of this disclosure of God to Himself is summed up in the opening lines of Ibn Arabi's most commented text, *Fusûs al-hikam.* The chapter entitled "The Ringstone of the Wisdom of Divinity in the Word of Adam" (*Fass hikmat ilâhiyya fî kalimat âdamiyya*) begins:

> The Real willed, glorified be He, in virtue of His Beautiful Names, which are innumerable, to see their identities (*a'yân*)—if you so wish you can say: to see His Identity (*'ayn*)—in a comprehensive being that comprises the entire affair due to its having taken on existence. His Mystery is manifest to Himself through it. The vision a thing has of itself in itself is not like the vision a thing has of itself in another thing, which will serve as a mirror for it.[29]

Man alone reflects back to the Absolute all, and not just some, of the Divine qualities; it is for this reason that man is the "valid interlocutor", the receptacle and the mirror of the Divine qualities, the "other" to whom and through whom these qualities are revealed. The function, then, of an apparent "other", at the level of Divine self-disclosure of itself to itself, is to make possible a particular mode of self-knowledge. One recalls here the holy utterance, or *hadîth qudsî*,[30] so fundamental to Sufi spirituality: "I was a hidden

28. "The term *self-disclosure* (*tajallî*)—often translated as 'theophany'—plays such a central role in Ibn al-Arabi's teachings that, before he was known as the great spokesman for *wahdat al-wujûd,* he had been called one of the Companions of Self-Disclosure (*ashâb al-tajallî*)" (W. C. Chittick, *The Self-Disclosure of God* [Albany, 1998], p. 52).
29. This is cited from a new translation of the *Fusûs al-Hikam* by Caner Dagli, which is due to be published by Kazi Press, Chicago, in 2001, and which is the most accurate and reliable commented translation of this major text in the English language.
30. That is, a saying in which God speaks in the first person, on the tongue of the Prophet, but which is not part of the Quran.

treasure, and I loved to be known (*fa ahbabtu an u'raf*), so I created the world." If the creation of the world springs from a Divine love for a distinct mode of self-knowledge, the Quran indicates that the differentiation, within mankind, in respect of gender, tribe, and race, likewise serves an essentially cognitive function:

> O mankind, truly We have created you male and female, and have made you nations and tribes that ye may know one another. Truly the most noble of you, in the sight of God, is the most Godfearing (49:13).

Distinction and difference are here affirmed as Divinely willed,[31] and as means by which knowledge is attained. One should note that the word used in the phrase "that ye may know one another" is *ta'ârafû*; and the word for being "known" in the *hadîth* of the "hidden treasure" is *u'raf*—both words being derived from the same root, *'arafa*. There is thus a clear connection with *ma'rifah*, spiritual knowledge or gnosis, the essence of which is expressed in the famous *hadîth*, "Whoso knows himself knows his Lord" (*man 'arafa nafsahu faqad 'arafa rabbahu*). Thus, knowledge of self, knowledge of the other, and knowledge of God are all interwoven, and should be seen as complementary and mutually reinforcing, each element having a role to play in the plenary attainment of *ma'rifah*.

The verse cited above is often given as a proof-text for upholding the necessity of dialogue, establishing the principle of peaceful coexistence, and indicating the divine ordainment of human diversity. Now while it does indeed support such principles, the import of the verse is deepened, its message is made the more compelling, and its scope more far-reaching insofar as it is consciously related to the metaphysical principle of self-knowledge through self-disclosure. Thus, dialogue here-below—a dialogue rooted in the sincere desire for greater knowledge and understanding both of "the other" and of oneself—can be seen as a reflection of, and participation in, the very process by which God knows Himself in distinctive, differentiated mode; that is, not in respect of His unique, eternal essence, but in respect of the manifestation of the "treasure" comprised or "hidden" within that essence, yielding the perpetually renewed theophanies of Himself

31. Cf. "And of His signs is the creation of the heavens and the earth, and the differences of your languages and colors. Indeed, herein are signs for those who know" (30:22).

to Himself through an apparent "other", the "seeing of Himself as it were in a mirror".

Another Quranic verse that can be given as a support for this perspective on the cognitive function of creation is the following:

> I only created the jinn and mankind in order that they might worship Me (51:56).

In his *Kitâb al-Luma'*, Abu Nasr al-Sarraj (d. 378/988) reports the comment on this verse given by Ibn Abbas: the word "worship" here means "knowledge" (*ma'rifah*), so that the phrase *illâ li-ya'budûni* (except that they might worship Me) becomes *illâ li-ya'rifûni* (except that they might know Me).[32] This interpretation is given also by several other prominent Sufi authorities, as well as some exoteric scholars.[33] The very purpose of the creation of man thus comes to be equated with that knowledge of God which constitutes the most profound form of worship. But it is not just man that, in coming to know God, participates in the Divine dialogue, that is, the Divine self-disclosure of itself to itself; in fact, there is nothing in creation that does not obey the ontological imperative of "making known" the Divine treasure, even if it is the prerogative of man alone to "know" the Divine treasure, which he does in two ways: through correctly reading all the signs of God or the manifestations of the "hidden treasure"; and through knowing the essence of his own soul:

> We shall show them Our signs on the horizons and in their own souls, so that it become clear to them that He is the Real (41:53).

As regards the objective signs on the horizons, the Quran refers repeatedly to the universal law of "making known" the hidden treasure, doing so in reference to a broadly conceived notion of praise and glorification:

> All that is in the heavens and the earth glorifieth God; and He is the Mighty, the Wise (57:1).

32. *Kitâb al-Luma'*, p. 40 (of the Arabic text). Ed. R. A. Nicholson, E. J. Gibb Memorial Series XXII (London, 1963).
33. See for example Hujwiri's (d. 456/1063) *Kashf al-Mahjûb*, one of the most definitive of the classic manuals of early Sufism, trans. R. A. Nicholson (Lahore, 1992), p. 267; and Qushayri (d. 465/1074) in his famous *Risâla*, trans. B. R. von Schlegell as *Principles of Sufism* (Berkeley, 1990), p. 316. As regards exoteric scholars, Fakhr al-Din al-Razi, for example, cites the *hadîth* of the "hidden treasure", as well as the interpretation *illâ li-ya'rifûni*, at the end of his commentary on 51:56. See *Tafsîr al-kabîr* (Beirut, 2001), vol. 10, p. 194.

> The seven heavens and the earth and all that is therein praise Him, and there is not a thing but hymneth His praise, but ye understand not their praise (17:44).
>
> Hast thou not seen that God, He it is Whom all who are in the heavens and the earth praise; and the birds in flight: each verily knoweth its prayer and its form of glorification (24:41).
>
> He is God, the Creator, the Shaper out of naught, the Fashioner. His are the most beautiful names. All that is in the heavens and the earth glorifieth Him, and He is the Mighty, the Wise (59:24).[34]

Thus we see that in the Quranic perspective, every single thing, by dint of its very existence, "praises" and "glorifies" its Creator: its existence constitutes its praise. Every created thing bears witness to, and thus "praises", its Creator; the existence of every existent "glorifies" the bestower of existence. But, more fundamentally, the existence of every existing thing is not its own; this existence "belongs" exclusively to that reality for which it serves as a locus of theophany (*mazhar*); there is no "sharing", "partnership", or "association" in being—no ontological *shirk*, in other words. Thus we return to the metaphysics of oneness: nothing is real but God. Each thing in existence has two incommensurable dimensions: in and of itself a pure nothingness; but in respect of that which is manifested to it, through it, by means of it—it is real. This is the import of the interpretation given by Ghazzali to the verse cited above, "Everything is perishing except His Face" (28:88). It is worth dwelling on the commentary he provides upon this verse; for it contains, arguably, some of the most radically esoteric ideas of his entire corpus, and also sums up many of the themes expressed thus far.

The commentary comes in his treatise entitled *Mishkât al-anwâr* ("The Niche of Lights"), which takes as its point of departure the famous "light verse":

> God is the light of the heavens and the earth. The similitude of His light is as a niche wherein is a lamp. The lamp is in a glass. The glass is as it were a shining star. [The lamp is] kindled from a blessed olive tree, neither of the East nor of the West, whose oil would almost glow forth though no fire touched it. Light upon light. God guideth to His light whom He will. And God striketh similitudes for mankind. And God knoweth all things (24:35)

34. This theme is expressed in several other verses. See for example, 13:13; 59:1; 61:1; 62:1; 64:1, *et passim.*

Ghazzali's commentary on this verse identifies the one, true light of God as the one, true Being: darkness is nonexistence. The following statement on the nature of existence forms the backdrop for the commentary on 28:88, which is our focus here:

> Existence can be classified into the existence that a thing possesses in itself, and that which it possesses from another. When a thing has existence from another, its existence is borrowed and has no support in itself. When the thing is viewed in itself, and with respect to itself, it is pure non-existence. It only exists inasmuch as it is ascribed to another. This is not a true existence. . . . Hence the Real Existent is God, just as the Real Light is He.[35]

Then comes the section entitled *Haqîqat al-haqâ'iq* ("The Reality of realities"), which describes the ascent of the gnostics, the knowers of God, "from the lowlands of metaphor to the highlands of Reality". They are given a direct vision of the truth

> that there is none in existence save God, and that everything is perishing except His Face. [It is] not that each thing is perishing at one time or at other times, but that it is perishing from eternity without beginning to eternity without end. It can only be so conceived since, when the essence of anything other than He is considered in respect of its own essence, it is sheer nonexistence. But when it is viewed in respect of the "face" to which existence flows forth from the First, the Real, then it is seen as existing not in itself but through the face turned to[36] its giver of existence. Hence the only existent is the Face of God. Each thing has two faces: a face toward itself, and a face toward its Lord. Viewed in terms of the face of itself, it is nonexistent; but viewed in terms of the Face of God, it exists. Hence nothing exists but God and His Face.[37]

Ghazzali then makes an important distinction within the category of these gnostics who "see nothing in existence save the One, the Real". One group is said to arrive at this vision "*irfânan 'ilmiyyan*, that is, as a mode of cognitive knowledge; and another group pos-

35. Al-Ghazali, *The Niche of Lights*, trans. David Buchman (Provo, Utah, 1998), p. 16.
36. We are following Hermann Landolt's translation of *yalî* as "turned to" rather than Buchman's "adjacent to". See Landolt, "Ghazali and 'Religionswissenschaft': Some Notes on the *Mishkât al-Anwâr* for Professor Charles J. Adams", *Études Asiatiques*, XLV, No. 1, 1991, p. 60. Kashani refers to two faces of the heart: the *sadr* (the breast) as the "face of the heart which is turned to (*yalî*) the soul, just as the *fu'âd* is the face of the heart which is turned to the spirit" (*Tafsîr*, Vol. I, p. 17).
37. *The Niche of Lights*, pp. 16-17.

sess this vision *dhawqan*, that is, as a mystical state of "tasting".[38] The essential vision is the same, but the depth of assimilation, the mystical attunement to the reality perceived, differs. This distinction helps to underscore the epistemological value of affirming principles of a metaphysical and mystical order, even if the plenary realization of those principles eludes the rational faculty. Reflection and meditation on the principles alluded to can bring about at least some degree of cognitive apprehension of the ultimate realities in question; realities that remain ineffable inasmuch as they are predicated on the extinction of the individuality, and thus on the transcendence of all modes of cognition proper to the individual subject as such. Ghazzali continues with a description of those who experience this transcendent extinction. Plurality disappears for them, as they are plunged in "sheer singularity" (*al-fardâniyyat al-mahda*):

> They become intoxicated with such an intoxication that the ruling authority of their rational faculty is overthrown. Hence one of them says, "I am the Real!" (*ana'l-Haqq*), another, "Glory be to me, how great is my station!"[39]. . . When this state gets the upper hand, it is called "extinction" in relation to the one who possesses it. Or rather, it is called "extinction from extinction", since the possessor of the state is extinct from himself and from his own extinction. For he is conscious neither of himself in that state, nor of his own unconsciousness of himself. If he were conscious of his own unconsciousness, then he would [still] be conscious of himself. In relation to the one immersed in it, this state is called "unification" (*ittihâd*) according to the language of metaphor, or is called "declaring God's unity" (*tawhîd*) according to the language of reality.[40]

We return to the relationship between *fanâ'* and *tawhîd*, between extinction and, not only "declaring God's unity", which is but one aspect of *tawhîd*, but, more essentially, the "making one", according to the literal meaning of the verbal noun *tawhîd*. One might also translate *tawhîd* as "the realization of oneness", the "making real" of the actual reality of oneness, through the elimination of all multiplicity.

38. *Ibid.*, p. 17.
39. See Ernst, *Words of Ecstasy*, for a good discussion of these *shathiyyât*, or theopathic utterances, by Hallaj and Bayazid al-Bastami, respectively.
40. *The Niche of Lights*, pp. 17-18.

Earlier, the divinely willed plurality within the human race was referred to: it is God who divided mankind up into nations and tribes, "so that ye may know one another". Is there not a contradiction, it might be asked, between the extinction of phenomenal multiplicity presupposed by the deepest level of *tawhîd,* and the affirmation of human plurality called forth by the will of God? One way of transforming this apparent contradiction into an expression of spiritual profundity is by returning to the notion of the "face" within each thing that constitutes the real being of that thing. Those Sufis who are extinguished to their own particular "face"—extinguished from their own non-existence—come alive to the Divine face that constitutes their true reality, the immanence of God's presence within them, and also within all that exists: "Wherever ye turn there is the Face of God." Now it is precisely that Divine aspect—in all things, and in all other nations and tribes—that comes into focus when this level of *tawhîd* is grasped aright. One does not have to experience the grace of mystical annihilation to comprehend this principle; as Ghazzali put it, one can arrive at this principle not only *dhawqan,* by way of "taste", or mystical experience, but also *'irfânan 'ilmiyyan,* as a mode of cognitive knowledge. If the mystical realization of this principle bestows a "taste" of *tawhîd,* we might say, following on from Ghazzali, that an intellectual assimilation of the principle bestows a "perfume" of *tawhîd.* As Ibn Arabi puts it, the gnostics cannot explain their spiritual states (*ahwâl*) to other men; they can only indicate them symbolically to those who have begun to experience the like.[41] A conceptual grasp of these deeper aspects of *tawhîd* might be said to constitute just such a beginning. If the ultimate, mystical degree of *tawhîd* is realized only through extinction, the lower, conceptual degrees imply at least that "beginning" or prefiguration of mystical extinction, which consists in self-effacement, in humility. Now an intellectual assimilation of this vision of unity, together with a moral attunement to the humility that it demands, is certainly sufficient to dissolve the egocentric knots that constitute the stuff of *ta'assub,* of all forms of fanaticism.

41. We have slightly modified this sentence, which Nicholson translates in *The* Tarjumán al-Ashwáq, p. 68. The sentence is part of Ibn Arabi's commentary on one of the poems.

Elsewhere, Ghazzali gives this telling description of *ta'assub*. He writes that it "usually comes together with man's disregard of his neighbor, and of his opinions, and the taking root in his heart of certain ideas which become so much a part of him that he fails to distinguish between right and wrong".[42] What results, on the contrary, from an apprehension of the deeper implications of *tawhîd* is a heightened, spiritual discernment: that is, not just a moral judgment between right and wrong, but also a presentiment both of one's own nothingness before the Divine reality, and also of the innate holiness, the Divine "face", within the neighbor. The transcendent, Divine reality before which one is extinguished is known to be mysteriously present within the "other". One observes here the spiritual underpinning of that crucial relationship, so often stressed in Sufi ethics, between humility and generosity, between self-effacement and self-giving; the first being a kind of *fanâ'* in moral mode, and the second being a moral application of *tawhîd*. Respect for one's neighbor is thus deepened in the very measure that one is aware of the Divine Presence, which is at once within and beyond oneself, and within and beyond the neighbor. Herein, one might say, resides one of the spiritual foundations of *adab*, or "courtesy", understanding by this word the profound respect, if not reverence, for the "other" that constitutes the true substance of all outward, socially conditioned forms of etiquette, good manners, and propriety towards the neighbor. One sees that it is not so much "religious pluralism" as "metaphysical unity" that establishes a deep-rooted and far-reaching tolerance, one which is not only formulated as a rule, to be obeyed or broken as one will, but which is organically related to an awareness of the Divine Presence in all things, an apprehension of the inner holiness of all that exists.

Islam: Quintessential and Universal Submission

In this second part of the paper we would like to begin by stressing one aspect of the meaning of the word "Islam", its literal meaning, that of submission, and to show how, from a Sufi perspective on the Quran, this meaning is tied to a conception of the essence of reli-

42. Quoted by H. Lazarus-Yafeh, *Studies in Ghazzali* (Jerusalem, 1975), pp. 197-198.

gion, or to "religion as such",[43] which takes precedence over such and such a religion.

According to one of the most highly regarded translators of the Quran, Muhammad Asad, the word "Islam" would have been understood by the hearers of the word at the time of the revelation of the Quran in terms of its universal, and not communal, meaning. In a note on the first use of the word *muslim* in the chronological order of the revelation (68:35), he writes:

> Throughout this work, I have translated the terms *muslim* and *islam* in accordance with their original connotations, namely, "one who surrenders [or "has surrendered"] himself to God", and "man's self-surrender to God". . . . It should be borne in mind that the "institutionalized" use of these terms—that is, their exclusive application to the followers of the Prophet Muhammad—represents a definitely post-Quranic development and, hence, must be avoided in a translation of the Quran.[44]

He asserts that when the Prophet's contemporaries heard the words *islam* and *muslim*, they would have understood them in this original sense, "without limiting these terms to any specific community or denomination".[45] This meaning emerges clearly from many verses containing the words *muslim* and *islam*. In the following verse, the principle of universal submission is equated with the religion of God:

> Seek they other than the religion of God (*dîn Allâh*), when unto Him submitteth whosoever is in the heavens and the earth, willingly or unwillingly? And unto Him they will be returned (3:83).

Kashani helps to situate with the utmost clarity the nature of this religion of God. He does so in his esoteric exegesis on two sets of verses. First, in relation to a verse which declares that the religion bestowed upon the Prophet Muhammad was the very same religion which was bestowed upon his predecessors:

> He hath ordained for you of religion (*min ad-dîn*) that which He commended unto Noah, and that which We reveal to thee [Muhammad], and that which We commended unto Abraham and

43. A key distinction, stressed throughout his works by Frithjof Schuon.

44. *The Message of the Qur'an: Translated and Explained* by Muhammad Asad (Gibraltar, 1984), p. 885, n. 17.

45. *Ibid.*, p. vi.

> Moses and Jesus, saying: Establish the religion, and be not divided therein (42:13).

Kashani comments:

> He hath ordained for you of the religion, [that is] the absolute religion (*ad-dîn al-mutlaq*), which God charged all the prophets to establish, and to be unanimous, not divided, with regard to it. This is the principle and root of religion (*asl ad-dîn*), that is, *tawhîd*, justice, and knowledge of the Resurrection, as expressed by [the phrase] "faith in God and the Last Day". This is other than the details of the revealed Laws, by which they [the prophets] differentiate this [root of religion]; this differentiation occurs in accordance with what is most beneficial in [the different situations]—such as the prescription of acts of obedience, worship, and social intercourse. As God Most High says, "For each We have appointed from you a Law and a Way (5:48).[46]

The difference between the "absolute" or unconditional religion (*ad-dîn al-mutlaq*) and the different forms this unique essence may take is then described by Kashani in terms of permanence and immutability. He continues: "So the right religion (*ad-dîn al-qayyim*) is tied to that which is immutable within knowledge and action; while the revealed Law is tied to that which alters in respect of rules and conditions." The nature of this unchanging religion, together with its essential connection with the primordial nature of the human soul, the *fitrah*, is expounded by Kashani in an illuminating commentary on the following crucial verse:

> So set thy purpose for religion as one with pure devotion—the nature [framed] of God, according to which He hath created man. There is no altering God's creation. That is the right religion (*ad-dîn al-qayyim*), but most men know not (30:30).

Kashani comments:

> So set thy purpose for the religion of *tawhîd*, and this is the path to the Real . . . or religion in the absolute sense (*ad-dîn mutlaqan*). That which is other than this is not "religion", because of its separation from the [way which leads to] attainment of the goal. The purpose [or "face", *al-wajh*, in the verse being commented on] refers to the existent essence, with all its concomitants and accidental properties; and its being set for religion is its disengagement from all that which is other than the Real, its being upright in *tawhîd*, and stopping with the Real, without heeding its own soul

46. Kashani, *Tafsîr*, Vol. II, p. 109.

> or others, so that his way will be the way of God; and his religion and his path will be the religion and path of God, for he sees nothing but Him in existence.[47]

Then follows this comment on the primordial nature, the *fitrah*, fashioned by God:

> That is, they cleave to the *fitrat Allâh*, which is the state in accordance with which the reality of humanity was created, eternal purity and disengagement, and this is the right religion (*ad-dîn al-qayyim*) in eternity without beginning or end, never altering or being differentiated from that original purity, or from that intrinsic, primordial *tawhîd*.[48]

The *fitrah* is described as being the result of the "most holy effusion" (*al-fayd al-aqdas*) of the Divine Essence; and no one who remains faithful to this original nature can deviate from *tawhîd*, or be veiled from God's reality by the presence of phenomena. Kashani cites the *hadîth*, "Every baby is born according to the *fitrah*; its parents make it a Jew, a Christian." But then he adds this important point: "It is not that this underlying reality changes in itself, such that its essential state be altered, for that is impossible. This is the meaning of His words: there is no altering God's creation. That is the right religion, but most men know not."

The following verse (30:31) reads: "Turning to Him; and do your duty to Him, and establish worship and be not of those who ascribe partners." The "turning" to God implies for Kashani a turning away from all otherness, from the "demons of fancy and imagination" and from "false religions"; it implies also the disengagement and detachment from the "shrouds of created nature, bodily accidents, natural forms, psychic properties". As regards the last part of the verse, he comments as follows: "'Be not of those who ascribe partners [or 'be not of the polytheists']. . . . through the subsistence of the *fitrah*, and the manifestation of I-ness (*zuhûr al-anâ'iyyah*) in its station."[49] Here the ontological limitation of the *fitrah* and its "station" is indicated by Kashani. For the *fitrah* presupposes an individual soul, of which it is the most fundamental model, pattern, or prototype; as such, it cannot but uphold that I-ness or egoic nucleus that must, from the point of view of absolute oneness,

47. *Ibid.*, Vol. II, p. 131.
48. *Ibid.*, Vol. II, p. 132.
49. *Ibid.*, Vol. II, p. 132.

be transcended; and it is only transcended by *fanâ'*. Despite this ontological shortcoming attendant upon the operative presence of the *fitrah*, it is clear that for Kashani it is only through fidelity to the *fitrah* that one can open oneself up to that ultimate form of Islam which is constituted—or rather sublimated—by *fanâ'*.

At the level of human knowledge, however, the *fitrah* is conceived as a fundamental, or "constitutional", affinity between the deepest dimension of the human soul and the ultimate realities expressed through Divine revelation; it is the purest texture of the substance of the soul that resonates harmoniously with the most profound truths conveyed by the revealed word. This harmonious reverberation translates spiritual affinity into mystical unity—the realization, through *fanâ'*, of the ultimate degree of *tawhîd*, as described above in reference to Ghazzali's exegesis of "everything is perishing except His Face" (28:88).

The mystery of this affinity between primordiality and revelation—between the knowledge divinely embedded *a priori* within the soul, and the knowledge divinely bestowed *a posteriori* upon the soul—seems to be alluded to in the following verse: "Truly there hath come unto you a Prophet from yourselves" (9:128). The literal meaning here, as addressed to the immediate recipients of the revelation, is that the Prophet is one of them: a man, not an angel, an Arab, not a foreigner, and so forth. But the word *minkum*, "from you", also carries a deeper significance. One also has this verse: "The Prophet is closer to the believers than their own selves" (33:6) Again, the literal meaning refers to the precedence of the Prophet, his greater right or claim over the believers than they have over themselves. But the deeper meaning emerges as a different, and equally legitimate, reading of the word *minkum*. The word also appears, as noted earlier, in a verse with a similar import: "For each We have appointed from you a Law and a Way (*shir'atan wa minhâjan*)" (5:48). Not only the Prophet, but the revealed Law and the spiritual Way he brings—all seem already to be, in essence, within the human soul. To follow the Prophet, to abide by the Law, to follow the Way he traces out is to follow, not some rules arbitrarily imposed from without, but a call from within; it is to follow one's own deepest nature. It is for this reason that the Quran refers to itself in several places as a "reminder" or as a remembrance (*dhikr*):

> And it is nothing but a reminder to creation (68:52 and 81:27).

We have not revealed unto thee this Quran that thou shouldst be distressed, but as a reminder unto him that feareth (20:2-3).

Nay, verily this is a reminder, so whoever will shall remember it (74:54-55).

This understanding of the meaning of the word *minkum* is a possible but by no means exclusive one. It does flow naturally, however, from a fundamental principle of Sufi spirituality. For our purposes here it suffices to cite the engaging simile offered by Rumi, by which he explains the verse:

In the composition of man all sciences were originally commingled so that his spirit might show forth all hidden things, as limpid water shows forth all that is under it . . . and all that is above it, reflected in the substance of water. Such is its nature, without treatment or training. But when it was mingled with earth or other colors, that property and that knowledge was parted from it and forgotten by it. Then God Most High sent forth prophets and saints, like a great, limpid water such as delivers out of darkness and accidental coloration every mean and dark water that enters into it. Then it remembers; when the soul of man sees itself unsullied, it knows for sure that so it was in the beginning, pure, and it knows that those shadows and colors were mere accidents. Remembering its state before those accidents supervened, it says, This is that sustenance which we were provided with before.[50] The prophets and the saints therefore remind him of his former state; they do not implant anything new in his substance. Now every dark water that recognizes that great water, saying, "I come from this, and I belong to this", mingles with that water. . . . It was on this account that God declared: Truly there hath come unto you a Prophet from yourselves.[51]

Near the end of the *Discourses*, this theme is expressed again, this time in more intimate terms:

Those who acknowledge the truth see themselves in the prophet and hear their own voice proceeding from him and smell their own scent proceeding from him. No man denies his own self. Therefore the prophets say to the community, "We are you and you are we; there is no strangeness between us."[52]

50. 2:25. This verse is given as the words uttered by the souls in Paradise upon being given fruits of the heavenly garden.
51. We have slightly modified Arberry's translation of 2:25 and of 9:128, which concludes the paragraph from Rumi's *Discourses*, pp. 44-45.
52. *Ibid.*, p. 227.

It is clear from these passages that Rumi, referring to the prophets in the plural, regards the prophetic mission as one and the same, despite the different forms taken by that message. In the *Mathnawî*, this principle is expressed in many different places. One striking example is his poetic comment upon the words of the Quranic verse "We make no distinction between any of them [God's prophets] (2:136; and at 3:84). Under this verse as a heading come the following couplets:

> If ten lamps are present in (one) place, each differs in form from the other:
>
> To distinguish without any doubt the light of each, when you turn your face toward their light, is impossible.
>
> In things spiritual there is no division and no numbers; in things spiritual there is no partition and no individuals.[53]

*

* *

The conception of essential or absolute religion, explicitly affirmed by Kashani and implicit in so much of Rumi's writing, is predicated on a clear vision of the spirit of faith which transcends all the forms that religious traditions assume. Before elaborating upon this vision with reference to particular Quranic verses, it is important to mention very briefly the Quranic encounter between Moses and the mysterious personage, not mentioned by name in the Quran, but identified by tradition with al-Khidr. Even in its literal aspect, the story alludes to the distinction between the form of religion and its transcendent essence, between exoteric and esoteric knowledge. In this encounter certain forms of the law and social convention are violated by al-Khidr, who is questioned and criticized as a result by Moses. After committing three acts that flout outward norms, al-Khidr tells Moses of the realities hidden beneath the surface of each of the situations in which the acts take place, realities revealed to al-Khidr by direct, Divine inspiration.[54]

53. *Mathnawî*, trans. R. A. Nicholson (London, 1926), Book I, 678-679. Nicholson does not include the heading, consisting of the verse, which is given in the Persian. See the edition by Abd al-Hamid Mashayikh Tabataba'i, published by Nashr-i Tulû', in Tehran (n.d.), p. 35.
54. See 18:60-82.

One of the uses to which Ibn Arabi puts this story reinforces its already esoteric nature. Al-Khidr becomes the personification of the station of nearness (*maqâm al-qurba*), a station which is identified with plenary sanctity (*walâyah*),[55] while Moses personifies the law-giving prophet, or prophecy as such (*nubuwwah*). In Ibn Arabi's perspective, sanctity as such is superior to prophecy as such, because, as he explains in the chapter of the *Fusûs* under the heading of Seth, "The message (*ar-risâlah*) and prophecy (*an-nubuwwah*)—that is, law-giving prophecy and its message—come to an end, but sanctity (*al-walâyah*) never comes to an end."[56] Sanctity is higher because the knowledge proper to it is universal, and prophecy is lower insofar as the knowledge comprised within it is delimited by a particular message: "Know that *walâyah* is the all-encompassing sphere, thus it never comes to an end, and to it belong [the assimilation and communication of] universal tidings; but as for law-giving prophecy and the message, they terminate."[57] But it is a question of principial priority and not personal superiority: sanctity is more universal than prophecy, but the prophet is always superior to the saint. For, on the one hand, the prophet's sanctity is the source of the sanctity of the saint; and on the other, every prophet is a saint, but not every saint is a prophet:

> When you observe the prophet saying things which relate to what is outside the law-giving function,[58] then he does so as a saint (*walî*) and a gnostic (*'ârif*). Thus his station as a knower and a saint is more complete and more perfect than [his station] as a messenger or as a legislative prophet. . . . So if one says that that the saint is above the prophet and the messenger, he means that this is the case within a single person, that is: the messenger, in respect of his being a saint, is more complete than he is in respect of his being a prophet or messenger.[59]

55. This station "represents the ultimate point in the hierarchy of the saints" (M. Chodkiewicz, *Seal of the Saints: Prophethood and Sainthood in the Doctrine of Ibn 'Arabî*, trans. Liadain Sherrard [Cambridge, 1993], p. 58).
56. *Fusûs*, p. 34. See R. Austin's translation, *The Bezels of Wisdom*, p. 66.
57. *Fusûs*, p. 167; in *Bezels*, p. 168.
58. Kashani comments on the domain which is said to lie beyond the scope of the law-giving function: "The explanation of 'adornment of the soul with the qualities of God' (*takhalluq bi akhlâq Allâh*), the proximity [attained through] supererogatory and obligatory devotions; and the stations of trust, contentment, submission, realizing oneness, attaining singularity, extinction, union and separation, and the like" (*Fusûs*, p. 168).
59. *Fusûs*, p. 168; *Bezels*, pp. 168-169.

According to Ibn Arabi, then, the encounter between Moses and al-Khidr is understood microcosmically: al-Khidr represents a mode of universal consciousness within the very soul of Moses, one which surpasses his consciousness *qua* prophet, whence the disapproval by the prophet of the antinomian acts of the saint: "He [al-Khidr] showed him [Moses] nothing but his [Moses's] own form: it was his own state that Moses saw, and himself that he censured."[60] Ibn Arabi's conception of *walâyah* is a complex and controversial one, but it does cohere with the esoteric implications of the Quranic narrative of the encounter between Moses and the mysterious person who was given "knowledge from Us". This narrative, together with its amplification in Ibn Arabi's conception of sanctity, clearly alludes to the relativity of the outward law in the face of its inner spirit, and the limitations proper to the law-giving function as opposed to the universal dimensions of sanctity. There is a clear and important relationship between this universal function of sanctity and the "absolute" or "unconditional" religion referred to above, that religion which is above and beyond all the particular forms—legal, confessional, social, cultural, and psychological—that it may assume.

Now, to consider more explicit Quranic verses describing or alluding to this quintessential religion:

> Say: We believe in God and that which is revealed unto us, and that which is revealed unto Abraham and Ishmael and Isaac and Jacob and the tribes, and that which was given unto Moses and Jesus and the prophets from their Lord. We make no distinction between any of them, and unto Him we have submitted (3:84).

Then comes this verse:

> And whoso seeketh a religion other than Islam, it will not be accepted from him, and he will be a loser in the Hereafter (3:85).

Now whereas this last verse is understood, from a theological point of view, as upholding the exclusive validity of "Islam", defined as the religion revealed to God's last Prophet, and, as will be discussed below, as abrogating other verses which point to a different conclusion, it can also be seen as confirming the intrinsic validity of all the

60. *Al-Futûhât al-Makkiyya*, II. 261. See the French translation of the chapter on the station of nearness (Chapter 161) by Denis Gril in "Le terme du voyage" (pp. 339-347) in *Les Illuminations de La Mecque*, ed. M. Chodkiewicz (Paris, 1988).

revelations brought by all the prophets mentioned in the previous verse. "Islam" thus encompasses all revelations, which can be seen as so many different facets of essentially one and the same self-disclosure of the Divine reality. Both senses can in fact be maintained as "valid" interpretations, according to a key hermeneutical principle of Ibn Arabi: namely, that it is not tenable to exclude the validity of an interpretation of a verse which is clearly upheld by the literal meaning of the words.[61] It is one of an indefinite number of meanings that are all "intended" by God to be derived from the words of the verse. No one interpretation is right and true to the exclusion of all others. Furthermore, applying a distinctively Akbarian metaphysical principle, we could say that to exclude the exclusivist reading is in turn to fall into a mode of exclusivism.[62] Thus a truly inclusivist metaphysical perspective must recognize the validity of the exclusivist, theological perspective, even if it must also—on pain of disingenuousness—uphold as more compelling, more convincing, and more "true", the universalist understanding of Islam.

This universalist conception of religion is linked to the innate knowledge of God within all human souls, or within the soul as such, and to the universal function of revelatory "remembrance"—that innate knowledge which is re-awakened within the forgetful soul by Divine revelation. The following verse establishes with the utmost clarity the fact that knowledge of the Divine is inscribed in the very substance of the human soul at its inception, and is thus an integral dimension of the *fitrah*:

61. As M. Chodkiewicz writes, in his excellent study of Ibn Arabi's hermeneutics, "Given the extremely rich polysemy of Arabic vocabulary, rigorous fidelity to the letter of Revelation does not exclude but, on the contrary, implies a multiplicity of interpretations. Ibn al-Arabi insists on this point on a number of occasions, emphasizing that there is a general rule applicable to all the revealed Books: 'Any meaning of whatever verse of the Word of God—be it the Qur'ân, the Torah, the Psalms, or the Pages—judged acceptable by one who knows the language in which this word is expressed represents what God wanted to say to those who interpreted it so.' As a corollary, none of these meanings is to be rejected. To deny the validity of this rule is to limit divine knowledge" (*An Ocean Without Shore: Ibn Arabi, the Book, and the Law*, trans. D. Streight [Albany, 1993], p. 30).
62. This accords with the principle, expressed in a variety of paradoxical ways throughout the Akbarian corpus, that "part of the perfection of being is the existence of imperfection within it; for were it otherwise, the perfection of being would be imperfect because of the absence of imperfection within it" (*The Sufi Path of Knowledge*, p. 296).

> And when thy Lord brought forth from the Children of Adam, from their reins, their seed, and made them testify of themselves [saying], Am I not your Lord? They said: Yea, verily. We testify. [That was] lest ye say on the Day of Resurrection: Truly, of this we were unaware (7:172).

At the dawn of creation, then, knowledge of the Divine lordship, the reality of the Absolute, and all essential truths deriving therefrom is infused into the human soul—into all human souls, all Children of Adam, without exception. Another way of presenting this universal fact, with the stress on the spiritual substance of these principial truths, is given in these verses:

> And when thy Lord said unto the angels: Verily I am creating a mortal from clay of black mud, altered. So, when I have made him and have breathed into him of My Spirit, fall ye down, prostrating yourselves before him (15:28-29).[63]

Thus, it is this spirit of God, breathed into man, that constitutes, according to the Quran, the fundamental, irreducible substance of the human soul. It is for this reason that the angels are commanded to prostrate to him. The act not only proceeds from obedience to the command of God, but also is an acknowledgement of the breath of God that articulates the Adamic substance—the reason for the command, one might say.

One can understand the truths comprised within the Divine Spirit, which is "breathed" into the soul, in terms of the "names" taught to Adam by God, in virtue of which his knowledge transcends that of all other beings, including the angels. The story of the creation of Adam, the transcendent knowledge proper to the human soul, the Fall, and the means of overcoming the consequences of the Fall—all these fundamental principles are given in the following verses in a manner which succinctly presents both the universality and necessity of Divine revelation:

> And when thy Lord said unto the angels: Verily I am placing a viceroy (*khalîfah*) on earth, they said: Wilt Thou place therein one who will do harm therein and will shed blood, while we, we hymn Thy praise and sanctify Thee? He said: Surely I know that which ye know not.

63. Identical to 38:72. Cf. also the verse "Then He fashioned him and breathed into him of His Spirit" (32:9).

> And He taught Adam all the names, then showed them to the angels, saying: Inform Me of the names of these, if ye are truthful.
>
> They said: Be Thou glorified! We have no knowledge save that which Thou hast taught us. Truly Thou, only Thou, art the Knower, the Wise.
>
> He said: O Adam, inform them of their names, and when he had informed them of their names, He said: Did I not tell you that I know the secret of the heavens and the earth? And I know that which ye disclose and that which ye hide.
>
> And when We said unto the angels: Prostrate yourselves before Adam, they fell prostrate, all save Iblis. He refused and waxed proud, and so became a disbeliever.
>
> And We said: O Adam, dwell thou and thy wife in the Garden, and eat freely thereof where ye will; but come not near this tree lest ye become wrong-doers.
>
> But Satan caused them to slip therefrom, and expelled them from the state they were in. And We said: Fall down, one of you a foe unto the other! There shall be for you on earth a habitation and provision for a time.
>
> Then Adam received words from his Lord, and He relented toward him; verily He is ever-Relenting, all-Merciful.
>
> We said: Go down, all of you, from hence; but verily there cometh unto you from Me a guidance; and whoso followeth My guidance, no fear shall come upon them neither shall they grieve.
>
> But they who disbelieve, and deny Our revelations, such are rightful owners of the Fire. They abide therein (2:30-39).

Adam is therefore not just the first man, but also the first prophet, the first to have received words from his Lord. The guidance promised by God—the means by which the primordial human condition is restored to its plenary state—is, it is to be noted, immediately defined in terms of Our revelations, or Our signs, that is, *âyâtinâ*. One is given a sense here of a single religion, Divine guidance, which comprises diverse forms of expression, different "signs".

The universality of this guidance through revelation is clearly stressed in the following verses. First, "For every community (*ummah*) there is a Messenger" (10:48). As noted above, the Quran makes explicit reference to several prophets, but the scope of prophetic guidance extends far beyond those mentioned, for "Verily, We sent Messengers before thee; among them are those about whom We have told thee, and those about whom We have not told thee" (40:78). Moreover, that which was revealed to the Prophet in the Quran does not differ in essence from what was revealed to all the prophets:

> And We sent no Messenger before thee but We inspired him [saying]: There is no God save Me, so worship Me (21:25).
>
> Naught is said unto thee [Muhammad] but what was said unto the Messengers before thee (41:43).[64]

This single, unique message of guidance is always revealed to the Messenger in the language of his folk (14:4).

To appreciate more fully the relationship between the substance of the message and its form, one can benefit from a distinction found in Ibn Arabi's writings. This is the distinction, within the Speech of God, between the "necessary Speech" (*al-qawl al-wâjib*), which is not subject to change, and the "accidental Speech" (*al-qawl al-ma'rûd*), which is subject to change.[65] It is the former, the necessary Speech, which one can identify with the unchanging substance of the Divine message. This view is articulated more explicitly in the following comment on the oneness of the religious path. It is, he writes,

> that concerning which Bukhari wrote a chapter entitled, "The chapter on what has come concerning the fact that the religions of the prophets are one". He brought the article which makes the word "religion" definite, because all religion comes from God, even if some of the rulings are diverse. Everyone is commanded to perform the religion and to come together in it. . . . As for the rulings which are diverse, that is because of the Law which God assigned to each one of the messengers. He said, "To every one (of the Prophets) We have appointed a Law and a Way; and if God willed, He would have made you one nation" (5:48).[66] If He had done that, your revealed Laws would not be diverse, just as they are not diverse in the fact that you have been commanded to come together and to perform them.[67]

64. Cf. "Say: I am no innovation among the Messengers" (46:9).
65. See "Le Livre du Nom de Majesté", trans. M. Valsan, *Études Traditionelles,* No. 272, December, 1948, p. 345.
66. We quote here Chittick's rendition of the verse. Our preferred translation of the first part of the verse is: "For each We have appointed from you a Law and a Way". The importance of translating the phrase literally, together with the mysterious word *minkum,* "from you", has been noted above in connection with Rumi's illuminating comments.
67. Quoted in Chittick, *Sufi Path,* p. 303.

Thus, on the basis of scriptural and exoteric orthodoxy, Ibn Arabi points to the substantial content of religion, which both transcends and legitimizes the various revelations; the key criteria of this substance are centered on two elements: Divine command and human response. In other words, however diverse the particular rulings pertaining to the different religions may be, the substance or principle of these rulings remains the same: to submit to that which has been divinely instituted. The inner reality of religion is thus unfolded for the individual, of whatever religion, in the course of his submission to God and the practice of the worship enjoined upon him.

Returning to the verse "We never sent a Messenger save with the language of his folk", one can apply Ibn Arabi's distinction and assert that the essence of the message, the necessary Speech, is one, whereas the "languages", the accidental Speech, are many. Needless to say, the distinction in question is not to be understood as relating to a merely linguistic difference with identical semantic content, but rather by "language" should be understood the whole gamut of factors—spiritual, psychological, cultural, and linguistic—that go to make the message of the supra-formal Truth intelligible to a given human collectivity. Herein lies an important aspect of the message conveyed by Ibn Arabi's *Fusûs al-hikam*: the nature of the jewel (Revelation) is shaped according to the receptivity—conceptual, volitive, affective—of the bezel (*fass*, singular of *fusûs*), that is, the specific mode of prophetic consciousness as determined by the particular human collectivity addressed by the Revelation.

The above considerations lead one to posit the distinction between religion as such, on the one hand, and such and such a religion, on the other. While such and such a religion is distinct from all others, possessing its own particular rites, laws, and spiritual "economy", religion as such can be discerned within it and within all religions—religion as such being the exclusive property of none, as it constitutes the inner substance of all. It must be carefully noted here that this view of a religious essence that at once transcends and abides within all religions does not in the least imply a blurring of the boundaries between the different religions on the plane of their formal diversity; rather, the conception of this "essential religion" presupposes formal religious diversity, regarded not so much as a regrettable differentiation but a divinely willed necessity. The following verses uphold this calibrated conception, which recognizes the inner substance of religion inherent in all revealed religions, on the one hand, and affirms the necessity of abiding by the dictates of one particular religion, on the other:

> For each We have appointed from you a Law and a Way (*shir'atan wa minhâjan*). Had God willed, He could have made you one community. But that He might try you by that which He hath given you [He hath made you as you are]. So vie with one another in good works. Unto God ye will all return, and He will inform you of that wherein ye differed (5:48).

> Unto each community We have given sacred rites (*mansakan*) which they are to perform; so let them not dispute with thee about the matter, but summon them unto thy Lord (22:67).[68]

These diverse laws, paths, and rites, however, ought not obscure the fact that the religion ordained through the last Prophet is, in essence, the very same religion as that ordained through all previous prophets:

> He hath ordained for you of the religion (*min ad-dîn*) that which He commended unto Noah, and that which We reveal to thee [Muhammad], and that which We commended unto Abraham and Moses and Jesus, saying: Establish the religion, and be not divided therein (42:13).

This is the verse quoted by Ibn Arabi in the citation above; after quoting it, Ibn Arabi refers to a passage in the Quran which mentions the prophets Abraham, Isaac, Jacob, Noah, David, Solomon, Job, Joseph, Moses, Aaron, Zachariah, John, Jesus, Elias, Ishmael, Elisha, Jonah, and Lot, and which ends with the words: "Those are they whom God guideth, so follow their guidance" (6:91). Ibn Arabi adds: "This is the path that brings together every prophet and messenger. It is the performance of religion, scattering not concerning it and coming together in it."[69] Again, what is being stressed here is quintessential religion, *ad-dîn*.

The "Islam" revealed to the Prophet Muhammad is unique, and thus a religion; but at the same time, it is identical in its essence to all religions, and is thus *the* religion; in other words, it is both such and such a religion, and religion as such. "Establish the religion, and be not divided" (42:13), for "naught is said unto thee

68. Cf. "And each one hath a goal (*wijha*) toward which he turneth" (2:148).
69. Quoted in Chittick, *Sufi Path*, p. 303.

[Muhammad] but what was said unto the Messengers before thee" (41:43). In another important verse, used above as our epigraph, we are given a succinct definition of what constitutes this inner, essential religion. The verse also stands out as one of the most significant proof-texts in the Quran for upholding the principle that access to salvation is not the exclusive preserve of the particular religion of Islam, that is, the specific Law and Way ordained through the last Prophet. On the contrary, the description given here of that which is necessary for salvation gives substance to the universal definition of Islam that we are trying to bring out here:

> Truly those who believe, and the Jews, and the Christians, and the Sabeans—whoever believeth in God and the Last Day and performeth virtuous deeds—surely their reward is with their Lord, and no fear shall come upon them, neither shall they grieve (2:62).

It was seen above that the number of prophets is given indefinite extension by verses which mention several by name and then add, "We sent Messengers before thee; among them are those about whom We have told thee, and those about whom We have not told thee" (40:78). Likewise, in the preceding verse, the explicit mention of four distinct groups—those who believe, referring to Muslims in the particular sense, alongside the Jews, the Christians, and the Sabeans—is indefinitely prolonged by the universal category comprising "whoever believeth in God and the Last Day and is virtuous". In a moment, we shall return to this crucial, and controversial, position, one which holds out the possibility of salvation beyond the confines of Islam *qua* particular religion. At this point, however, attention should remain focused on the ramifications of this "essential religion" of faith in God and in the Hereafter, allied to virtue.

The following verse is akin to a veritable creedal affirmation:

> The Messenger believeth in that which hath been revealed unto him from his Lord, and [so do] the believers. Every one believeth in God and His angels and His scriptures and His Messengers—we make no distinction between any of His Messengers (2:285).[70]

What should be underscored here is the fact that belief in all the revealed scriptures is followed by the declaration that no distinction

70. The phrase "We make no distinction between any of His Messengers" also comes earlier in the same *Sûrah*, at 2:136, which we cite below.

can be made between any of God's Messengers. Again, there is the recognition of the formal diversity of revelation combined with the affirmation of a unique message.

In the Quran, this universal religion, or religion as such, which resists any communal specification, is often referred to as the religion of Abraham, *al-hanîf*, "the devout".[71] Abraham stands forth as both the symbol and the concrete embodiment of pure, monotheistic worship: "he was not one of the idolators". In the following verse, also from the *Sûrat al-Baqara*, we read:

> And they say: Be Jews or Christians, then ye will be rightly guided. Say Nay but [we are of] the religious community (*millah*) of Abraham, the devout (*hanîfan*), and he was not one of the idolators (2:135).

Then, in the verse immediately following this one, one finds a description of what affiliation to this *millah*, or religious community, entails:

> Say: We believe in God, and that which was revealed unto Abraham, and Ishmael, and Isaac, and Jacob, and the tribes, and that which was given unto Moses and Jesus and the prophets from their Lord. We make no distinction between any of them, and unto Him we have submitted (2:136; this verse is almost identical to 3:84).

After this comes another important verse, which reinforces the interpretation of religion as universal submission:

> And if they believe in the like of that which ye believe, then they are rightly guided. But if they turn away, then they are in schism (2:137).

The next verse is also highly relevant to our theme. It begins, mysteriously, with a reference to the color of God (*sibghat Allâh*). Pickthall renders the verse thus, making explicit what he sees as intended by the ellipse: "[We take our] color from God; and who is

71. We translate this word as "devout" on the basis of the following explanation of Asad: "The expression *hanîf* is derived from the verb *hanafa*, which literally means 'he inclined [towards a right state or tendency]'. Already in pre-Islamic times, this term had a definitely monotheistic connotation, and was used to describe a man who turned away from sin and worldliness and from all dubious beliefs, especially idol-worship; and *tahannuf* denoted the ardent devotions, mainly consisting of long vigils and prayers, of the unitarian God-seekers of pre-Islamic times" (*The Message of the Qur'an*, p. 28, note 110 on 2:135).

better than God at coloring? And we worship Him" (2:138).[72] The verses immediately following this one suggest what this "color" might mean:

> Say: Dispute ye with us concerning God, when He is our Lord and your Lord? Ours are our works, and yours your works. We are devoted purely to Him.
>
> Or say ye that Abraham, and Ishmael, and Isaac, and Jacob, and the tribes were Jews or Christians? Say: Do you know best or doth God? (2:139-140).

Here we are given a strong sense of the need to view religious affiliation in the light of absolute values, rather than allowing religious affiliation to determine the "color" or nature of the Absolute: "We are devoted purely to Him"; it is not religion, but God Who is worshipped. "And we worship Him." One is reminded here of the image given by Junayd, and so often quoted by Ibn Arabi: "Water takes on the color of the cup."[73] The imperative of 'transcending the gods of belief', mentioned earlier, can be seen as concordant with the need to go beyond the "color" imparted by religious dogma or affiliation, to the pure Absolute, at once surpassing all color and assuming every color. As Rumi puts it:

> Since colorlessness (pure Unity) became the captive of color (manifestation in the phenomenal world), a Moses came into conflict with a Moses.
>
> When you attain unto the colorlessness which you possessed, Moses and Pharaoh are at peace.[74]

And again:

> The religion of Love is separate from all religions: for lovers, the religion and creed is—God.[75]

It might be objected here that the Quranic verses cited above could just as easily be interpreted as an affirmation of Islamic exclu-

72. The Arabic here is *nahnu lahu 'âbidûn*, which can also be translated as "we are His worshippers"; the strong implication, in both senses of the phrase, is that God is the sole object of worship, and that for this reason true worshippers "belong" to God alone, this being made explicit in the verses which follow 2:138.
73. See *Sufi Path*, pp. 149, 229, 341-344.
74. *Mathnawî*, I, 2467-8.
75. *Mathnawî*, II, 1770.

sivism, the "Islam" revealed by the Quran being the purest form of that primordial religion of Abraham that was subsequently distorted by the Jews and the Christians. It must readily be conceded that such a view would indeed be upheld, in differing degrees, and with varying implications, not only by traditional theological and exoteric authorities, but also by their mystical and esoteric counterparts, including those cited here, Ibn Arabi, Rumi, Kashani, and Ghazzali. For all such Sufis—those belonging to what one might call the "normative" Sufi tradition, in which the *Sharî'ah* is scrupulously upheld—Islam in the particular sense would be regarded as the most complete religion, *qua* religion, and thus the most appropriate one to follow.[76] This belief, however, on the plane of religious form, does not translate into chauvinism, and still less, intolerance. For the metaphysical vision of the religious essence that transcends all forms leads directly to an appreciation of the possibility of salvation and sanctification through diverse, and unequal, religious forms. Even if other religious forms be regarded as less "complete" than Islam, or in a certain sense superseded by it, all believers in God can nonetheless be regarded as belonging to the same community, the same *umma* defined in terms of essential faith, rather than as a confessionally delimited community. In the *Sûrah* entitled "The Prophets", the following verse is given, after mention is made of several prophets, finishing with a reference to the Virgin Mary: "Truly, this, your *umma*, is one *umma*, and I am your Lord, so worship Me" (21:92). Just as our God and your God is one,[77] so all believers, whatever be the outward, denominational form taken by their belief, are judged strictly according to their merits, and not according to some artificial religious label:

> And those who believe and do good works, We shall bring them into Gardens underneath which rivers flow, wherein they will abide forever—a promise of God in truth; and who can be more truthful than God in utterance? (4:122).

76. For example, Kashani, after pointing out the flaws in the religions of Judaism and Christianity, avers that Islam is "altogether true; indeed, it is the truth of truths. It is the supreme and most brilliant truth" (cited in Lory, *Commentaires ésoteriques*, p. 132).
77. The verse in which these words are given is as follows: "And only discourse with the People of the Book in a way that is most excellent, save with those who do wrong. And say: We believe in that which hath been revealed to us and revealed to you. Our God and your God is one, and unto Him we surrender" (29:46). We shall return to this verse below.

Lest one think that the category of "those who believe and do good works" refers only to the Muslims in the specific sense—one possible reading, admittedly—the very next verse establishes the universal scope of the promise. This verse, indeed, is of the utmost importance for the perspective or "reading" being expounded here:

> It will not be in accordance with your desires, nor the desires of the People of the Scripture. He who doth wrong will have the recompense thereof (4:123).

One can read this verse as implying that insofar as the Muslim "desires" that salvation be restricted to Muslims in the specific, communal sense, he falls into exactly the same kind of exclusivism of which the Christians and Jews stand accused: "And they say: None entereth paradise unless he be a Jew or a Christian. These are their own desires" (2:111). It should be noted that the very same word is used both for the "desires" of the Jews and the Christians, and the "desires" of the Muslims, *amâniyy*. As noted above, the logic of these verses clearly indicates that one form of religious prejudice or chauvinism is not to be replaced with another form of the same, but with an objective, unprejudiced recognition of the inexorable and universal law of Divine justice. This universal law is expressed with the utmost clarity in the following two verses, which complete this important passage from the *Sûra al-Nisâ'*:

> And whoso doeth good works, whether male or female, and is a believer, such will enter paradise, and will not be wronged the dint of a date-stone.
>
> Who is better in religion than he who submitteth his purpose to God (*aslama wajhahu li'Llâh*), while being virtuous, and following the religious community of Abraham the devout? (4:124-125).

In these four verses, taken as a whole (4:122-125), the Divine "promise" of salvation is starkly contrasted with confessional "desires"; on the one hand, there is an objective and universal criterion of wholehearted submission to God, and on the other, a subjective and particularistic criterion of formal attachment to a specific community. To return to the verse cited above, one should note the riposte that follows the unwarranted exclusivism of the People of the Book:

> And they say: None entereth paradise unless he be a Jew or a Christian. These are their own desires. Say: Bring your proof if ye are truthful.

> Nay, but whosoever submitteth his purpose to God, and he is virtuous, his reward is with his Lord. No fear shall come upon them, neither shall they grieve (2:111-112).

Verse 112 thus comes as a concrete rebuttal of unwarranted exclusivism. It does not contradict the exclusivist claims of the Jews and the Christians with an exclusivism of its own, that is, with a claim that only "Muslims", in the specific sense, go to Paradise. Access to salvation, far from being further narrowed by reference to the privileged rights of some other "group", is broadened, and in fact universalized: those who attain salvation and enter paradise are those who have submitted wholeheartedly to God and are intrinsically virtuous. Faithful submission, allied to virtue: such are the two indispensable requisites for salvation. Thus it is perfectly justified to argue that the verse does not respond "in kind" to the exclusivism of the People of the Book, but rather pitches the response on a completely different level, a supra-theological or metaphysical level, which surpasses all reified definitions, confessional denominations, communal allegiances, and partisan affiliations.

It is also important to note that the words cited earlier, "Unto God belong the East and the West, and wherever ye turn, there is the Face of God", come two verses later, at 2:115. This verse is referred to by Ibn Arabi at the end of the following well-known warning to Muslims against restricting God to the form of one's own belief, a warning that is entirely in accordance with the thrust of the Quranic discourse:

> Beware of being bound up by a particular creed and rejecting others as unbelief! Try to make yourself a prime matter for all forms of religious belief. God is greater and wider than to be confined to one particular creed to the exclusion of others. For He says, Wherever ye turn, there is the Face of God.[78]

78. Quoted by T. Izutsu in his *Sufism and Taoism* (Berkeley, 1983), p. 254. We have modified somewhat Izutsu's translation of this passage from the *Fusûs* (pp. 135-16). In particular, the word *'aqîda*, should, we believe, be translated as "creed" and not, as Izutsu has it, "religion". Izutsu's translation nonetheless adequately conveys the clear intention behind this warning to believers not to restrict God to the form of their own belief, whether this is a doctrinal form *vis-à-vis* other possible forms within the same religion, or a religious belief *vis-à-vis* the beliefs of other religions. But, as has been discussed in the previous section, for Ibn Arabi, there is but one religion, which comprises diverse modes of revelation and different rulings, according to the requirements of different human collectivities addressed by the one and only Divinity.

We can also turn to Ibn Arabi for a useful Sufi means of overcoming one of the obstacles to wholesome dialogue between Muslims and members of other faiths: the traditional legal notion of the abrogation of other religions by Islam. Before doing so, however, it is important to situate the principle of abrogation in relation to the verse cited above, 2:62, in which salvation is promised not just to Muslims in the specific sense, but also to Jews and Christians and Sabeans, whoever believeth in God and the Last Day and performeth virtuous deeds. A great deal hinges on the meaning attributed to this verse. Its literal meaning is clear enough: all believers who act virtuously, in consequence of their faith, are promised that their reward is with their Lord, and "no fear shall come upon them, neither shall they grieve". But it is held by many of the traditional commentators, based on a report from Ibn Abbas, that this verse is abrogated by 3:85—"And whoso seeketh a religion other than Islam, it will not be accepted from him, and he will be a loser in the Hereafter." Among the classical commentators, however, it is noteworthy that Tabari (d. 310/923) and the Shi'ite commentator Tabarsi (d. 548/1153) both reject the idea that the verse can be subject to abrogation. In general, as regards the principle of abrogation (*naskh*), Tabari writes, in his commentary on verse 2:106—"We abrogate no verse, nor do We cause it to be forgotten, but that We bring one better than it or like it":

> Thus, God transforms the lawful into the unlawful, and the unlawful into the lawful, and the permitted into the forbidden, and the forbidden into the permitted. This only pertains to such issues as commands and prohibitions, proscriptions and generalizations, preventions and authorizations. But as for reports (*akhbâr*), they cannot abrogate nor be abrogated.[79]

In regard to verse 2:62, he writes that the literal meaning of the verse should be upheld, without being restricted in its scope by reference to reports of its abrogation, "because, in respect of the bestowal of reward for virtuous action with faith, God has not singled out some of His creatures as opposed to others".[80] Tabarsi, in his commentary *Majma' al-bayân fî tafsîr al-qur'ân*, argues that "abrogation cannot apply to a declaration of promise. It can be allowed

79. *Jâmi' al-bayân 'an ta'wîl ay al-qur'ân* (Beirut, 2001), Vol.1, p. 546.
80. *Ibid.*, Vol.1, p. 373.

only of legal judgments which may be changed or altered with change in the general interest".[81]

Nonetheless, as regards the specifically juristic point of view, it is almost universally upheld that Islam "abrogates" the previous dispensations, in the sense that its revealed law supersedes the laws promulgated in pre-Quranic revelations, with the concomitant that it is no longer permissible for Muslims to abide by those pre-Quranic revealed laws, the *Sharî'ah* brought by the Prophet being henceforth normative and binding. How, then, can a Muslim today, concerned with dialogue, reconcile the idea of salvation being accessible to non-Muslims who faithfully follow their religions, on the one hand, with the principle that Islam abrogates or supersedes all previous religions? One answer is given by Ibn Arabi, for whom the fact of abrogation does not imply the nullification of those religions which are superseded, nor does it render them salvifically inefficacious. In a brilliant dialectical stroke, Ibn Arabi transforms the whole doctrine of abrogation from being a basis for the rejection of other religions into an argument for their continuing validity. For one of the reasons for the pre-eminence of Islam is precisely the fact that Muslims are enjoined to believe in all revelations and not just in that conveyed by the Prophet of Islam:

> All the revealed religions are lights. Among these religions, the revealed religion of Muhammaḍ is like the light of the sun among the lights of the stars. When the sun appears, the lights of the stars are hidden, and their lights are included in the light of the sun. Their being hidden is like the abrogation of the other revealed religions that takes place through Muhammad's revealed religion. Nevertheless, they do in fact exist, just as the existence of the lights of the stars is actualized. This explains why we have been required in our all-inclusive religion to have faith in the truth of all the messengers and all the revealed religions. They are not rendered null [*bâtil*] by abrogation—that is the opinion of the ignorant.[82]

81. Quoted by M. Ayoub, *The Qur'ân and Its Interpreters* (Albany, 1984), Vol. I, p. 110. In the contemporary period, both Rashid Rida and Allamah Tabataba'i likewise uphold the literal meaning of the verse, and reject the possibility that it is subject to abrogation. See the discussion of this issue in Farid Esack, *Qur'ân, Liberation and Pluralism* (Oxford, 1997), pp. 162-166; and in Abdulaziz Sachedina, *The Islamic Roots of Democratic Pluralism* (Oxford, 2001), pp. 29-34.
82. Cited by W. C. Chittick, *Imaginal Worlds: Ibn al-Arabi and the Problem of Religious Diversity* (Albany, 1994) p. 125.

Finally, one has to address the fact that the Quran not only contains verses that clearly assert the Divine ordainment of religious diversity, the exhortation to engage in dialogue, and the presence of piety and righteousness in religions other than Islam; it also contains verses of a polemical nature. For example:

> O ye who believe, take not the Jews and the Christians for guardians. They are guardians one to another. He among you who taketh them for guardians is (one) of them. Truly, God guideth not wrongdoing folk (5:51).

> And the Jews say: Ezra is the son of God, and the Christians say: The Messiah is the son of God. That is their saying with their mouths. They imitate the saying of those who disbelieved of old. God fighteth them. How perverse are they! (9:30).

There are numerous such verses, which demonstrate the formal contradictions between different theological perspectives, and the consequent difficulties attendant upon the effort to engage in effective dialogue on the basis of theological perspectives alone. They also indicate, albeit indirectly, the necessity of elevating the mode of discourse to a metaphysical, supra-theological level, from the vantage point of which those formal contradictions are rendered less decisive as determinants of dialogue. The contradictions remain on their own plane; but the more challenging question is to determine the significance of that plane, and to make an effort to discern within the text of the Quran itself those openings that warrant a transition to a higher plane. This is what has been attempted in this paper, with the help of Sufi metaphysical perspectives on the Quran.

But one must also respond to the specific question: in the concrete context of interfaith dialogue, how is one to relate to the verses that severely criticize the dogmatic errors of the People of the Book? Apart from pointing out the need to examine carefully each such verse, to contextualize it, and to examine the degree to which the error in question is attributable to the orthodox theologies apparently being censured, one would respond immediately by referring to the following verse: "Call unto the way of thy Lord with wisdom and fair exhortation, and hold discourse with them [the People of the Book] in the finest manner" (16:125). One is urged to use one's judgment, one's own "wisdom" to debate with the "other" in the most appropriate manner, taking into account both the particular conditions in which the dialogue is being conducted, and the principial priority that must be accorded to universal realities—so clearly affirmed in the Quran—over historical, communal, and even theological contingencies. In other words, insofar as one's orientation to the religious "other" is determined by spiritual, rather than theological or legal considerations, one should give priority to those verses which are of a clearly principial or universal nature, as opposed to those which are clearly contextual in nature.[83] By "contextual" is meant those verses which relate to the plane of theological exclusivism or inter-communal conflict, the very plane that is transcended by the vision that unfolds from the verses stressed and commented upon above.

Secondly, there is no warrant, even with an exclusivist reading of the Quran, for any brand of religious intolerance, and still less, persecution of non-Muslims. Far from it. In fact the Muslims are enjoined to defend churches and synagogues, and not just mosques—all being described by the Quran as places "wherein the name of God is much invoked" (22:40). One should also cite in this connection the historically recorded acts of tolerance manifested by the Prophet himself: for example, the treaty of Medina, in which the Jews were given equal rights with the Muslims;[84] the treaty signed with the monks of St Catherine's monastery on Sinai;[85] and,

83. It should be noted that this stress on certain verses—those which are universal in content, and which promote peace and harmony between the different faith communities, as opposed to those which are more aggressive in tone, and which reflect particular historical situations or specific theological controversies—is not totally unrelated to Ghazzali's principle of the "variance in the excellence of the Quranic verses". See his *Jewels of the Quran: Al-Ghazali's Theory*, trans. M. Abul Quasem (London and Boston, 1983), pp. 64-5. Needless to say, for Ghazzali, the Quran in its entirety is of a revealed substance, so each verse is equal to all others in respect of revelation; but some verses are of more profound import and of greater theurgic value than others, as attested to by the Prophet in many sayings. Ghazzali refers to the "light of insight" that helps us to see "the difference between the Verse of the Throne (2:255) and a verse concerning giving and receiving loans, and between the *Sura* of Sincerity (112) and the *Sura* of Destruction (111)" (p. 64).

84. See the useful discussion of the first Constitution of Medina in S. H. M. Jafri, *Political and Moral Vision of Islam* (Lahore, 2000), pp. 11-41.

85. A copy of the document is displayed to this day in the monastery itself, which is the oldest continually inhabited monastic establishment in Christendom, and which—it is of considerable interest to note—includes within its precincts a mosque, constructed by the monks for the local Bedouins. See J. Bentley, *Secrets of Mount Sinai* (London, 1985), pp. 18-19.

especially, the highly symbolic fact that, when the Christian delegation arrived from Najran to engage the Prophet in theological debate, principally over the Divine nature of Christ, they were permitted by him to perform their liturgical worship in his own mosque.[86]

One observes here a perfect example of how disagreement on the plane of dogma can co-exist with a deep respect on the superior plane of religious devotion. This example of the prophetic *sunnah* or conduct is a good background against which one can evaluate the following important passage from the *Discourses* of Rumi. In one part of the book, he clearly takes to task a Christian, Jarrah, for continuing to believe in certain Christian dogmas, in particular, the idea that Jesus is God,[87] but this disagreement on the plane of dogma does not blind Rumi from his majestic vision of the spirit above all religious forms—a vision so often evoked in his poetry—nor does it preclude discourse with Christians, or mutual inspiration. In Rumi's words:

> I was speaking one day amongst a group of people, and a party of non-Muslims was present. In the middle of my address they began to weep and to register emotion and ecstasy. Someone asked: What do they understand and what do they know? Only one Muslim in a thousand understands this kind of talk. What did they understand, that they should weep? The Master [*i.e.*, Rumi himself] answered: It is not necessary that they should understand the form of the discourse; that which constitutes the root and principle of the discourse, that they understand.[88] After all, every one acknowledges the Oneness of God, that He is the Creator and Provider, that He controls everything, that to Him all things shall return, and that it is He who punishes and forgives. When anyone hears these words, which are a description and commemoration (*dhikr*) of God, a universal commotion and ecstatic passion supervenes, since out of these words come the scent of their Beloved and their Quest.[89]

86. See A. Guillaume, trans., *The Life of Muhammad: A Translation of Ibn Ishâq's Sîrat Rasûl Allâh* (Oxford, 1968), pp. 270-277.
87. *Discourses*, pp. 135-136.
88. We have taken the liberty of substantially altering Arberry's translation in this sentence. He translates the Persian *nafs-e în sukhan* as "the inner spirit of these words"; whereas Rumi's contrast between the *nafs* of the "words" and the *asl* of the "words" makes it clear that the latter is in fact the "inner spirit" and the former is something relatively superficial, the formal correlate of the *asl*, the supra-formal principle, or the "inner spirit".
89. *Discourses*, p. 108.

In this passage the notion of creative, spiritual dialogue is given clear definition. Receptivity to innate spirituality, such as is rooted in the *fitrah*, constitutes the inalienable substance of the human soul; and this innate spirituality recognizes no confessional boundaries. Rumi is not so much denying the fact that Muslims and non-Muslims disagree over particular dogmas, as affirming the ever-present validity of spiritual dialogue, a mode of dialogue which bears fruit despite theological disagreement, and which serves to limit the negativity arising out of that disagreement, while turning to spiritual account the underlying, devotional orientation to the transcendent Reality that defines the essential reality of all believers.

This mode of dialogue is possible because the receptivity proper to spiritual substance is of infinitely greater import than the limitations that circumscribe all mental conceptions. This is how one can understand the following statement, in which both faith and infidelity are transcended by something more fundamental than the plane on which this dichotomy exists: "All men in their inmost hearts love God and seek Him, pray to Him and in all things put their hope in Him, recognizing none but Him as omnipotent and ordering their affairs. Such an apperception is neither infidelity nor faith. Inwardly it has no name."[90] This perspective is reinforced by the following statements from the same work. Prayer, Rumi says, changes from religion to religion, but "faith does not change in any religion; its states, its point of orientation, and the rest are invariable."[91] "Love for the Creator is latent in all the world and in all men, be they Magians, Jews, or Christians."[92]

Now, to return to the polemical verses that the Quran contains, in addition to all that has been said above, one has also to counterbalance such verses with the Quranic order to engage in constructive dialogue, and to avoid disputation—an order which is given added depth by affirmations of the presence of piety and faith in other religious traditions. For example:

> They are not all alike. Of the People of the Scripture there is a staunch community who recite the revelations of God in the watches of the night, falling prostrate.

90. *Ibid.*, p. 109.
91. *Ibid.*, p. 43. Arberry translates the word *qibla* as locus; but we prefer to translate this word as "point of orientation" in the above sentence.
92. *Ibid.*, p. 214.

> They believe in God and the Last Day, and enjoin right conduct and forbid indecency, and vie with one another in good works. These are of the righteous.
>
> And whatever good they do, they will not be denied it; and God knows the pious (3: 113-114).
>
> Thou wilt find the nearest of them [the People of the Scripture] in affection to those who believe to be those who say: Verily, we are Christians. That is because there are among them priests and monks, and they are not proud (5:82).
>
> I believe in whatever scripture God hath revealed, and I am commanded to be just among you. God is our Lord and your Lord. Unto us our works and unto you your works; no argument between us and you. God will bring us together and unto Him is the journeying (42:15).
>
> And only discourse with the People of the Book in a way that is most excellent, save with those who do wrong. And say: We believe in that which hath been revealed to us and revealed to you. Our God and your God is one, and unto Him we surrender (29:46).

And finally, it is worth repeating the following verse, which can justifiably be put forward as altogether definitive in respect of dialogue:

> Call unto the way of thy Lord with wisdom and fair exhortation, and hold discourse with them in the finest manner (16:125).

For those wishing to engage in dialogue with other faiths and their representatives, the key question devolves upon the way in which one understands that which is "finest", "most excellent", or "most beautiful", the word *ahsan* comprising all these meanings. One is urged to use one's own intelligence, one's own "aesthetic" feel for what accords most harmoniously with the conditions of one's own "dialogical" situation. The verse also links the "call" to the way of God with holding discourse with adherents of other belief-systems. Thus dialogue can itself be seen, not as contrary to the Muslim duty of bearing witness to his faith, but as an aspect of that duty, and perhaps, in the modern world, the wisest way of performing that duty. In an age when, in the words of Frithjof Schuon, "the outward and readily exaggerated incompatibility of the different religions greatly discredits, in the minds of most of our contemporaries, all religion",[93] a "call to God" which is based on

93. F. Schuon, *The Transcendent Unity of Religions* (Wheaton, IL, 1993), p. xxxiii.

universal inclusivity rather than dogmatic exclusivity is much more likely to be heeded. The Quranic discourse explicitly refers to the fragility and illogicality of confessional or denominational exclusivity, and affirms truths of a universal nature, doing so, moreover, with an insistence and in a manner that is unparalleled among world scriptures. It is therefore uniquely situated, in intellectual terms, to assist in the resolution of the contemporary crisis precipitated by mutually exclusive religious claims.

Wisdom is explicitly called for in the verse we have cited above; and wisdom, by definition, is not something that can be laid down in advance of all the concrete and unique situations in which wisdom needs to be applied, as if it were a formal rule or a blueprint. On the contrary, it is, on the one hand, a Divine bestowal, and on the other, a quality that can be developed and cultivated only through intellectual, moral, and spiritual effort. In the Quran, wisdom is described as a gift from God: "He giveth wisdom to whom He will; and he to whom wisdom is given hath been granted great good" (2:269). But it is also a quality which can be cultivated, acquired, or learned, and this is implied in the following verse, where the Prophet is described as one who teaches and imparts not just the formal message, but the wisdom required to understand and creatively apply that message: "He it is Who hath sent among the unlettered ones a Messenger of their own, to recite unto them His revelations and to make them grow [in purity], and to teach them the Scripture and wisdom" (62:2).

One of the most important aspects of wisdom taught by the scripture of the Quran and the conduct of the Prophet is tolerance of those with belief-systems different from one's own, a tolerance grounded in a consciousness of the Reality which transcends all systems of belief, one's own included, but which is also mysteriously present in the depths of each human soul. Authentic dialogue emerges in the measure that this presence of God in all human beings is respected. For Muslims living at a time when the alternative to dialogue is not just diatribe but violent clash, the imperative of highlighting that which unites the different religions, of upholding and promoting the common spiritual patrimony of mankind, is of the utmost urgency. As we have seen, there is ample evidence in the Quranic text itself, and in the compelling commentaries on these verses by those most steeped in the spiritual tradition of Islam, to demonstrate that the Quran not only provides us with a universal vision of religion, and thus with the means to contemplate all revealed religions as "signs" (*âyât*) of God, but also opens up paths of creative, constructive dialogue between the faithful of all the different religious communities, despite their divergent belief-systems. It provides us with the basis for dialogue and mutual enrichment on aspects of religious life and thought that go beyond the outward forms of belief, yielding fruit in the fertile fields of metaphysical insight, immutable values, contemplative inspiration, and spiritual realization.

Chapter 8

A Unity with Distinctions: Parallels in the Thought of St Gregory Palamas and Ibn Arabi

Peter Samsel

The interrelation of Orthodox Christianity and Islam has—throughout their shared history—too often been one of political contention and tragedy conjoined with dogmatic theological rejection. Politically, the conquest and hegemony of the Ottoman Turks in the Levant was a cultural disaster for the Byzantines, despite the religious tolerance shown by the Ottomans. Even in present times, in such regions as Cyprus and the former Yugoslavia, the tensions of previous generations continue to persist. While, in a sense, such difficulties have largely conformed to the typical historical pattern of neighboring cultures and civilizations everywhere, they have also served to aggravate the already substantial inherent barriers to mutual comprehension. These barriers have been predominantly religious in nature, centering on the question of the nature and role of both Jesus and Muhammad as understood in each tradition.

Christianity, historically antecedent and conceived as a universal mission, has little "theological space" for Islam in its scriptural and apostolic sources. With the rise of Islam, the Christian self-understanding regarding the nature of Christ as the incarnate Son of God and His associated universal salvific role precluded any theological admission of validity to Muhammad, even on the level of the Hebraic prophets. Islam, historically subsequent and not—despite the preeminence granted to its founder and the disputed question of abrogation—conceived as a universal mission, has, in contrast, considerable "theological space" for Christianity. In particular, the Quran holds an unfailingly positive view of Jesus and a generally positive one of Christians. However, the Quranic understanding of Christianity is not the same as the Christian self-understanding. The figure of the Prophet Isa (Jesus) in the Quran reinforces the Quranic self-understanding regarding the unity of God, the nature of revelation, and the role of prophecy, and thus differs in significant ways from the Christ of the Gospels.

Clearly, if any substantial mutual comprehension is to be achieved—assuming of course that such an achievement is desirable—it must be built on bases other than those of raw politics or dogmatic polemics. Perhaps the most fertile basis for such comprehension lies in the respective spiritual paths, Hesychasm and Sufism, that are found at the heart of each of these traditions. Within these spiritual paths, one of the soundest points of intersecting concern is the mutual witness of those saints and friends of God who have achieved holiness and nearness to the Divine. Such individuals are figures of universal attraction, and it is relatively easy to conceive of a mutual sympathy and regard manifesting between such figures as Elder Joseph the Hesychast[1] and Shaykh Ahmad al-Alawi,[2] contemporaries to one another and near contemporaries to ourselves. The remarkable congruence of spiritual method, particularly the practice of continual invocatory prayer of the heart, as represented in the Hesychast Prayer of Jesus and the Sufi remembrance of God (*dhikr*), forms another natural point of convergent concern between Orthodoxy and Islam.[3] A third point of intersection, one that has perhaps not been sufficiently well explored, is that of doctrinal similarity in what might be termed the "mystical theologies" of Hesychasm and Sufism. Such an exploration is particularly important in that these mystical theologies represent the highest self-understanding of each respective tradition. As such, the discovery of real similarities can address dogmatic polemicisms on an intellectual level, and with a greater force and directness than similarities of either sanctity or praxis.

The two figures that form the focus of this paper, Gregory Palamas and Ibn Arabi, are, with little qualification, the pre-eminent mystical theologians within their respective traditions. This description—"mystical theologians"—while somewhat ill-fitting, has the virtue of capturing the essential nature of their thought. Both were "mystical" in the sense that neither were mere theoreticians,

1. Elizabeth Theokritoff, trans., *Elder Joseph the Hesychast* (Mount Athos: The Holy and Great Monastery of Vatopaidi, 1999).
2. Martin Lings, *A Sufi Saint of the Twentieth Century* (Berkeley: University of California Press, 1971).
3. Seyyed Hossein Nasr, "The Prayer of the Heart in Hesychasm and Sufism", *Greek Orthodox Theological* Review, Vol. 31, No. 1-2 (1986).

but rather were intensely engaged in spiritual practice and had partaken of the Divine illumination granted through such practice. In addition, both were deeply concerned to articulate and defend the nature and validity of spiritual practice and mystical experience to their philosophically and rationally oriented detractors. Both were "theologians" in the sense that, although they were remarkably creative, they were at the same time deeply faithful to the sources of their respective traditions, to which their thought always circles and returns. For Palamas, these sources comprise the Gospels, the Apostolic Epistles, and the writings of the earlier Church Fathers; for Ibn Arabi, they comprise the Quran, the sayings of the Prophet (*hadîth*), and the writings of the earlier Sufis. Both might be termed philosophic as well, as neither were strangers to philosophic argumentation and explication. Yet for both, such philosophic reasoning is no more than a tool to be used in the service of cogent expression, rather than as a primary means to Truth. Although neither were systematic theologians, they were at once synthetic and decisive in that they encompassed everything that came before them and shaped everything that came after.

Gregory Palamas (1296-1359), Athonite monk and abbot, archbishop of Thessalonika, eminent theologian and saint, was the most significant spiritual and intellectual figure of Orthodox Byzantium. He was drawn into theological explication through the controversy surrounding the validity of Hesychast spirituality that was instigated by the Greek Italian philosopher Barlaam the Calabrian. Hesychasm, the eremitic way of life dedicated to contemplation and continual prayer, claimed as its fruits the attainment of "quietude" (*hesychia*) of the passions and the experience of the uncreated light, the same light witnessed by the chosen Apostles on Mt Tabor. Barlaam, arguing philosophically, attacked the theological foundations of Hesychasm, denying that such an experience could be a real knowledge of God. Palamas arose to defend his Athonite brothers and, in the Councils of 1341, successfully defeated Barlaam. His major theological work, *Triads in Defense of the Holy Hesychasts,* although composed as a polemical defense, represents a primary witness to both the content and meaning of Christian experience.[4] To quote Vladimir Lossky:

4. John Meyendorff, ed., *Gregory Palamas: The Triads.* Classics of Western Spirituality (New York: Paulist Press, 1983), p. 8.

> It is very difficult to separate the personal doctrine of St. Gregory Palamas from the common patrimony of the Orthodox Church because the very aim of Palamas's work was a dogmatic expression of the foundation of that mystical life which is proper to the Orthodox Church.[5]

Ibn Arabi (1165-1240), the most influential proponent of intellectual Sufism in Islamic history, was known as the "Greatest Spiritual Master" (*ash-shaykh al-akbar*) and the "Revivifier of Religion" (*muhyî ad-dîn*). An intensely prolific author, his magnum opus, *The Meccan Openings*, encompasses a vast array of Islamic disciplines: Quranic commentary, Prophetic *hadîth*, jurisprudence, theology (*kalâm*), philosophy (*falsafah*), and Sufism. This work bears witness to his deep loyalty to the foundations of the Islamic tradition; not only is its content deeply marked by the Quran and *hadîth*, but the very architectural structure of the work relates in the most intricate fashion to that of the Quran as well.[6] Although attacked by Islamic exoterists such as Ibn Taymiyya and his followers, his influence was and continues to be extraordinarily broad among Muslims concerned with the spiritual and intellectual life. To quote William Chittick, "In the Islamic world itself, probably no one has exercised deeper and more pervasive influence [than Ibn Arabi] over the intellectual life of the community during the past seven hundred years."[7]

Although not broadly recognized, the thought of these two figures exhibits remarkable parallels, not only in the topics that they address—including the nature of the Divine essence, its articulation towards and creation of the world, the paradoxical transcendence/immanence of God in the creation, the nature and potentiality of the human being, and the interplay of Divine revelation and human consummation—but also in the answers and descriptions that they provide. Although their vocabularies and means of expression differ, the close parallelism between them suggests that the vision that each grasps, through the contextual lenses of their respective traditions, is in fact the same vision of the Real. In this

5. Clement Lialine, "The Theological Teaching of Gregory Palamas on Divine Simplicity", *Eastern Churches Quarterly*, Vol. VI (1946), p. 283.
6. Michel Chodkiewicz, *An Ocean Without Shore: Ibn Arabi, the Book, and the Law* (Albany: State University of New York Press, 1993), pp. 59-100.
7. William C. Chittick, *The Sufi Path of Knowledge: Ibn al-'Arabî's Metaphysics of Imagination* (Albany: State University of New York Press, 1989), p. x.

respect, it may be useful to bear in mind a phrase that Palamas was fond of repeating: "Our religion is not a question of words, but of realities."[8]

The Essence in Itself

The root of comparative exploration between these two figures should, it seems, begin with the very Root of All. Ontologically prior to any manifestation and disclosure, the Divine in its Essence stands alone. The Essence in Itself is beyond any possible relationship, knowing or dependence. As the preface to the Eucharistic canon of the Orthodox liturgy states, "Thou art God, ineffable, invisible, incomprehensible."[9] St Gregory describes the situation as:

> The supra-essential nature of God is not a subject for speech or thought or even contemplation, for it is far removed from all that exists and more than unknowable is incomprehensible and ineffable to all forever. There is no name whereby it can be named, neither in this age nor in the age to come, nor word found in the soul and uttered by the tongue, nor contact whether sensible or intellectual, nor yet any image which may afford any knowledge of its subject, if this be not that perfect incomprehensibility which one acknowledges in denying all that can be named.[10]

This Essence in Itself, or super-essence (*hyperousios*), as Palamas often terms it, is not only unknowable, but also simple,[11] independent and "self generating" (*authyparktos kai autopator*),[12] to the extent that it can be described in any positive terms at all.

For Ibn Arabi, the situation might be most simply stated thus: "God is, and nothing is with Him."[13] He further elaborates:

> He is independent of the worlds (Quran 3:97), and this belongs to no existent essence save the Essence of the Real—no engendered thing is tied to the Essence, no eye perceives It, no limit encompasses It, and no demonstration gives knowledge of It.[14]

8. John Meyendorff, *A Study of Gregory Palamas* (Crestwood, NY: St. Vladimir's Seminary Press, 1998), p. 239.
9. *The Triads*, p. 14.
10. George C. Papademetriou, *Introduction to Saint Gregory Palamas* (New York: Philosophical Library, 1973), p. 33.
11. Lialine, p. 276.
12. *Introduction to Saint Gregory Palamas*, p. 32.
13. *The Sufi Path of Knowledge*, p. 131.
14. *Ibid.*, p. 64.

God, in the absolute unity of His Essence (*dhât*)—the One as such—is inaccessible: "He who awaits the meeting with his Lord, let him not associate the One (*al-ahad*) with adoration of his Lord." "Unity (*al-ahadîyyah*) ignores and refuses you."[15]

The Articulation of the Essence

The Essence in Itself might be termed the interiority of God, but God in His Essence also possesses certain modalities of being and expression. For St Gregory, these modalities comprise the Trinity, the three *prosopa* or *hypostases*, each expressing a distinct face and aspect of the Divine being.[16] The articulation of the modalities of the Essence finds its generative principle in the *hypostasis* of the Father, which is the sole principle of Divinity (*theotetos arche*), its source (*pege*) and cause (*aiton*).[17] Although the Father is "prior" to the other *hypostases*, it is only in this sense that He may be said to be above them: "He [the Father] is greater than the Son and the Spirit, but only in as much as He is their cause."[18] The three *prosopa*, the Persons or faces of the Divinity, are not distinct and separate elements, even less distinct centers of consciousness:[19]

> We worship one true and perfect God in three true and perfect Persons, not a threefold God—far from it—but a simple God. For there is not a threefold goodness nor a trinity of goodnesses, but one, holy, revered and adored Trinity, the supreme Goodness, continually pouring out of itself into itself, and divinely existing in itself from all eternity.[20]

As the Hesychast Council of 1351—which Palamas presided over—stated, "God is not only in three hypostases, but He is also the All-powerful One (*pantodunamos*)."[21] This unity extends to the domain of the will and operation, or "energy", of the persons: "God is always like Himself, for the three divine *hypostases* possess one another nat-

15. *An Ocean Without Shore*, p. 40.
16. Kallistos Ware, "The Human Person as an Icon of the Trinity", *Sobornost*, Vol. 8, No. 2 (1986), p. 14.
17. *Introduction to Saint Gregory Palamas*, p. 37.
18. M. Edmund Hussey, "The Persons-Energy Structure in the Theology of St Gregory Palamas", *St Vladimir's Theological* Quarterly, Vol.18, No. 1 (1974), p. 34.
19. "The Human Person as an Icon of the Trinity", p. 14.
20. "The Persons-Energy Structure in the Theology of St Gregory Palamas", p. 29.
21. Vladimir Lossky, *Orthodox Theology: An Introduction* (Crestwood, NY: St. Vladimir's Seminary Press, 1978), p. 157.

urally, totally, eternally, and indivisibly, but also without mixture or confusion, and they co-penetrate each other in such a way that they only possess one energy."[22] As the Divine operations stem from a single source, so do the multifarious relationships between the Divinity and creation: "The Father, Son, and Holy Spirit are one source and Lord relative to creation, one Creator, one God and Father, Provider, Custodian, and all the rest."[23]

Although the Persons do not break the unity of the Divinity, they nevertheless possess distinct modalities. At the level of the Essence, the Father is ungenerated (*agennetos*), the Son is generated (*gennetos*), and the Holy Spirit proceeds (*ekporeuetai*).[24] In relation to the Divine activities and operations, "We see the individual effect of each of the three persons."[25] More specifically, the one work of creation is "from the Father through the Son in the Spirit".[26] A perspicacious commentator on Palamas has glossed this by saying that "the Father is the source and initiator, the Son is the effecting agent, and the Spirit is the completing touch of all Divine activity".[27]

In Ibn Arabi's short collection of mystical odes, *The Interpreter of Desires*, there appears a remarkable verse: "My Beloved is three although He is One, even as the [three] Persons [of the Trinity] are made one Person in essence." He interprets the verse this way: "Number does not beget multiplicity in the Divine Substance, as the Christians declare that the Three Persons of the Trinity are One God, and as the Quran declares: 'Call on God or call on the Merciful; however ye invoke Him, it is well, for to Him belong the most excellent Names' (Quran 17:110)."[28] Given the isolated appearance and allusive nature of this fragment, it would be dangerous to interpret it broadly, and yet the primary insight that the Divine substance is articulated while remaining one is representative of his thought. It is worth noting, in this regard, that the Quranic criticism of the doctrine of the Trinity seems oriented more towards early heretical

22. *A Study of Gregory Palamas*, p. 216.
23. "The Persons-Energy Structure in the Theology of St Gregory Palamas", p. 28.
24. *Introduction to Saint Gregory Palamas*, p. 38.
25. "The Persons-Energy Structure in the Theology of St Gregory Palamas", p. 41.
26. *Ibid.*, p. 32.
27. *Ibid.*, p. 41.
28. Reynold A. Nicholson, trans., *The* Tarjuman al-Ashwaq (London: Theosophical Publishing House, 1978), p. 70.

positions than the developed understanding of the later Christian councils.[29]

In discussing the externalization of the Essence, the Shaykh uses the term "Level" (*martabah*). It is at the Level that one may speak of Allah ("God") as the Divinity or Lord—terms implying relationship. He writes:

> In respect of His Essence, He belongs to His Essence, but in respect of what is named "God" ["Allah"], He seeks the cosmos. The cosmos knows nothing of the Real save the Level, that is, the fact that He is a God, a Lord. So the cosmos has nothing to say about Him except concerning these relations and attributes.[30]

According to the Quran, God's "mercy embraces all things" (7:156), while it is the All-Merciful who "sat upon the Throne" (20:5). For Ibn Arabi, the All-Merciful (*ar-Rahmân*), because of its all-embracing nature, is the predominant face presented by God and is bound up with the very act of creation: "Since God was kind toward us through the name 'All-merciful', He brought us out from evil, which is nonexistence, to good, which is existence."[31] Closely associated with the All-Merciful is the Divine Breath, through which God speaks the cosmos into existence: "God attributed a Breath to Himself, ascribing it to the name 'All-merciful', only to tell us 'that mercy comprises and includes all things'."[32] Ibn Arabi states further:

> The Breath of the All-merciful (*nafas ar-Rahmân*) bestows existence upon the forms of the possible things, just as the human breath bestows existence upon letters. Hence the cosmos is the words of God in respect to his Breath.[33]

This understanding is very close to one of the Psalms: "By the word of the Lord the heavens were made, and all the host of them by the breath of His mouth" (Ps 33:6). St Athanasius, referring to this text, explicitly identifies the breath with the Spirit (*pneuma*).[34]

29. See, for example, Geoffrey Parrinder, *Jesus in the Qurân* (Oxford: Oneworld Publications, 1995), pp. 133-41.
30. William C. Chittick, *The Self Disclosure of God: Principles of Ibn al-'Arabî's Cosmology* (Albany: State University of New York Press, 1998), p. 194.
31. *The Sufi Path of Knowledge*, p. 290.
32. *Ibid.*, p. 130.
33. *Ibid.*, p. 131.
34. Vladimir Lossky, *The Mystical Theology of the Eastern Church* (Crestwood, NY: St Vladimir's Seminary Press, 1976), p. 100.

Ibn Arabi also refers to the reality denoted by the Breath of the All-Merciful in other terms: the Real Through Which Creation Occurs, the Supreme *Barzakh*, the Cloud, and the Reality of the Perfect Man, or Muhammadan Reality.[35] The term "Cloud" stems from a *hadîth*—evocative of the verse of the Psalms "clouds and darkness surround Him" (Ps 97:2)—in which the Prophet was asked, "Where was our Lord before he created the creatures?", to which he replied, "He was in a Cloud."[36] The Muhammadan Reality that proceeds from the Divine name "the All-Merciful" (*haqîqah muhammadiyyah rahmâniyyah*)[37] denotes the preexistent essence of the Prophet and fountainhead of all prophetic activity.[38] This understanding derives from a number of Prophetic *hadîths*: "I was a prophet while Adam was still between water and clay."[39] "The first thing that God created was my spirit."[40] "I am the first man to have been created and the last to have been sent [as a prophet]."[41] Also relevant is the *hadîth qudsî* (extra-Quranic revelation) "If you [Muhammad] had not been, I would not have created the spheres".[42] Ibn Arabi did not introduce the concept denoted by the Muhammadan Reality, which has a long traditional history, particularly as symbolized by the "Muhammadan Light" (*nûr muhammadî*).[43] For instance, the early Sufi Sahl al-Tustari wrote, "God created the light of Muhammad out of His own Light. After it, He created the creatures."[44]

Although these articulations—the All-Merciful, the Breath, *etc.*—are distinct modalities of Being, they do not break the Divine unity: "God declares the unity [of the Real Through Which Creation Occurs] despite the fact that it proceeds from Him. People are bewildered because it pluralizes Him, for there is nothing but He."[45]

35. *The Sufi Path of Knowledge*, p. 125.
36. *The Self Disclosure of God*, p. 435.
37. Michel Chodkiewicz, *Seal of the Saints: Prophethood and Sainthood in the Doctrine of Ibn Arabî* (Cambridge: Islamic Texts Society, 1993), p. 68.
38. Annemarie Schimmel, *And Muhammad is His Messenger: The Veneration of the Prophet in Islamic Piety* (Chapel Hill, NC: University of North Carolina Press, 1985), p. 132.
39. Claude Addas, *Quest for the Red Sulphur: The Life of Ibn Arabî* (Cambridge: Islamic Texts Society, 1993), p. 76.
40. *And Muhammad is His Messenger*, p. 130.
41. *Seal of the Saints*, p. 63.
42. *And Muhammad is His Messenger*, p. 130.
43. *Seal of the Saints*, p. 61.
44. *Ibid.*, p. 65.
45. *The Self Disclosure of God*, p. 78.

The Articulation of the Attributes and Acts

Ontologically subsequent to the articulation of the Essence, the attributes and acts of God describe the modalities of His operative nature and activity as He descends to the created order. For St Gregory, these modalities are collectively termed the energies (*energeia*); they are subsequent to the Essence and are its natural manifestations, but are external to the very being of the Trinity,[46] being referred to as *ta peri auton* –the things that surround Him.[47] The energies are "uncreated", neither coming into being, nor ceasing to be.[48]

Although the term "energy" or "energies" is encountered most frequently in St Gregory's writings, he also uses such equivalent terms as "work" and "virtue",[49] as well as "grace, power, energy, radiance, kingdom and incorruption",[50] to denote God's eternal, uncreated activity.[51] The modalities of the energies are indicated by the names attributed to God in Scripture.[52] Among these, St Gregory explicitly mentions goodness, eternal will, providence, wisdom, power, divinity, majesty,[53] life, immortality, simplicity, immutability, infinity, blessedness and holiness.[54] Among those Fathers that he cites most frequently, St Maximus the Confessor and the Pseudo-Dionysius stand out particularly. The Pseudo-Dionysius, in *The Divine Names,* provides a considerable listing:

> they give it many names, such as "I am being", "life", "light", "God", the "truth". These same wise writers, when praising the Cause of everything that is, use names drawn from all the things caused: good, beautiful, wise, beloved, God of gods, Lord of lords, Holy of Holies, eternal, existent, Cause of the ages. They call him source of life, wisdom, mind, word, knower, possessor beforehand of all the treasures of knowledge, power, powerful, and King of Kings,

46. *The Mystical Theology of the Eastern Church,* p. 81.
47. *The Triads,* p. 147.
48. *Introduction to Saint Gregory Palamas,* p. 46.
49. *The Triads,* p. 147.
50. Kallistos Ware, "God Hidden and Revealed: The Apophatic Way and the Essence-Energies Distinction", *Eastern Churches* Review, Vol. 7, No. 2 (1975), p. 131.
51. "The Persons-Energy Structure in the Theology of St. Gregory Palamas", p. 30.
52. *Orthodox Theology,* p. 41; *The Mystical Theology of the Eastern Church,* p. 80.
53. *Introduction to Saint Gregory Palamas,* pp. 44-5.
54. Hierotheos Vlachos, *St Gregory Palamas as a Hagiorite* (Levadia, Greece: Birth of the Theotokos Monastery, 1997), p. 306.

> ancient of days, the unaging and unchanging, salvation, righteousness and sanctification, redemption, greatest of all and yet the one in the still breeze.[55]

In language remarkably similar to that used by Ibn Arabi in describing the All-Merciful, the Pseudo-Dionysius singles out the name "Good" as being preeminent, on the strength of Christ's teaching, "Why do you call Me good? No one is good but One, that is, God" (Mt 19:17, Lk 18:19):

> Let us move on now to the name "Good", which the sacred writers have preeminently set apart for the supra-divine God from all other names. They call the Divine subsistence itself "goodness". This essential Good, by the very fact of its existence, extends goodness into all things.[56]

Although Palamas does not discuss the relationships between the Essence and the various energies in detail, he does distinguish between those energies that are intrinsic to the Essence and independent of the creation and those that may only manifest in activity in relation to the creation:

> The wise Maximus [the Confessor] thus rightly says that "existence, life, holiness, and virtue are works of God that do not have a beginning in time. There was never a time when virtue, goodness, holiness, and immortality did not exist".[57]

He continues, "There are, however, energies of God which have a beginning and an end, as all the saints will confirm."[58] These energies, such as creative power or prescience, may have a beginning or end in their external operations, though not as pre-existent in the mind of God.[59] Ultimately, the names and their correlative energies are innumerable, with only some of them known to us through Scripture.[60]

For Ibn Arabi, the attributes and acts of God are articulated through the Breath of the All-Merciful.These modalities are designated by the Most Beautiful Names—those names, traditionally

55. Colm Luibheid, trans., *Pseudo-Dionysius: The Complete Works*. Classics of Western Spirituality (New York: Paulist Press, 1987), p. 55.
56. *Ibid.*
57. *The Triads,* p. 95.
58. *Ibid.*, p. 96.
59. *Ibid.*, p. 148.
60. *The Mystical Theology of the Eastern Church,* p. 80.

ninety-nine in number, attributed to God in the Quran, although in their entirety they are beyond enumeration.[61] "God discloses Himself (*tajallî*) in His Most Beautiful Names."[62] A number of them appear in the following Quranic passage:

> There is no god but He, Knower of the absent and the witnessed, and He is the All-Merciful, the Compassionate. He is God, there is no god but He, the King, the Holy, Peace, the Faithful, the Guardian, the Exalted, the All-Dominating, the Self-Great, the Creator, the Author, the Form-Giver. To Him belong the Most Beautiful Names (59:23-24).[63]

Of the names mentioned in the Quran, the names Alive, Knowing, Desiring, Powerful, Speaking, Generous, and Just are often cited as being the most fundamental.[64] However, the names Allah and All-Merciful are even more significant, given their polysemous nature. These names are both Divine attributes as well as articulations of the Essence:

> God says, "Call upon Allah or call upon the All-Merciful; whichever you call upon to Him belong the most beautiful names" (Quran 17:110). Here God makes the Most Beautiful Names belong equally to both Allah and the All-Merciful. But notice this subtle point: Every name has a meaning (*ma'nâ*) and a form (*sûrah*). "Allah" is called by the name's meaning, while the "All-Merciful" is called by the name's form. This is because the Breath is ascribed to the All-Merciful, and through the Breath the Divine words become manifest.[65]

The name Allah is the "all comprehensive name" (*al-ism al-jâmi'*) in that it brings together every Divine quality, designating God as He is with the greatest possible inclusiveness.[66]

Ibn Arabi often categorizes the names in terms of incomparability (*tanzîh*) and similarity (*tashbîh*), the former including such names as Independent and One, the latter including such names as Compassionate and Forgiving:[67]

61. William C. Chittick, *Imaginal Worlds: Ibn al-'Arabî and the Problem of Religious Diversity* (Albany: State University of New York Press, 1994), p. 21.
62. *The Sufi Path of Knowledge,* p. 43.
63. *The Self Disclosure of God,* p. 171.
64. *Imaginal Worlds,* p. 21.
65. *The Sufi Path of Knowledge,* p. 34.
66. *The Self Disclosure of God,* p. 171.
67. *The Sufi Path of Knowledge,* p. 58.

> There are two kinds of Divine attributes: Divine attributes which require the declaration of incomparability, like All-great and All-high, and Divine attributes which require the declaration of similarity, such as the Magnificent, the Self-exalted, and everything by which the Real described Himself and by which the servant is also qualified.[68]

Although he does not use a separate term, such as energies, to distinguish between the actual operations of God and their denotations in the Quran, the Shaykh clearly distinguishes between the two: "You should know that the Divine names which we have are the names of the Divine names."[69]

The names form the *barzakh*—that which stands between two things, both separating them and conjoining them—between the Essence and creation:

> The divine names are the *barzakh* between us and the Named. They look upon Him since they name Him, and they look upon us since they bestow upon us effects attributed to the Named. So they make the Named known and they make us known.[70]

The Bringing Forth of the Created World

The operations of God, articulated from His Essence and in accordance with His creative will, act to bring forth the created order. For St Gregory, this will finds its ultimate motivation in the goodness and love of God: "God's love calls forth His energies, which disclose themselves in His creatures."[71] He writes further:

> Therefore we must look for a god who not only possesses his own end within himself, his own energy and his own deification, but who is a good God—for so it will not be enough for him just to exist in the contemplation of himself.[72]

God, through the shared will of the Persons of the Trinity,[73] has created all things by His uncreated energies.[74] The energies of God

68. *Ibid.*
69. *Ibid.*, p. 34.
70. *Ibid.*, p. 39.
71. *The Mystical Theology of the Eastern Church*, p. 75.
72. *A Study of Gregory Palamas*, p. 210.
73. *Introduction to Saint Gregory Palamas*, p. 58.
74. *The Mystical Theology of the Eastern Church*, p. 89.

penetrate the created universe,[75] forming the essential connection between the Essence and the creatures, which truly live only to the extent that they participate in the energies.[76] Although the energies permeate and support the creation, it does not thereby become infinite and coeternal with God.[77] Rather, it is characterized by limitation and determination, finitude, and contingency.[78] What is created is the effect (*energethen*), not the energy (*energeia*).[79]

The energies, in their multiplicity and differentiation, enter into the creation in diverse ways appropriate to the diversity of created beings:

> All created beings participate in God's energy, but in different ways. Some share only in the creative Divine energy and not in that which confers life. Others participate in the life-conferring energy as well but lack the wisdom-conferring Divine power in which rational beings participate. Finally, only the good angels and godly men have a share in the deifying energy and grace of God, by means of which they approach and resemble their creator. Thus, even though all created things partake of Divine energy, only angels and saints are sharers in the Divine life, and as a result only these can be seen as truly participators in Divinity.[80]

The created beings themselves, given existence through the abiding and enlivening of the uncreated energies, are located prior to the creation as the words (*logoi*) in the knowledge of God.[81] These *logoi* are not created, and yet they are not part of the Essence. They are the non-existents to which God gives existence *ex nihilo*.[82] As St Paul writes, God "calls those things which do not exist as though they did" (Rom 4:17). Differing with the earlier Fathers on this point, St Gregory conflates the *logoi* with the energies themselves—uncreated, and yet distinct from the Essence.[83] He comments:

> How could the manifold Divine thoughts, and the images of beings to come which these thoughts reflect... be themselves the

75. *Ibid.*
76. *The Triads*, p. 150.
77. *The Mystical Theology of the Eastern Church*, p. 74.
78. *Ibid.*, p. 89.
79. *Introduction to Saint Gregory Palamas*, p. 44.
80. Georgios I. Mantzaridis, *The Deification of Man* (Crestwood, NY: St. Vladimir's Seminary Press, 1984), pp. 107.
81. *A Study of Gregory Palamas*, p. 223.
82. *Introduction to Saint Gregory Palamas*, p. 58.
83. *A Study of Gregory Palamas*, p. 223.

essence? In fact through them God is in relation with beings, whereas, by essence, He is outside all relation.[84]

For Ibn Arabi, God's underlying love as the motivating cause of creation is expressed most decisively in the famous *hadîth qudsî*: "I was a Treasure but was not known, so I loved to be known; I created the creatures and made Myself known to them, so they came to know Me."[85] He comments, "The Breath [of the All-Merciful] emerges from a root, which is Love for the creatures, to whom He desired to make Himself known, so that they might know Him."[86] He remarks, with respect to human beings, "His love for His servants is identical with the origination of their engendered existence."[87]

Within the Breath, or the Cloud, the created order is brought forth: "Within the Cloud, God opened up the forms of everything of the cosmos beside Himself."[88] This bringing forth is governed by the Divine command "Be!": "Our only word to a thing, when We desire it, is to say to it 'Be!'" (Quran 16:40). The created beings come into manifestation through conjoining with the properties of the Divine names. These properties, manifested within the created beings—such as life, compassion, or knowledge—can be traced back to the Divine attributes.[89] The created beings are, in fact, nothing other than the properties or effects of the Divine names.[90] "To God belong the Most Beautiful Names, and to the cosmos belongs manifestation through the names by assuming their traits."[91] The Shaykh explains further: "No property becomes manifest within existence without a root in the Divine Side by which it is supported."[92] "The 'Divine support' is the fact that the Divine names are the support for the *loci* (*mahâll*) [created beings] wherein their own effects exist, so that the levels of the names may become designated."[93]

84. *Ibid.*, p. 224.
85. *The Self Disclosure of God*, p. 21.
86. *The Sufi Path of Knowledge*, p. 128.
87. *The Self Disclosure of God*, p. 22.
88. *Ibid.*, p. 337.
89. *Ibid.*, p. 53.
90. *The Sufi Path of Knowledge*, p. 86.
91. *Ibid.*, p. 284.
92. *Ibid.*, p. 39.
93. *Ibid.*

Although the Divine names enter into creation, it is nevertheless characterized by imperfection and poverty relative to the Real:

> When He made the creatures manifest, He bestowed upon them those names which He willed to bestow and actualized the creatures through them. Creation stands in the station of imperfection because of its possibility and its poverty toward someone to give preponderance [to its existence over its nonexistence].[94]

The created beings, or existent things, given existence and manifestation by God, are known to Him prior to the creation as the immutable entities (*a'yân thâbitah*) or possible things (*mumkin*).[95] Ibn Arabi finds a reference to this in the Quranic passage, "There is no thing whose treasuries are not with Us" (15:21). For the Shaykh, these "treasuries" are the immutable entities,[96] existent in God's knowledge but nonexistent in the creation: "Although the possible thing exists, it has the property of the nonexistent thing."[97] It is these entities that are given existence by God and form the entire created order through being the *loci* for the properties of the Divine names: "Every entity was nonexistent in itself and known to Him, and He loved to bring it into existence."[98]

Between Unknowability and Disclosure

Although God in the interiority of His Essence is never known, He is known to His creatures through the disclosure of His nature in their own properties. Although God has made Himself multiple, through the articulation of His Essence, His operations, and His creatures, He remains singular and undivided. God embraces, in a mysterious and antinomic manner, the extremes of identity and real difference, of presence with His creatures and absence in His interiority.

The Gospels themselves give voice to this mystery: "No one has seen God at any time" (Jn 1:18), but "the pure in heart . . . shall see God" (Mt 5:8). St John writes in one and the same Epistle: "No one has seen God at any time" (1 Jn 4:12), and "we shall see Him as He

94. *Ibid.*, p. 43.
95. *Ibid.*, p. 84.
96. *Ibid.*, p. 87.
97. *The Self Disclosure of God*, p. 30.
98. *Ibid.*, p. 22.

is" (1 Jn 3:2). How are these statements to be reconciled? For St Gregory, "It is right for all theology which wishes to respect piety to affirm sometimes one and sometimes the other when both affirmations are true."[99] He explains further:

> The Divine nature must be called at the same time incommunicable and, in a sense, communicable; we attain participation in the nature of God, and yet he remains totally inaccessible. We must affirm both things at once and must preserve the antinomy as the criterion of piety.[100]

Expressing the full paradox of the situation, he writes: "He is being and not being; He is everywhere and nowhere; He has many names and cannot be named; He is both in perpetual movement and immovable; He is absolutely everything and nothing of that which is."[101]

Despite the apparent differentiation of God into hierarchy and multiplicity, He remains singular. Palamas, upholding the doctrine of the Divine simplicity, repudiates any suggestion that God's nature could be "composite" (*synthetos*).[102] He writes, "God is one; He is at the same time incomprehensible (*akataleptos*) in His essence, and comprehensible in His energies, by the creature."[103] Explaining further, he remarks, "God does not lose his simplicity either because of the division and distinction of the *hypostases* [of the Trinity], or because of the division and multiplicity of the powers and energies."[104] Because of His simplicity and singularity, His transcendence of the categories of whole and parts, He is not merely present in His *hypostates* and energies, but wholly and fully so:[105]

> Goodness is not one part of God, Wisdom another, and Majesty or Providence still another; God is wholly Goodness, wholly Wisdom, wholly Providence, and wholly Majesty; for He is one, without any division into parts, but, possessing in Himself each of these energies, He reveals Himself wholly in each by His presence and His action in a unified, simple and undivided fashion.[106]

99. *Orthodox Theology*, p. 157.
100. *Ibid.*, p. 156.
101. *A Study of Gregory Palamas*, p. 209.
102. "God Hidden and Revealed", p. 135; *The Deification of Man* , pp. 106-7.
103. *Introduction to Saint Gregory Palamas*, p. 34.
104. "God Hidden and Revealed", p. 135.
105. *Ibid.*, p. 136.
106. John Meyendorff, *St Gregory Palamas and Orthodox Spirituality* (Crestwood, NY: St Vladimir's Seminary Press, 1974), p. 121.

The antinomic tension between God's hidden and revealed nature can in no way be resolved through any partitioning of Him:

> That which is manifest, that which makes itself accessible to intellection or participation, is not part of God, for God is not thus subject to partition for our benefit; complete He manifests himself and does not manifest Himself, complete He is conceived and is inconceivable by the intelligence, complete He is shared and is imparticipable.[107]

Although God is simple by nature, there is no identity between His essence, on the one hand, and His energies and creation, on the other; otherwise, creatures would be gods by nature, and God would no longer be the One, but a many. However, there is not a real difference either; for then God would be cut off from the created order and no connection with Him would be possible.[108] Both positions must therefore be embraced: "In a certain sense, Essence and energy are identical in God, but in another sense, they are different."[109] Palamas makes use of a number of expressions to provide a glimpse of the situation, speaking of "a union without confusion, a distinction without division",[110] and of the "undivided division" (*adiaireton diairesin*).[111] Most typically, he speaks of the relationship between God's Essence and energies as a "real distinction" (*pragmatike diakrisis*), contrasting this to both a "real division" (*pragmatike diairesis*), which would destroy the Divine unity and simplicity, and a merely "rational distinction" (*diakrisis kat epinoian*), which would possess only subjective existence.[112]

Although the Divine Essence is incommunicable to the creatures, we should not conceive of it as being therefore absent from creation. In fact, it is present everywhere: "Everywhere there is present indivisibly something of the Divine Essence; the Divine energies are shared with the creatures. . . . the Divine nature is never shared."[113] "For the Divine nature is everywhere present, but it is incommunicable, for no created being . . . would be able to par-

107. *A Study of Gregory Palamas*, p. 214.
108. Vladimir Lossky, *The Vision of God* (Crestwood, NY: St Vladimir's Seminary Press, 1973), p. 159.
109. *A Study of Gregory Palamas*, p. 225.
110. "God Hidden and Revealed", p. 135.
111. "The Persons-Energy Structure in the Theology of St Gregory Palamas", p. 42.
112. *Introduction to Saint Gregory Palamas*, p. 47.
113. *Ibid.*, p. 44.

take of it."[114] In a remarkable passage, St Gregory describes how the Divine Essence "multiplies itself" and shares itself with the creatures, while remaining indivisible:

> There is therefore a reality between creatures and the imparticipable superessentiality; not one sole reality, but as many as the objects which share therein. I want to speak about these mediating realities; they are powers of the Superessentiality which, in a unique and unifying way, possesses by anticipation and resumes in itself all the multitude of the participable realities; because of this multitude, it multiplies itself in its manifestations and all creatures share in it, although it remains indivisibly within its imparticipability and unity.[115]

In this regard, it is worth noting that this sense of multiplicity in unity extends to the Divine energies as well, where Palamas writes of the Divine energies both in the singular and in the plural; the singular "energy" relating to the Essence as its source of manifestation, and the plural "energies" relating to the multiple created beings that they participate in.[116]

The Quran also expresses the inherent paradox of God's relationship to His creation in many verses—such as "He is the First and the Last, the Manifest and the Non-manifest" (57:3)—but perhaps most remarkably in the combined verse "Nothing is like Him, and He is the Hearing, the Seeing" (42:11). Ibn Arabi comments:

> He declares Himself similar (*tashbîh*) in one place and incomparable (*tanzîh*) in another. He declares Himself incomparable through His words "Nothing is like Him" and similar through His words "And He is the Hearing, the Seeing" (42:11). Hence thoughts of similarity were dispersed, and thoughts of incomparability were scattered.[117]

Explaining the situation further, he describes in blunt philosophical terms how God embraces both incomparability and similarity, nondelimitation and delimitation:

> He is not declared incomparable in any manner that will remove Him from similarity, nor is He declared similar in any manner that will remove Him from incomparability. So do not declare Him

114. *Ibid.*, p. 47.
115. *A Study of Gregory Palamas*, p. 221.
116. David Coffey, "The Palamite Doctrine of God: A New Perspective", *St Vladimir's Theological Quarterly*, Vol. 32, No. 4 (1988), pp. 331-2.
117. *The Sufi Path of Knowledge*, p. 112.

> non-delimited and thus delimited by being distinguished from delimitation! For if He is distinguished, then He is delimited by His non-delimitation. And if He is delimited by His non-delimitation, then He is not He.[118]

Most typically, the Shaykh uses the term *wujûd*, meaning being, existence, and finding, to designate how God may be found, both to Himself and in the creation.[119] Just as God is One, so is *wujûd*, whether in reference to the divine Being or the existence of the created things. He asserts the unicity of *wujûd* in various ways: "There is nothing in *wujûd* but He, and *wujûd* is acquired only from Him. No entity of any existent thing becomes manifest except through His self-disclosure."[120] "The Real says, 'There is no thing to which I manifest Myself, because I am identical with each thing.'"[121] "The Entity is one in *wujûd*, but the relations pertain to nonexistence, and in them the diversity occurs."[122] And yet, while all might be said to be *wujûd*, *wujûd* itself carries distinctions, being both uncreated and created:

> Concerning the entities of the cosmos, it is said that they are neither identical with the Real, nor other than the Real. On the contrary, *wujûd* is all Real. However, some of what is Real is described as created, and some is described as not created, while all of it is existent.[123]

Ibn Arabi often uses the phrase "He/not He" (*huwa lâ huwa*)[124] to describe the ambiguity of the cosmos; everything is and is not God. Citing a Quranic verse, "You did not throw when you threw, but God threw" (8:17), which refers to the Prophet's symbolic throwing of sand in the direction of the enemy at the battle of Badr, the Shaykh comments:

> There is none in *wujûd* [Being/existence] but God. But the clear formulation of this question is terribly difficult. Verbal expression falls short of it and conceptualization cannot define it, because it quickly escapes and its properties are contradictory. It is like his words "You did not throw", so He negated, "when you threw", so

118. *Ibid.*
119. *Ibid.*, p. 6.
120. *The Self Disclosure of God*, p. 15.
121. *Ibid.*, p. 41.
122. *Ibid.*, p. 72.
123. *The Sufi Path of Knowledge*, p. 133.
124. *Ibid.*, p. 113.

> He affirmed, "but God threw", so He negated the engendered existence (*kawn*) of Muhammad and affirmed Himself as identical (*'ayn*) with Muhammad, since He appointed for him the name "God".[125]

Although ambiguously present, He is everywhere so. Just as the Quran testifies that "He is with you wherever you are" (57:4) and that "He is nearer than the jugular vein" (50:16), so Ibn Arabi remarks that "since the Being of the Real permeates the cosmos, no one denies Him".[126] God, in entering into creation, remains One, while becoming paradoxically multiple. The Shaykh describes the situation thus:

> Though Being is One Entity, the entities of the possible things have made It many, so It is the One/Many (*al-wâhid al-kathîr*).... Without Him, we would not be found, and without us, He would not become many through the many attributes and the names diverse in meaning which He ascribes to Himself.[127]

And yet His very multiplicity devolves to Unity, even in the context of the Divine names, in which God multiplies Himself into various aspects and properties. In discussing the Divine names, Ibn Arabi remarks that the names—denoting various aspects of *wujûd*'s perfections—have no independent existence, since they are merely relationships between *wujûd* and the nonexistent things: "The cosmos is restricted to entities and relations. The entities pertain to *wujûd*, while the relations are intelligible and pertain to nonexistence. This is everything other than God."[128]

The Divine Image

Among all the created beings, all the many *loci* of manifestation, the human being is utterly unique, endowed with characteristics that render him both more "like God" and more comprehensive in his nature than anything else in the cosmos. In Genesis, we find, "So God created man in His own image, in the image of God He created him; male and female He created them" (Gen 1:27). The Church Fathers express a diversity of understandings of the sense in which man may

125. *Ibid.*
126. *Ibid.*, p. 81.
127. Ibid., p. 214.
128. *The Self Disclosure of God*, p. 39.

be taken to be the "image" of God. For St Maximus the Confessor, man as "image" is characterized by "being" and "eternity";[129] for St Gregory of Nyssa, the primary characteristics are "intellect" and "free will".[130] Palamas substantially agrees with the latter view, identifying the "image" with man's noetic faculties and the freedom which he possesses to obtain moral perfection.[131] He writes:

> For that which is in the image resides not in the body but in the intellect, which is the highest aspect of human nature. If there was something else still higher, that which is in the image would reside in that.[132]

And yet, although the intellect is preeminent, the body also represents something of the image: "The word Man is not applied to either soul or body separately, but to both together, since together they have been created in the image of God."[133] As image, man was made a microcosm (*mikrokosmos*), in which is summarized and recapitulated all the rest of creation. As such, man embraces and beautifies both the visible and the invisible worlds.[134]

In the same passage of Genesis, there appear the words "Let us make man in our image, after our likeness" (Gen 1:26). Here, the Fathers often distinguish "image" as a granted state from "likeness", which implies a state *in potentia* but not yet achieved.[135] Specifically for St Gregory, as for the Fathers generally, the "image" represents man's potentiality to attain perfection in God, while the "likeness" is the condition of attained perfection.[136] He writes, "All men are in the image of God, and perhaps also in His likeness."[137] The likeness is, in fact, equivalent to the deification (*theosis*) of man.[138]

According to a *hadîth* of the Prophet, "God [Allah] created Adam upon His own form (*sûrah*)."[139] Here, Ibn Arabi finds signifi-

129. *The Triads,* p. 18.
130. *The Deification of Man,* p. 16.
131. *Introduction to Saint Gregory Palamas,* pp. 60-1.
132. *The Deification of Man,* p. 17.
133. *The Mystical Theology of the Eastern Church,* p. 116.
134. *Introduction to Saint Gregory Palamas,* p. 58; *The Deification of Man,* p. 20.
135. *Ibid.,* p. 21.
136. *Introduction to Saint Gregory Palamas,* pp. 60-1.
137. *The Deification of Man,* p. 22.
138. *St Gregory Palamas as a Hagiorite,* p. 350.
139. William C. Chittick, "Ethical Standards and the Vision of Oneness: The Case of Ibn al-'Arabî", in Robert A. Herrera, ed., *Mystics of the Book: Themes, Topics, and Typologies* (New York: Peter Lang Publishing, 1993), p. 364.

cance in the mention of the name "Allah", the all-comprehensive name: "For the Prophet reported that God created Adam in His form, and the human being has brought together the whole cosmos."[140] By virtue of this all-comprehensiveness, "There is no Divine name of which we do not possess a portion."[141] The "form" is bound closely with another concept, man's "primordial nature" (*fitrah*): "God's primordial nature (*fitrah*), in keeping with which He brought forth (*fatara*) human beings" (Quran 30:30). The Shaykh comments:

> When God created the human spirit, he created it perfect, fully developed, rational, aware, having faith in God's unity (*tawhîd*), admitting His lordship. This is the primordial nature (*fitrah*) according to which God created human beings.[142]

Being created in the all-comprehensive form, man is the microcosm, possessing in a concentrated manner all the properties of the cosmos:

> God created the cosmos outside of the human being only as the striking of a likeness for the human being, that he might know that everything that becomes manifest in the cosmos is within himself and that the human being is the Intended Entity. He is the totality of the wisdoms, and for his sake were created the Garden and the Fire, this world and the last world, all the states, and the hownesses. Within him becomes manifest the totality of the Divine names and their traces.[143]

To manifest the form fully is to honor fully the "Trust" (*amânah*) granted to man by God.[144] The Quran obliquely describes the obligation imposed by the Trust: "God commands you to deliver trusts back to their owners" (4:58). Commenting on the verse, the Shaykh writes that "the attributes of the Real are a trust with the servant".[145] To honor and deliver the Trust is precisely to manifest fully the all-comprehensive form.[146] He writes:

140. *The Self Disclosure of God*, p. 28.
141. *The Sufi Path of Knowledge*, p. 276.
142. William C. Chittick, "Between the Yes and the No: Ibn al-'Arabî on *Wujûd* and the Innate Capacity", in Robert K. C. Forman, ed., *The Innate Capacity: Mysticism, Psychology, and Philosophy* (Oxford: Oxford University Press, 1998), p. 97.
143. *The Self Disclosure of God*, p. 189.
144. See Quran 33:72.
145. *The Sufi Path of Knowledge*, p. 317.
146. *Ibid.*, p. 275.

> God created Adam upon His own form. Hence He ascribed to him all His Most Beautiful Names. Through the strength of the Form he was able to carry the offered Trust. The reality of the Form did not allow him to reject the Trust in the way that the heavens and the earth refused to carry it.[147]

Divine Initiative and Human Transformation

Although we, as human beings, are cast in the Divine mold or stamp, our capacity to manifest and unite ourselves with the Divine qualities in the fullest possible way must be brought from a state of potentiality to one of completion. However, we in ourselves are incapable of such a transformation; this is precisely the role of Divine initiative and guidance. For St Gregory and the Fathers, Christ, by becoming incarnate as man, is absolutely fundamental to such a possibility of transformation. Christ, quoting the Psalms, declared, "I say, 'You are gods'" (Jn 10:34), and St Athanasius, inspired by these words, summarized the purpose of the Incarnation with the phrase "He was made man, that we might be made god".[148]

Palamas, affirming this same truth, holds that the main purpose of the Incarnation is the "union" (*henosis*) of the Divine with the human.[149] In the incarnation, the "first fruits of our substance" were deified: "He renewed, not our *hypostasis* [unique to each person], but our nature, which He assumed, united to it in His own *hypostasis.*"[150] Christ also acts as teacher and guide:

> Salvation is through the Logos. The Logos, who is God the Son, became man to make us like Him through repentance and by counseling (*symboulen*). We are as far away from the Kingdom of God "as the heavens are from the earth", but the union (*henosis*) is made possible by the willingness of the Incarnate Logos.[151]

The guidance of Christ, "through repentance and by counseling", a guidance that both encompasses and internalizes the Mosaic Law, is essential to our transformation: "I did not come to destroy [the Law] but to fulfill [it]" (Mt 5:17). St. Gregory explains:

147. *Ibid.*, p. 276.
148. *The Deification of Man,* p. 7.
149. *Introduction to Saint Gregory Palamas,* p. 54.
150. *The Deification of Man,* p. 30.
151. *Introduction to Saint Gregory Palamas,* p. 52.

> Did He not deign to make His dwelling in man, to appear to him and speak to him without intermediary, so that man should be not only pious, but sanctified and purified in advance in soul and body by keeping the Divine commandments, and so be transformed into a vehicle worthy to receive the all-powerful Spirit?[152]

Yet the most significant means by which man becomes transformed are the sacraments, the created media that convey the uncreated and deifying grace of God.[153] Of the sacraments, the two that Palamas considers the most decisive are Baptism and the Eucharist:[154] "On these two acts [Baptism and the Eucharist] depends our entire salvation, for in them is recapitulated the whole of the divine-human economy."[155] In Baptism, the Holy Spirit regenerates human nature, purifying man "in the image" and granting him the power, lost by the fall, to achieve "likeness" to God.[156] St Paul attests to this power: "For as many of you as were baptized into Christ have put on Christ" (Gal 4:7). Whereas Baptism purifies man's "image", the Eucharist brings about his advance towards the "likeness".[157] Through partaking of the Eucharist, the sacramental union with Christ, man, in his individual *hypostasis*, attains a real union with His deifying grace and energy:[158]

> The Son of God, in His incomparable love for man, did not only unite His Divine *hypostasis* with our nature, by clothing Himself in a living body and a soul gifted with intelligence . . . but also united Himself . . . with the human *hypostases* themselves, in mingling Himself with each of the faithful by communion with his Holy Body.[159]

This union with Divine energy and grace in the Eucharist finds its pre-figuration in the witnessing of the uncreated light by the Apostles on Mt Tabor: "And He was transfigured before them. His face shone like the sun, and His clothes became as white as the light" (Mt 17:2). Palamas continues:

> For on the day of the Transfiguration, that Body, source of the light of grace, was not yet united with our bodies; it illuminated

152. *The Triads*, p. 21.
153. *The Deification of Man*, p. 41.
154. *A Study of Gregory Palamas*, p. 161.
155. *Introduction to Saint Gregory Palamas*, p. 63.
156. *The Deification of Man*, p. 46.
157. *Ibid.*, p. 51.
158. *Ibid.*, p. 53.
159. *The Triads*, p. 19.

from outside those who worthily approached it, and sent the illumination into the soul by the intermediary of the physical eyes; but now, since it is mingled with us and exists in us, it illuminates the soul from within.[160]

In Islam, God's Word does not become incarnated, but it is "inlibrated"; it is the descent of the Quran to the Prophet and his community that forms the proper parallel for consideration to the incarnation of Christ. This descent is not associated with a direct regeneration of human nature, as man is not considered to be in a state of fall, but rather is predominantly associated with guidance, since the fundamental problem of man is persistent human forgetfulness and heedlessness. As the human being is called upon by the Trust to manifest fully the all-comprehensive form of his creation, the guidance provided must be similarly all-comprehensive. Just as "Allah" is the all-comprehensive name of God, the very name of the Book, *qur'ân*, signifies "gathering" and "bringing together".[161] Ibn Arabi comments, "The Quran is one book among others except that, to the exclusion of all other books, it alone possesses all-comprehensiveness (*jam'iyyah*)."[162]

This all-comprehensiveness of the Quran is shared by the nature of the Prophet himself, who is the perfected *locus* of manifestation for the Divine name "Allah".[163] The Shaykh remarks, "Muhammad was the greatest *locus* of Divine self-disclosure . . . since he was given the all-comprehensive words."[164] The association of the nature of the Prophet with the Quran finds further definition in the *hadîth* in which Aisha, the wife of the Prophet, stated, "Surely the character of the Prophet was the Quran"[165]—a character that the Quran describes as "tremendous". Ibn Arabi explains:

God says, "Surely thou [Muhammad] art upon a tremendous character (*khuluqin 'azîm*)" (68:4). . . . When Aisha was asked about the character of the Messenger of God, she answered, "His character was the Quran." She said that because he was unique in character, and that unique character had to bring together all noble character traits. God described that character as being "tremendous",

160. *Ibid.*
161. *The Sufi Path of Knowledge*, p. 239.
162. *Ibid.*
163. *Ibid.*, p. 241.
164. Ibid., p. 240.
165. *Ibid.*, p. 241.

> just as He described the Quran in His words "the tremendous Quran" (15:87). So the Quran is his character. If a person in the community of the Messenger who has not met the Messenger of God desires to see him, let him look upon the Quran. When he looks upon it, there is no difference between looking upon it and looking upon God's Messenger. It is as if the Quran takes the configuration of a corporeal form which is named Muhammad ibn Abdallah ibn Abd al-Muttalib.[166]

It is the *sharî'ah,* the Divine Law derived from the teaching of the Quran and the example of the Prophet, that codifies the all-comprehensive guidance that human beings stand in need of if they are to attain felicity, even more so if they are to deliver fully the Trust. For Ibn Arabi, the *sharî'ah* is not merely the pointer to or symbol of the *haqîqah* (the Real, the Divine Truth); it is the *haqîqah.*[167] The traveler to God must cling to its rulings and guidance: "He must move forward according to the scale of knowledge derived from the revealed Law."[168] "Beware lest you throw the Scale of the Law from your hand."[169] Although the Law is silent on certain subjects, this silence is in fact an aspect of its all-comprehensiveness and plenitude;[170] as the Quran states, "Do not ask us about those things that, if they were shown to you, would bring you wrong" (5:101).

Of the prescriptions set down by the Law, none is more central than the *salât,* the ritual prayer. Two *hadîth*s speak of the remarkable depths contained in this activity, an activity associated in the Quran with God Himself: "It is He who does *salât* over you" (33:43). "Each of you, when you pray, has an intimate talk with the Lord",[171] and "Prayer is the ascension (*mi'râj*) of the believer." In this second *hadîth,* the *salât* is compared to the heavenly ascension of the Prophet during the Night Journey,[172] in the course of which the *salât* itself was instituted by God.[173] As the Quran states, attesting to the intimacy inherent in the ritual prayer, "Bow in prostration and draw near" (96:19).

166. *Seal of the Saints,* p. 71.
167. *An Ocean Without Shore,* p. 57.
168. *The Sufi Path of Knowledge,* p. 256.
169. *Ibid.,* p. 257.
170. *An Ocean Without Shore,* p. 56.
171. *Ibid.,* p. 107.
172. See Quran 17:1.
173. *An Ocean Without Shore,* p. 112.

The recitation of the Quran, which forms a fundamental part of the ritual prayer, is an arena of intimacy in which God and His Word are made present in the heart of the believer: "When the Quran . . . descends upon the heart, it is then He Whose Word the Quran is that descends with it."[174] The Shaykh explains further in a remarkable passage:

> It is I, He says, who recite My Book for him with his tongue while he listens to Me. And that is My nocturnal conversation with him. That servant savors My Word. But if he binds himself to his own meanings, he leaves Me by his reflection and his meditation. What he must do is only lean toward Me and leave his ears receptive to My Word until I am present in his recitation. And just as it is I who recite and I who make him hear, it is also I who then explain My Word to him and interpret its meanings. . . . And he is at that moment a witness, present with Me; and it is I who take charge of his instruction.[175]

The Consummation of the Human Being

The human being, created with the potentiality for perfection and union, strengthened to that end through the grace and guidance of revelation, may come to manifest the Divine image in the fullest possible way through a union with the manifested Divine qualities. In Orthodoxy, the gifts of the Holy Spirit mentioned in Isaiah, "The spirit of wisdom and understanding, the spirit of counsel and might, the spirit of knowledge and of the fear of the Lord" (Isa 11:2), represent partial modalities of human perfection through grace. St Paul speaks of men having "gifts differing according to the grace that is given to us" (Rom 12:6), and adds that "there are diversities of gifts but the same Spirit" (1 Cor. 12:4). There is no special distinction between these gifts and grace itself.[176]

Man, although partaking of these partial gifts, may enter into a yet more complete union with the Divine. St Peter writes of the potentiality for human beings to become "partakers of the Divine nature" (2 Pet 1:4). St Gregory affirms that the saints participate in the Divine nature, but through union with the energies, and not the

174. *Ibid.*, p. 26.
175. *Ibid.*, p. 27.
176. *The Mystical Theology of the Eastern Church*, p. 162.

Essence;[177] they become "gods by grace", as he affirms, quoting St Maximus.[178] Elsewhere, St Maximus writes that "God and the saints had one and the same energy".[179] This union or deification (*theosis*) is taught by St Gregory and the Fathers to be both God's greatest gift to man and the ultimate goal of human existence.[180]

Through the life of holiness, the grace of the sacraments, and the action of continual prayer, man enters into a state of readiness for deification, which is completed through the active grace of God.[181] "By grace, God totally embraces those who are worthy, and the saints embrace God in his fullness."[182] This union with the energy is conjoined with its vision, where—as on Mt Tabor—the vision of the uncreated energy of God is perceived by the spiritual eye as light. Palamas explains:

> He who participates in the Divine energy himself becomes, to some extent, light; he is united to the light, and by that light he sees in full awareness all that remains hidden to those who have not this grace; thus, he transcends not only the bodily senses, but also all that can be known by the intellect . . . for the pure in heart see God . . . who being Light, dwells in them and reveals Himself to those who love Him, to His beloved.[183]

In another remarkable passage, he explains further how contemplation of the uncreated light is made possible only through union with it:

> Having separated itself from all other beings, it becomes itself all light and is assimilated to what it sees, or rather, it is united to it without mingling, being itself light and seeing light through light. If it sees itself, it sees light; or if it beholds the object of its vision, that too is light; and if it looks at the means by which it sees, again it is light. For such is the character of the union, that all is one, so that he who sees can distinguish neither the means nor the object not its nature, but simply has the awareness of being light and of seeing a light distinct from every creature.[184]

177. *The Triads*, p. 153.
178. *A Study of Gregory Palamas*, p. 175.
179. *Ibid.*
180. *The Deification of Man*, p. 12.
181. *St Gregory Palamas as a Hagiorite*, p. 178.
182. Vladimir Lossky, *In the Image and Likeness of God* (Crestwood, NY: St Vladimir's Seminary Press, 1974), p. 59.
183. *The Mystical Theology of the Eastern Church*, p. 224.
184. *The Triads*, pp. 65-6.

As mentioned previously, Palamas uses the terms "energy", "light", and "grace" nearly synonymously, but with distinct shades of meaning: energy refers generally to God's creative operation and manifestation, light refers to the contemplated manifestation of God in the experience of the saints, and grace refers to the operation of God in the salvific action of the Holy Spirit. As the saint explains, "The Divine and deifying illumination and grace are not the substance (*ousia*), but the energy of God."[185]

Since the Divine nature is infinite and inexhaustible, deification is in no way a state of static completion; man, even in a state of union, cannot encompass the whole of God.[186] In this sense, deification, while a real union, is not exhaustive: "Every man worthy of it participates differently in the great gift of the Spirit; this corresponds to the degree of his own purity, mingling with the harmony of that Beauty."[187] "What one receives is never more than a part of what is given; he who receives the Divine energy cannot contain the whole of it."[188] Additionally, deification is a dynamic participation and vision: "The contemplation of this light is a union, even though it does not endure with the imperfect."[189] "This contemplation has a beginning, and something follows on from this beginning, more or less dark or clear; but there is never an end, since its progress is infinite."[190]

The man who is deified becomes "uncreated" by grace through participation in the uncreated energy of God. At the same time, he does not cease to be a creature, nor does he lose his natural identity. Rather, he acquires a new condition, that of being a sharer in the Divine life.[191] Palamas provides a glimpse into the nature of such a state:

> Do you not see that these Divine energies are in God, and remain invisible to the created faculties? Yet the saints see them, because they have transcended themselves with the help of the Spirit. As we read: "He who has been found worthy to enter into God will per-

185. *Introduction to Saint Gregory Palamas*, p. 47.
186. *The Triads*, p. 135.
187. *A Study of Gregory Palamas*, p. 167.
188. *Ibid.*, p. 166.
189. *The Triads*, p. 65.
190. *Ibid.*
191. *A Study of Gregory Palamas*, p. 178; "The Persons-Energy Structure in the Theology of St Gregory Palamas", p. 26.

ceive preexisting in God all those inner principles of created things, through a simple and indivisible knowledge."[192]

In a remarkable passage, he explains how the Trinity, paradoxically inseparable from the energies and present in them,[193] becomes indwelling in the deified man:

> Let us not, then, turn aside incredulous before the superabundance of these blessings; but let us have faith in Him, who has participated in our nature and granted it in return the glory of His own nature, and let us seek how to acquire this glory and see it. How? By keeping the Divine commandments. For the Lord has promised to manifest Himself to the man who keeps them, a manifestation He calls His own indwelling and that of the Father, saying, "If anyone loves Me, he will keep My word, and My father will love him, and We will come to him and will make our abode with him" (Jn 14:23), and "I will manifest Myself to him" (Jn 14:21).[194]

For Ibn Arabi, the path to God is bound up with the assimilation of the Divine qualities or "character traits" (*akhlâq*), as indicated by the Divine names. He approves of a saying often attributed to the Prophet, "Assume the character traits of God", adding, "that is Sufism".[195] In a sense, man already possesses the traits, since he was created upon the Divine form: "The fact is that all of the Divine character traits are found in man's innate disposition."[196] The task imposed by the Trust is to bring the traits into manifestation, fullness, and harmony. Given the multiplicity of qualities, assuming them in an appropriate balance is not without difficulties: "Without doubt, putting noble character traits into practice is difficult, since doing so . . . involves the meeting of opposites."[197] The principle by which the proper harmony may be achieved is the Divine Law, as the Shaykh explains: "In your every motion in respect to every existent thing, look at the ruling of the Law. . . . Then in all of that you will be secure and honored with God, and you will possess a Divine light."[198]

192. *The Triads*, p. 107.
193. *The Mystical Theology of the Eastern Church*, p. 86.
194. *The Triads*, p. 61.
195. *The Sufi Path of Knowledge*, p. 283.
196. *Ibid.*, p. 287.
197. *Ibid.*, p. 288.
198. *Ibid.*

As the spiritual traveler proceeds on the path back to God, he may be granted a tasting (*dhawq*), unveiling (*kashf*), or opening (*fath*), through which God illuminates the heart and enables him to perceive something of the unseen world. Although such a perception most typically takes a visionary form,[199] the perception of spiritual reality as light is a fundamental mode of unveiling. The association of light with both God and existence runs throughout the Islamic tradition. According to the famous "Light Verse" of the Quran, "God is the light of the heavens and the earth" (24:35), while the Prophet said of God, "He is a light."[200] For Ibn Arabi, light is associated with *wujûd* itself: "God says, 'And to whomsoever God assigns no light, no light has he' (Quran 24:40). The light 'assigned' to the possible thing is nothing other than the *wujûd* of the Real."[201] In the two passages below, the Shaykh describes the unveiling of light in the heart, both as enabling the perception of visionary forms, and as perception of light itself:

> But when man applies himself to the mirror of his heart and polishes it with invocation [*dhikr*] and the recitation of the Quran, he thereby gains some light. And God possesses a light called the "light of existence", which is deployed over all existent things. When these two lights come together, unseen things are unveiled as they are in themselves and as they occur in existence.[202]

> If the seeker desires the Divine *loci* of witnessing and lordly sciences, he should multiply his nightly vigils and continually multiply within them his concentration (*jam'iyyah*). If scattered lights should appear to him such that between each light darkness is interspersed, and if those lights have no subsistence but disappear quickly, this is one of the first marks of acceptance and opening. Those noble lights will never cease becoming manifest to him through his acts of spiritual struggle (*mujâhadah*) and his striving until a greatest light is unveiled for him. Then the obstructions which prevent people from reaching these knowledges will be removed and mysteries of which he had nothing in himself and by which he was not described will be unveiled for him in their stations.[203]

The end of the spiritual path is to become a full *locus* of disclosure for the totality of the Divine qualities, as represented in the all-

199. *Ibid.*, p. 220.
200. *Ibid.*, p. 217.
201. *Ibid.*, p. 214.
202. *Ibid.*, p. 222.
203. *Ibid.*, p. 223.

comprehensive name "Allah". The perfected human being, or "perfect man" (*al-insân al-kâmil*), is the one who has fully realized the Trust, and the only one who may truly be called a vicegerent of God. As Ibn Arabi remarks:

> Man possesses an eminence over everything in the heaven and earth. He is God's sought-after goal among the existent things, since it is he whom God has taken as a locus of self-disclosure. I mean by "man" perfect man, since he is perfect only through God's form.[204]

The perfect man is the "Possessor of the Two Eyes" (*dhu'l-'aynayn*).[205] Through the one, he sees God as incomparable: "He sees Him neither in any thing nor in himself."[206] Through the other, he sees Him as similar: "He sees His Being permeating all things."[207] In either case, he witnesses nothing but God.

In the station of all-comprehensiveness, of the perfect disclosure and equilibrium of the totality of Divine qualities, no particular attributes delimit the perfect man. Rather, he stands in the station of "no station" (*lâ maqâm*): "The highest of all human beings are those who have no station."[208] The Shaykh explains further:

> The most all-inclusive specification is that a person not be delimited by a station whereby he is distinguished. So the Muhammadan [*i.e.*, the possessor of no station] is distinguished only by the fact that he has no station specifically. His station is that of no station.[209]

Such a station is not one of stasis, but rather involves a dynamic equilibrium characterized by constant fluctuation at each instant. "In every breath, in every moment, and in every state he takes the form which is required by that breath, moment and state."[210] Similarly, even in this station, there is no end to unveiling or self-disclosure, and thus no end to knowledge of God: "In every state the knower says, 'My Lord, increase me in knowledge!' (Quran 20:114)."[211]

204. *Ibid.*, p. 368.
205. *Ibid.*, p. 367.
206. *Ibid.*, p. 368.
207. *Ibid.*
208. *Ibid.*, p. 376.
209. *Ibid.*, p. 377.
210. *Ibid.*

Perfect man, through being a perfected *locus* of Divine self-disclosure, embraces, in his own qualities, perfect servanthood, perfect poverty, and even, paradoxically, perfect nonexistence. "There can be no sheer servanthood, uncontaminated by any lordship whatsoever, except in perfect man alone."[212] "The returners to God are "destitute" of everything other than God."[213] "The final end and ultimate return of the gnostics (*'ârifûn*)—though their entities remain immutably fixed—is that the Real is identical with them, while they do not exist."[214] While they never embrace God in His Essence, which remains transcendent for every aspect of the created order, their situation becomes that described by the well-known *hadîth qudsî*:

> My servant draws near to Me through supererogatory works until I love him. Then, when I love him, I am his hearing through which he hears, his sight through which he sees, his hand through which he grasps, and his foot through which he walks.[215]

Conclusion

The shoal on which so much polemical furor and ecumenical fervor has run aground is the assumption that the truth or validity of another faith rests largely on its degree of exoteric identity with one's own. While attractive for obvious reasons, it nevertheless places limits upon God, who is presumed to have revealed Himself once, or at least best, in one's own faith. But God is not exhausted by a given revelatory disclosure, nor does He disclose Himself in the same way twice.[216] In respect of God's distinct revelatory disclosures, we cannot expect to overcome uniqueness and difference, precisely because the disclosures revealed by God are distinct. Only in respect of their Source, God, who is one and singular, can such differences in His revelatory disclosures be overcome. As we cannot stand at such a level, what we may attempt instead is to grasp,

211. *Ibid.*, p. 345.
212. *Ibid.*, p. 372.
213. *Ibid.*, p. 378.
214. *Ibid.*, p. 375.
215. *Ibid.*, p. 325.
216. *Ibid.*, p. 103; see also *Imaginal Worlds*, particularly the last section, for Ibn Arabi's views on religious diversity.

through the offered parallels that lie at the heart of His multiple disclosures, a vision of their unique underlying Source.

When, in his old age, Palamas was captured by the Turks during a sea voyage and made to stay nearly a year in Asia Minor, the captive archbishop engaged in amicable theological debates with, among others, the son of the Emir. One hope that he harbored during these debates was that "a day will soon come when we will be able to understand each other".[217] Let us hope that that day, so long overdue, may dawn for us all.

217. *St Gregory Palamas and Orthodox Spirituality*, p. 101.

Chapter 9

Hesychia: An Orthodox Opening to Esoteric Ecumenism

James S. Cutsinger

> The smallest creaturely image that ever forms in you is as great as God is great. Why? Because it comes between you and the whole of God. As soon as the image comes in, God and all His Divinity have to give way. But as the image goes out, God goes in.
>
> Meister Eckhart

When I first began planning this conference nearly two years ago, I never imagined that its theme would prove so timely. Had we any doubts before, the events of this past September 11th and their continuing repercussions throughout the world have proven conclusively that interfaith understanding is today more important than ever, and that no discussion is more urgently needed than that between Christians and Muslims. We know that during his captivity in Asia Minor in the 14th century, the Orthodox archbishop St Gregory Palamas, greatly impressed by the tolerance and kindness of the Muslims he met, became close friends with the son of the Turkish Emir, with whom he had many conversations, and in one of the letters which he wrote at that time, St Gregory expressed his hope that "a day will soon come when we shall be able to understand each other".[1] Now, nearly seven hundred years later, one prays all the more for such a day. But what exactly is the understanding we seek, and what kind of dialogue are we called to engage in?

Christianity and Esoteric Ecumenism

There are those for whom inter-religious understanding means doctrinal compromise. It is assumed in this case that religions are the creation of man, that dogmas are the lingering effects of a credu-

1. Quoted in John Meyendorff, *St Gregory Palamas and Orthodox Spirituality* (Crestwood, NY: St Vladimir's Seminary Press, 1974), p. 106.

lous and uncritical age, and that the surest way to tolerance and peace lies in the elimination, or humanistic reconstruction, of teachings that have served as the excuse for divisiveness and hatred in the past. Thus there are Christians, to pick the most obvious example from my own tradition, who insist that the only way to honor the convictions of other religious people is to jettison the idea of Christ's Divinity, an idea often joined to the belief that Christianity is uniquely true and salvific. Because traditional faith in the Only-Begotten has so often been confused with an ideology of the "only correct", it has seemed to these liberal ecumenists that the dogma must be discarded, and it is no surprise, given the reductionist tenor of religious conversation in the West, that such Christians have enjoyed a certain amount of success in promoting this method of dialogue with their counterparts in other traditions. Jesus was a preacher and a gifted teacher, they say, but there was nothing about Him of a supernatural or miraculous order: no virgin birth, no walking on the water or exorcism of demons, and no physical resurrection from the dead.

Now of course, a reductionist mindset is not the only explanation for the success of such ventures, and I do not mean to be simplistic. Clearly a considerable measure of good must come from the discovery, however occasioned, that people who practice different religions from our own are human too, and we would seriously err, especially in these turbulent and frightening days, to dismiss or belittle any well-intentioned effort to overcome prejudice and xenophobia. But we would also err if we ignored the fact that dialogue of the kind I have described so far, besides being based upon a lie about Christ, cannot help but contribute to the very problems it aims to solve. For it is in the very nature of things that pious believers will seize all the more strongly upon their convictions, and with all the more unthinking fervor, when they feel themselves threatened with a betrayal coming from within the ranks of their co-religionists. The ecumenism of the de-mythologizers is certainly not the only cause of religious retrenchment. Nevertheless liberal dialogues and exclusivist monologues remain like two sides of one coin, and it is only the shortest of steps from the substitution of a purely human teacher for the incarnate Second Person of the Holy Trinity to the insistence that a conscious and explicit commitment to Jesus Christ is the only means of salvation.

Is there any way out of this impasse? Is it possible, in other words, for people who follow different spiritual paths to acknowledge the presence of saving Truth in one other's religions, but without undermining the dogmatic foundations of their own? To refer specifically to the traditions represented at this conference, and to put my question in a yet more pointed way: is it possible for an Orthodox Christian like myself to respect Islam as a fully valid religion, revealed by the same God whom I worship, but without denying what my own tradition teaches me about the Divinity of Jesus Christ, even though (as we know) what Muslims believe concerning this same "Jesus, son of Mary" is so considerably different? I believe very firmly that the answer is yes. Indeed I would go further and say that an affirmative response to these questions is not simply possible; it is necessary. For Christian faith in Christ, if genuine and if pursued to its depths, is inseparable from the double precept that we should *touch* but not *cling*.

I have in mind Christ's words in John 20. Speaking on the one hand to Thomas, Jesus commands him to stretch forth his hand, to "place it in my side", and to "be not faithless, but believing"; and Thomas's response is the greatest of all the confessions in scripture: "My Lord and my God" (Jn 20:27-28). On the other hand, speaking to Mary Magdalene, Christ instructs her, "Do not hold me"—the Greek verb *haptô* means to bind something fast—"for I have not yet ascended to my Father; but go to my brethren and say to them, I am ascending to my Father and your Father, to my God and your God" (Jn 20:17). Taken together, these two commandments provide the model for every Christian's proper relation to Jesus: one is to reach out and touch Him as "*my* Lord and *my* God", acknowledging and embracing His true Divinity, but without clinging to the outward manifestation of that Divinity, and thus without binding Him in a way that would obstruct His ascent—and ours with Him—to *His* Lord and *His* God.

This double relationship between the Christian and Christ adumbrates, in the idiom of one religion, a more general relationship, found in all religions, between the outward or exoteric form and the inward or esoteric Truth which that form conveys, and it opens us to the possibility of a different kind of dialogue, one based upon a common understanding of the metaphysical essence of traditional teachings, and not limited by the letter of their dogmatic expressions. As many in my audience know, the Swiss philosopher and perennialist author Frithjof Schuon has described this approach as an "esoteric ecumenism",[2] and he insists throughout his many books that it is only esoterism which can avoid the dilemma that I was speaking of earlier. It is obvious, he writes, that the "narrowly literal belief" of exclusivist dogmatism, while "feasible within a closed system knowing nothing of other traditional worlds", has become "untenable and dangerous in a universe where everything meets and interpenetrates".[3] The solution, however, is not the "false ecumenism" of the liberals which "abolishes doctrine", and which (as Schuon sharply notes) in order "to reconcile two adversaries . . . strangles them both". No, a "true ecumenism" must honor and uphold the importance of traditional dogmas, irreconcilable as they may appear exoterically, while at the same time appealing, on the basis of prayer and contemplative insight, to "the wisdom that can discern the one sole Truth under the veil of different forms".[4]

What this means for our conference will perhaps be surprising to some. It means—again I am quoting from Schuon—that "the Christian must be really Christian and the Muslim really Muslim, however paradoxical this may seem in view of the spiritual communion that has to be established between them", for both parties, precisely for the sake of the mutual understanding they seek, are obliged to adopt "points of departure which are extrinsically and provisionally separative, not because they are separative or exclusive, but because, by their intrinsic veracity, they guarantee a true intuition of unity".[5]

For those not familiar with the perennialist perspective, this is a subtle, but extremely important point, and it needs to be emphasized. We are to take traditional doctrines seriously, not out of some

2. As in the title of his book *Christianity/Islam: Essays on Esoteric Ecumenism* (Bloomington, Indiana: World Wisdom Books, 1985).
3. *Logic and Transcendence*, trans. Peter N. Townsend (London: Perennial Books, 1975), p. 4.
4. *Logic and Transcendence*, p. 182.
5. *Logic and Transcendence*, pp. 223-24. "The inward and essential knowledge of a theologically exclusive Muslim," Schuon continues, "may be infinitely closer to the Christ-given mysteries than is the mental and sentimental universalism of a profane despiser of 'separatist dogmas'" (*Logic and Transcendence*, p. 224n). We may add, *mutatis mutandis*, that the mystical insight of a theologically exclusive Orthodox saint is doubtless much closer to the Sufic *tawhîd* or "union" than is the ecumenism of the modernist or liberal Christian, who has no qualms about destroying the very foundations of his religion in the interest of greater "understanding".

sentimental and ill-conceived nostalgia for the past, and certainly not with condescension toward those presumed to have a simpler and less intelligent faith than our own. One honors these teachings because they are *true*, and because they provide, each in its own way and within the symbolic and ritual context of a given tradition, an opening onto the Truth as such. It is only by conforming to "holy separation at the base", Schuon therefore writes, that we can realize "holy union at the summit; one can attain to the latter only by first perceiving the element of unity in the revealed form itself, and by loving this form as an expression of the Supraformal."[6] What this implies, concretely, is that in a dialogue such as ours the Christian interlocutor can expect to reach a sympathetic understanding of Islam only by a continued insistence that Christ was indeed God incarnate, and not merely a prophet. The Christian must embrace this teaching with his full conviction, stretching forth his hand, like Thomas, in worshipful reverence to Jesus, and communicating in His Divine body and blood, for it is by this means precisely that he will come to hear finally the words given to Mary, words spoken in the privacy and freshness of that first paschal garden: Do not hold Me back, but come with Me into the very heights of the only Real. *Lâ ilâha illâ'Llâh.*

Now of course, to place the central teachings of Christianity and Islam so closely side by side is bound to create something of a shock, and this juxtaposition will be especially shocking for traditional Christians, who will strongly resist the suggestion that the Jesus of the Gospels was Himself a witness to the Muslim *shahâdah,* and who may therefore find themselves from the start deeply suspicious of the dialogue I am here proposing. Surely, they will say, there is an unbridgeable difference between the belief that Christ was just one in a series of human messengers and the belief that He is God, and

6. *Logic and Transcendence,* p. 224. As examples of this "holy separation", Schuon notes the following: "St John Damascene held a high position at the court of the caliph in Damascus [where he "wrote and published, with the approval of the caliph, his famous treatise in defense of images, which had been prohibited by the iconoclast Emperor Leo III"]; yet he was not converted to Islam, any more than were St Francis of Assisi in Tunisia, St Louis in Egypt, or St Gregory Palamas in Turkey. ["While a prisoner of the Turks for a year, he had friendly discussions with the Emir's son, but was not converted, nor did the Turkish prince become a Christian"]. . . . Tradition tells that the Sufi Ibrahim ibn Adham had as his occasional master a Christian hermit, without either being converted to the other's religion" (*Christianity/Islam,* p. 91).

they may well suppose that the perennialists have done no less an act of violence to their religion than the liberals.

I have elsewhere undertaken a doctrinal response to these criticisms and have attempted to explain in some detail how the formal dogmas of Christology promulgated by the early Councils of the Church open up to precisely this esoteric equivalence.[7] Nor, as I have endeavored to show, is this a question simply of some contrived and Procrustean compatibility. For unless we choose to be heretics, the Christian tradition forbids us to think that the Second Person of the Trinity is the same as the first, or that His Divinity was confined to the historical individuality of Jesus alone. On the contrary, in contemplating the mystery of the two natures in the single Person of Christ, we must remember that it was not the Father who was incarnate in Jesus, nor was it some particular man, but man as such, who was hypostatically assumed into God. Indeed we ourselves are that man in our essential humanity, and the God who took us into Himself was the *Logos* or Word, whose Divinity is itself derived from a yet more ultimate Source: "The Father," as He Himself tells us, "is greater than I" (Jn 14:28). Jesus *is* most certainly God, and the perennialist would be among the first to defend the miraculous truth of that stunning ellipsis. But this does not mean that saving power was fully expended at a single moment of history, or that we should confuse the uniqueness of Him who was incarnate, *the only begotten Son of God*, with the human particularity of Jesus of Nazareth. There is only one eternal Son and one *Logos*, and "no man," He tells us, "comes to the Father except by Me" (Jn 14:6). But nowhere do the creeds oblige us to equate His transcendent uniqueness with a singularity of the factual or temporal order.[8]

Today, however, my topic is not doctrine but method. I would like to look once again at the Christological question, so as to understand better the inward unanimity between the Christian and

7. See "The Mystery of the Two Natures", *Sophia: The Journal of Traditional Studies*, Vol. 4, No. 2 (Winter 1998), pp. 111-141.

8. Schuon adduces the general principle: "A religion is a form—hence a limit—which contains the Limitless, if this paradox is permissible; every form is fragmentary because of its necessary exclusion of other formal possibilities." For this reason "it is contradictory to base a certitude that demands to be considered as total on the phenomenal order . . . while demanding an intellectual acceptance" (*Understanding Islam* [Bloomington, Indiana: World Wisdom Books, 1994], p. 174).

Muslim approaches to Christ, but I shall do so in a different and somewhat indirect way, by focusing our discussion on prayer. The goal is much the same, to encourage Christians, especially my fellow Orthodox, to keep their minds open to the possibilities of an esoteric ecumenism, but rather than examining the implications of traditional dogma as such, I wish to call your attention instead to the contemplative practice of the Christian East. "When a man seeks to escape from dogmatic narrowness," Schuon has written, "it is essential that it be 'upwards' and not 'downwards'",[9] for "truth does not deny forms from the outside, but transcends them from within".[10] As I shall suggest in what follows, there is no better way of understanding what this transcendence or inward ascent may involve for the Christian than to consider that distinctive method of prayer, described in the *Philokalia* and other traditional sources, which we know by the name of Hesychasm. Of course, in the emphasis that it places upon the mystical and interior life, the East itself is already a kind of ascent within the larger tradition, an opening in the Christian carapace to truths of a less formal and less juridical order. But the *hesychia* which has been sought by its masters as the final goal of their Way points us even further upward and inward, to an opening within the opening, inviting us into the very heart of a distinctively Christian esoterism.

Hesychia: Depths within Depths

It is customary for authorities on Eastern Christian spirituality to distinguish several senses of the term *hesychia*, a word often simply translated as "stillness", and in doing so they sometimes call attention to one of the *apothegmata* that we find among the *Sayings of the Desert Fathers*. We are told that when the Abba Arsenios was still living in the city, he prayed to God, asking to be shown the path to salvation, and in response a voice came to him from Heaven and said, "Arsenios, be solitary, be silent, be at rest. These are the roots

9. *Stations of Wisdom* (Bloomington, Indiana: World Wisdom Books, 1995), p. 4. "Dogmatic form is transcended," Schuon continues, "by fathoming its depths and contemplating its universal content, and not by denying it in the name of a pretentious and iconoclastic ideal of 'pure truth'."

10. *Spiritual Perspectives and Human Facts*, trans. Peter N. Townsend (London: Perennial Books, 1987), p. 118.

of a life without sin."[11] Only the last of these imperatives employs a cognate of the word *hesychia* itself, but it is traditionally understood, from the way in which the teaching is expounded in other Fathers, that the practice of Hesychasm includes all three of the dimensions contained in the answer to this Abba's prayer.

Corresponding to the three-fold structure of the human microcosm, there is first a physical or a bodily *hesychia*, which is apparent in the isolation of the hermit. "Be solitary" were the heavenly words. Thus, on the material and most external level of our being, we are Hesychasts when we retreat from the world and live alone, exchanging our life in society, or perhaps even the cenobitical life of a cloistered monk, for the life of an anchorite. This is the mode of *hesychia* that St Gregory of Sinai has in mind in teaching that "the practice of stillness is one thing and that of community life is another",[12] and it is in this same vein that Evagrios Pontikos (who was himself styled the Solitary) advises us, "If you cannot attain stillness where you now live, consider living in exile."[13] Second, there is a *hesychia* as it were of the soul, which one observes above all in refraining from speech. "Be silent", said the voice to Arsenios. In this case, we become Hesychasts, not in taking flight from the companionship of other men, but in guarding our tongues and in deliberately withdrawing, whether permanently or at certain set times, from verbal communication with our fellows. It is to this dimension of the method that St Thalassios the Libyan refers in warning that "only spiritual conversation is beneficial; it is better to preserve stillness than to indulge in any other kind".[14]

There remains, however, yet a third kind of stillness, *hesychia* proper, suggested to Arsenios by the words "be at rest"—*hesychaze* in Greek. This, we discover, is a spiritual stillness, a *hesychia* correspon-

11. Quoted by Bernard McGinn, *The Foundations of Mysticism: Origins to the Fifth Century*, Vol. I of *The Presence of God: A History of Western Christian Mysticism* (New York: Crossroad, 1997), p. 136. See *The Desert Christian: Sayings of the Desert Fathers*, trans. Benedicta Ward (New York: Macmillan, 1975), p. 9.
12. "On Prayer: Seven Texts", *The Philokalia*, trans. G. E. H. Palmer, Philip Sherrard, Kallistos Ware (London: Faber and Faber, 1995), Vol. IV, p. 279.
13. "Outline Teaching on Asceticism and Stillness in the Solitary Life", *The Philokalia*, trans. G. E. H. Palmer, Philip Sherrard, Kallistos Ware (London: Faber and Faber, 1979), Vol. I, p. 33.
14. "On Love, Self-Control, and Life in accordance with the Intellect: Written for Paul the Presbyter", *The Philokalia*, trans. G. E. H. Palmer, Philip Sherrard, Kallistos Ware (London: Faber and Faber, 1981), Vol. II, p. 311.

ding to the level of man's *nous* or intellect and distinguished (say the Fathers) by an inward state of complete serenity, immobility, and peace. By far the most difficult of all to attain, this truest and deepest form of Hesychasm consists in a solitude that is no longer contingent upon one's location in space and in a silence that is independent of speech. Reproving the monk who supposes that his desert cave is enough, St Symeon the New Theologian stresses that a "stillness" understood merely in terms of "withdrawal from the world" is of absolutely no benefit "if we are lazy and negligent",[15] and according to one of the most famous of the desert sayings, it was revealed to St Anthony the Great, called the father of monks, that there was a busy physician living in the midst of the city who was his spiritual equal.[16]

With these and similar texts in mind, Bishop Kallistos Ware has remarked that "solitude is a state of soul, not a matter of geographical location".[17] It seems from other sources, however, that we would be justified in extending his observation to a further level, adding that true silence is a state of the spirit, and not merely the absence of audible communication. Thus St John Cassian, warning about the wiles we must be on guard against in our battles with the demon of self-esteem, calls our attention to the fact that "when [this demon] cannot persuade [a man] to feel proud of his display of eloquence, it entices him through silence into thinking he has achieved stillness".[18] Such an admonition would obviously not be necessary if silence and stillness were exactly the same, nor if keeping our mouths closed were sufficient for entering into the perfection of peace. But no, even as solitude is no guarantee of silence, so silence is no guarantee of serenity. There is instead yet another, deeper, and considerably rarer level of *hesychia*, where one is no longer distracted even by an inward interlocutor and where the space of the heart remains unencumbered even by the conversations that we so often have with ourselves.

15. "On Faith", *The Philokalia*, Vol. IV, p. 19.
16. *Sayings of the Desert Fathers*, p. 6.
17. *The Inner Kingdom*, Vol. I of *The Collected Works of Kallistos Ware* (Crestwood, NY: St Vladimir's Seminary Press, 2000), p. 93. One is reminded of the Sufi *afrad* and his mysterious master Al-Khidr, whose *fard*—that is, isolation or singularity—is manifest with a special, if paradoxical, clarity when he is present among men.
18. "On the Eight Vices", *The Philokalia*, Vol. I, p. 91.

The Fathers of the *Philokalia* often describe this third form of stillness as a freedom from thoughts. As we read their writings, however, what we soon discover is that the term itself "thought" has several meanings, and that there are accordingly, even within the domain of this profoundest kind of *hesychia,* several distinct degrees of freedom, and so depths within depths. At a first and most superficial level, "thoughts"—*logismoi* is the term in the Greek—are taken to mean specifically bad thoughts or temptations, provoked by the demons, which attack a man through the two lower parts of his soul: either through the appetitive and desiring power, which when uncurbed gives rise to lust and gluttony, or through the incensive and irascible power, whence comes the temptation to anger. St Neilos the Ascetic seems to be speaking mainly of the former when he explains that "stillness will in time free the intellect from being disturbed by impure thoughts",[19] while in the Bible St Paul refers to thoughts proceeding from the latter source when he says that "in every place men should pray, lifting holy hands without anger or quarreling" (1 Tim 2:8).

As it happens, however, this same passage from scripture, 1 Timothy 2:8, provides the Hesychast with good reason for thinking that true stillness is something still deeper, involving more than just freedom from the obvious seductions of the world and their resulting passionate thoughts. For what St Paul actually says in the Greek of this verse is that men should pray without *dialogismos,* a word which can be translated as quarrel or argument, but which also means any mode of dialogue, conversation, or debate, whether taking an external or an internal form, and thus—even more fundamentally—any effect or operation of the mind. In order to pray as he ought, it is therefore essential for the Hesychast to undertake a much subtler detachment and to cultivate an inward state uncompromised by the sense-impressions, visual memories, and other conceptual contents which are at once the causes and the consequences of discursive consciousness. No longer are "thoughts" to be understood merely as the grosser images of sensuality, greed, and violence that dominate the thinking of the worldly man; the *logismoi* from which one is obliged to escape are instead the very apparatus of conceptual reasoning.

19. "Ascetic Discourse", *The Philokalia,* Vol. I, p. 230.

Here again, however, we find that there is more than one level, and different texts from the Fathers call attention to different dimensions of consciousness. On the one hand, certain passages are focused primarily on thoughts which flow from our perception of the physical world and which are responsible for giving shape to empirical data. When your intellect "withdraws from the flesh and turns away from all thoughts that have their source in sense-perception, memory, or the soul-body structure", says Evagrios, "then you may conclude that you are close to the frontiers of prayer".[20] Similarly St Hesychios the Presbyter counsels that we should pursue with all our strength "that perfect stillness of heart and blessed state of soul" that comes when the mind is "free from all images", a state—he is quick to add—which "is all too rarely found in man".[21] Meanwhile St Gregory of Sinai teaches that we have begun to attain to a state of pure *hesychia* only when "the intellect sees neither itself nor anything else in a material way. On the contrary"—he continues—"it is often drawn away even from its own senses by the light acting within it; for now it grows immaterial and filled with spiritual radiance."[22]

As this last formulation suggests, yet another level of withdrawal is possible, for there remains a final movement of inward ascent, one in which ideas as such are set aside and transcended, quite apart from any empirical or sensory basis. In this case, the *nous* or intellect, which is the seat of man's intuitive powers of apprehension and which, when activated through purgation, affords him an immediate knowledge of essences, becomes detached (says St Gregory) "even from its own senses", and the category of *logismoi* is thus expanded to include every object of consciousness, whether originating from a physical or a spiritual source. One notes, for example, that when St John Klimakos writes that "*hesychia* is a laying aside of

20. "On Prayer", *The Philokalia*, Vol. I, pp. 62-63. "Structure" is my term. The translation of Palmer *et al.* says "soul-body temperament".
21. "On Watchfulness and Holiness", *The Philokalia*, Vol. I, p. 182. St Philotheos of Sinai agrees concerning the exceptional nature of spiritual *hesychia.* Speaking about "the noetic work that is the true philosophy of Christ", he notes that "it is very rare to find people whose intelligence is in a state of stillness" ("Forty Texts on Watchfulness", *The Philokalia*, trans. G. E. H. Palmer, Philip Sherrard, Kallistos Ware [London: Faber and Faber, 1984], Vol. III, p. 17).
22. "On Commandments and Doctrines, Warnings and Promises; on Thoughts, Passions, and Virtues, and also on Stillness and Prayer", *The Philokalia*, Vol. IV, p. 239.

thoughts",[23] he does not qualify the term: it is not simply bad thoughts, or thoughts arising from the senses, or thoughts which take the form of visual images, but thoughts in themselves which must be placed in suspension. This teaching is reinforced by St Hesychios, who calls his reader to a "stillness of mind unbroken even by thoughts which appear to be good",[24] and St Gregory of Sinai takes the additional step of insisting that even thoughts which *are* good, and not merely those appearing that way, must be renounced by the true Hesychast, for "stillness means the shedding of all thoughts for a time, even those which are Divine and engendered by the Spirit; otherwise through giving them our attention because they are good we will lose what is better."[25]

What these spiritual masters are describing—at this deepest level of stillness—is the operative parallel to the doctrinal apophaticism for which Eastern Christianity is so well known, and which is so forcefully expressed in the works of St Dionysius the Areopagite. According to Dionysius, "the supra-essential being of God" is at "a total remove from every condition, movement, life, imagination, conjecture, name, discourse, thought, conception, being, rest, dwelling, unity, limit, infinity, the totality of existence", and it therefore follows, if we wish to approach this God in true prayer, that "we call a halt to the activities of our minds".[26] Just as Moses entered into darkness in his confrontation with God, so must we "leave behind everything that is observed," St Gregory of Nyssa agrees, "not only what sense comprehends but also what the intelligence thinks it sees".[27] For in this way, says St Dionysius again, "by an undivided and absolute abandonment of yourself and everything, shedding all and freed from all, you will be uplifted to the ray of the Divine shadow

23. Quoted by Ware, *The Inner Kingdom*, p. 96. Ware points out that St John is here "adapting an Evagrian phrase, 'Prayer is a laying aside of thoughts'".
24. "On Watchfulness and Holiness", p. 180.
25. "On Stillness", *The Philokalia*, Vol. IV, p. 270. Writes St Isaac the Syrian, "As the saints in the world to come no longer pray, their minds having been engulfed in the Divine Spirit, but dwell in ecstasy in that excellent glory; so the mind, when it has been made worthy of perceiving the blessedness of the age to come, will forget itself and all that is here, and will no longer be moved by the thought of anything" (quoted in Vladimir Lossky, *The Mystical Theology of the Eastern Church* [Crestwood, NY: St Vladimir's Seminary Press, 1976], p. 208).
26. *The Divine Names* in *Pseudo-Dionysius: The Complete Works*, trans. Colm Luibheid (New York: Paulist Press, 1987), pp. 54, 53.
27. *The Life of Moses*, trans. Abraham J. Malherbe and Everett Ferguson (New York: Paulist Press, 1978), p. 95.

which is above everything that is".[28] Many passages in the *Philokalia* underscore the necessity of this same final abandonment. "Do not think that avarice consists simply in the possession of silver or gold," writes St Peter of Damaskos. "It is present whenever our thought is attached to something,"[29] however noble and true. Therefore, as St Diadochos of Photiki teaches, true poverty—the *faqr* of the Sufis—can be attained only through a mode of "prayer, deep stillness, and complete detachment" in which "a man sets himself utterly at naught".[30]

Here we come finally to the innermost goal of our quest. In order to be truly still, we discover, it is not enough for a man to live alone, or to refrain from speaking, or to resist temptation, or to close his eyes, or to think without images. If he wishes to pray without *dialogismos*, like a true Hesychast, he must become—in the words of St Hesychios—"totally empty of form".[31]

No Other "Name"

Schuon has said that in an authentic esoterism, "truth does not deny forms from the outside, but transcends them from within", and we have been attempting to glimpse what this inward transcendence might involve for the Christian by tracing the depths within depths of Eastern teaching on stillness. But transcendence is not denial, and we would seriously err if we supposed that Hesychasm is meant to culminate in mental nebulosity, or in a collapse of con-

28. *The Mystical Theology* in *Pseudo-Dionysius: The Complete Works,* trans. Colm Luibheid (New York: Paulist Press, 1987), p. 135.
29. "A Treasury of Divine Knowledge: Obedience and Stillness", *The Philokalia,* Vol. III, p. 107.
30. "On Spiritual Knowledge and Discrimination", *The Philokalia,* Vol. I, p. 255. Lossky points out that "at the extreme height of the knowable, one must be freed from that which perceives as much as from that which can be perceived: that is to say, from the subject as well as from the object of perception" (p. 28). And Schuon observes that *hesychia* is thus "the exact equivalent of the Hindu and Buddhist *nirvana* and the Sufic *fana* (both terms signifying 'extinction'); the 'poverty' (*faqr*) in which 'union' (*tawhîd*) is achieved refers to the same symbolism" (*The Transcendent Unity of Religions,* trans. Peter Townsend [London: Faber and Faber, 1953], p. 181n).
31. "On Watchfulness and Holiness", p. 177. Similarly, in the continuation of *The Way of a Pilgrim,* we are told that "the spiritual and incomprehensible Being of God may be present to the mind and recognized in the heart in absolute 'formlessness'" (*The Pilgrim Continues His Way,* trans. R. M. French [San Francisco: Harper and Row, n.d.], p. 222).

centration and contemplative focus. On the contrary, as St Hesychios and other Fathers understood the process, becoming empty of form is not the same as having no outward form or support, and detachment from every object of consciousness must not be confused with an abandonment of consciousness as such. "Pure concentration also is prayer," writes Schuon, a concentration which is "none other than silence". But this silence can be of operative value, he adds, only "on condition that it have a traditional basis and be centered on the Divine".[32] The Hesychast masters were well aware of this principle, and while insisting that we should set aside every thought and go beyond every form, they never relinquished their fidelity to one particular thought nor their dependence on a central and indispensable form.

What I have in mind, of course, is their methodic use of the Name. The spirituality of the Christian East, in addition to its characteristic stress upon stillness, has also been distinguished historically by its practice of invocatory or monologic prayer. This is a method of contemplative orison, found also among the Sufis in their practice of *dhikr*, which involves the continual repetition of a single word or short formula as an aid to concentration. In the case of Hesychasm, the word in question is usually the Name of Jesus, which is pronounced either on its own or, more commonly, as part of a brief petition often called the Jesus Prayer, consisting of the words (or some slight variation) "Lord Jesus Christ, Son of God, have mercy upon us". A prayer of this kind can be used by the Christian in a variety of ways and on several levels, not the least important being as a personal plea for help in times of danger or trouble, or as an expression of devotion and love for the Person of the Savior. But for the spiritual masters, it also has a strictly contemplative or yogic purpose, which is to serve as a focus and a point of stability in our efforts to overcome distraction and to eliminate thoughts. "Let the remembrance of Jesus be united with your every breath," writes St John Klimakos, "and then you will know the value of stillness,"[33]

32. *Stations of Wisdom*, p. 124. This silence, Schuon continues, "has been called a 'Name of the Buddha' because of its connection with the idea of the Void", for "*Shunyâmûrti*, 'Manifestation of the Void', is one of the Names of the Buddha" (p. 125).
33. Quoted by Bishop Kallistos Ware, *The Power of the Name: The Jesus Prayer in Orthodox Spirituality* (Oxford: The Sisters of the Love of God, 1974), p. 11. St Hesychios offers an almost identical formulation: "The strength of the heart's

for through this remembrance, St Philotheus of Sinai explains, you can "concentrate your scattered intellect",[34] calming and unifying the turbulent and wandering mind.[35] In more recent times, St Theophan the Recluse has offered the same advice. If you wish "to stop the continual jostling of your thoughts", he writes, "you must bind the mind with one thought, or the thought of One only"[36]—namely, the thought of the Lord Jesus Christ.

Here, though, we encounter a paradox. As we have seen, the distinguishing aim of the Hesychast method of prayer, *hesychia* itself, consists in a freedom from all conceptual forms. Our goal is a state of radical simplicity and purity, in which the mind is no longer occupied with the thought of anything, even (say the Fathers) something good and Divine: a state of utter openness and emptiness that only God Himself, and no conception, can fill. In order that we might enter this state, however—so say the masters of this path to the heart—we must deliberately retain the thought of Jesus. But how is this possible? Is it not a contradiction to think that we can become genuine Hesychasts while at the same time keeping ourselves bound to the form of His Name?

It must be admitted that in many of the Eastern Christian fathers there *is* a contradiction, and that in spite of their continuing praise of contemplative stillness, what we find instead in their writings, whether in the *Philokalia* or elsewhere, is that a sentimental and devotional attachment to the incarnate Person of Christ has in fact taken center stage in their practice. There is little doubt, for example, that the purity of true *hesychia* has been severely compromised, or at least greatly mitigated, in the teaching of St Theodoros the Great Ascetic when he advises his reader to "think of the bless-

stillness, mother of all the virtues, is preserved in us through our being helped by the Lord. . . . Let the Name of Jesus adhere to your breath, and then you will know the blessings of stillness" ("On Watchfulness and Holiness", p. 179).

34. "Forty Texts on Watchfulness", p. 27.

35. We are told that the value of the practice comes at least partly from the fact that the Name itself carries within it a power and beauty with which our other thoughts are unable to compete. St Hesychios admits that it is extremely "difficult to still the mind so that it rests from all thoughts", and yet there lies close at hand a ready solution to this problem in the Name, for "he who through unceasing prayer holds the Lord Jesus within his breast will not tire in following Him", and "because of Jesus's beauty and sweetness, he will not desire what is merely mortal" ("On Watchfulness and Holiness", p. 188).

36. *The Inner Kingdom*, p. 101. The last phrase has been added by Bishop Kallistos.

ings which await the righteous: how they will stand at Christ's right hand, the gracious voice of the Master, the inheritance of the heavenly kingdom"—or again "that sweet light, the endless joy, never interrupted by grief, those heavenly mansions, life with the angels, and all the other promises made to those who fear the Lord". For—this same writer concludes—"unless a soul is strengthened with these thoughts, it cannot achieve stillness".[37] There is no denying, of course, that imaginative anticipations of this kind can be a powerful aid to a man's devotional piety, and one can have no objection to the important part they play in the discursive prayers of the Christian, nor indeed to their presence among the provisional and preparatory meditations of the Hesychast himself. And yet it is surely just as obvious that such thoughts as those described by this saint, motivated as they are by individual interest and colored by scriptural and other traditional images, cannot but clutter and distract the mind when it is seeking to enter into the deepest dimension of stillness. Clearly they must be set aside, at least at certain times, if this final goal is to be realized.

But how is this possible if one is praying the Jesus Prayer? Petitions by their very nature are constructed from concepts, they pertain to objects, and they express thoughts.[38] I have called into question the advice of St Theodoros, but one might well ask in his defense how *any* man, even one who guards his imagination more closely, can pray the Jesus Prayer without thoughtfully considering the words that he uses and without allowing his attention to be

37. "A Century of Spiritual Texts", *The Philokalia,* Vol. II, p. 25.
38. This is why some *startsi* recommend reducing the invocation to the name "Jesus" on its own. The Archimandrite Lev Gillet points out that "the name 'Jesus' forms the core and motive force" of the Jesus Prayer, and he adds that "the oldest, the simplest, and in our opinion the easiest formula is the word 'Jesus' used alone" (*The Jesus Prayer* [Crestwood, NY: St Vladimir's Seminar Press, 1987], p. 93). Speaking of *japa yoga* in general, Marco Pallis has observed that "the less the formula used lends itself to rational analysis, the better it will match the inward synthesis of which it is destined to become the operative support". Within the operative context of a contemplative method, the discursive meaning of an invocation, including the Jesus Prayer, is not the issue. On the contrary, "it is the Holy Name, sonorous presence of the Divine grace enshrined in the formula, that is both the source of its power to illuminate and a sharp sword to cut off ignorance and distraction at the root" ("Discovering the Interior Life", *The Sword of Gnosis: Metaphysics, Cosmology, Tradition, Symbolism,* ed. Jacob Needleman [London: Routledge and Kegan Paul, 1974], p. 195).

shaped by their meaning. How am I to bind my thoughts by this thought without thinking about it? It will perhaps be objected that I am exaggerating the difficulty of the method, and that in demanding from our minds a thoughtless thought, I have put the matter in too elliptical and problematic a fashion. Consider, however, the words of St Gregory of Sinai: "Unceasingly cry out: 'Lord Jesus Christ, Son of God, have mercy', *and* [he adds at once] do not allow yourself to retain any concept, object, thought, or form that is supposedly Divine, or any sequence of argument or any color."[39] But how can we do that? How are we to invoke a formula containing Christ's Name without our minds becoming enmeshed in its form?

The answer has to do with what is meant by the Name. Preaching the good news of Christ's redemptive death, in a much-quoted passage from the fourth chapter of Acts, the apostle Peter proclaimed that "there is no other Name under Heaven given among men by which we must be saved" (Acts 4:12). This of course is a text often cited by exclusivists in defense of their belief that a conscious commitment to Jesus is the only sure path to God. In their case, the word "name" is taken to mean a proper name, and the Name of Jesus is understood to be the appellation of a specific figure of history, Jesus of Nazareth, without whom salvation would not be possible. This, of course, is a perfectly legitimate and straightforward reading of the verse in question, for on one important and very obvious level, the Name "Jesus" surely *is* the name of Jesus. It is doubtless true also that when St Peter used the term "name" in this context, he was thinking specifically of the incarnate Son of God, the One who was "crucified, whom God raised from the dead" (Acts 4:10). Nevertheless it would be very wrong to assume that this is the only possible reference of the term, and to conclude therefore that the Name can mean only, or even that it does mean primarily, a given human name of the *Logos*.

Those who would have us restrict the word to this single level of reference have failed to consider at least four telling points. They have forgotten, first, that "Jesus" is but one of numerous ways of referring to the Son of God in the Scriptures, many of which clearly bear a more universal significance than the proper name of a man. St Gregory the Theologian provides this partial list of Christ's Biblical names: "Image, Vapor, Emanation, Effulgence, Creator, King,

39. "On Stillness", p. 270n.

Head, Law, Door, Foundation, Rock, Pearl, Righteousness, Sanctification, Redemption, Man, Servant, Shepherd, Lamb, High Priest, Sacrifice, Firstborn of Creation, Firstborn of the Dead".[40] It would obviously be absurd to suppose that the Divine Person thus described in these terms is deprived of His saving power when the specific name "Jesus" is not being used. The Name of Jesus, one begins to see, must be something more than these two syllables alone.[41]

Second, unless we wish to side with the heretical modalists, who suppose that the three distinct names of the Father, the Son, and the Holy Spirit apply alike to a single Person, we must admit that the name itself "Jesus" is not uniquely salvific, for, taking it strictly as a proper name, it clearly leaves *unnamed* the other two Hypostases of the Holy Trinity, upon whom salvation depends nonetheless, and whose own names must also be regarded as sacred. The Christian is reminded of this fact every time he prays the Lord's Prayer, asking that the Father's Name should be "hallowed". It is of considerable interest to note, by the way, that at least one early Christian

40. *Oratio* 40:4; quoted by Tomáš Špidlík, S.J., *The Spirituality of the Christian East: A Systematic Handbook* (Kalmazoo, MI: Cistercian Publications, 1986), p. 35. In his book *The Name of Jesus*, bearing the significant subtitle *The Names of Jesus Used by Early Christians*, Irénée Hausherr points out that while the name "Jesus" is "one of the names of the well-beloved Son", for "Hermas [author of the second century "Shepherd"] and others like him the very person of the Son was the name, the only name which perfectly expressed the Father" (Kalamazoo, MI: Cistercian Publications, 1978), p. 18.

41. This of course is not to deny the powerful symbolism of this name and its letters. Like every name of God, "Jesus" is rich in meanings, meanings which have been somewhat more elaborated in the West than in the East. Schuon observes that "it is not by chance that [St] Bernardino [of Siena] gave to his cipher of the Name of Jesus the appearance of a monstrance: the Divine Name, carried in thought and in the heart, through the world and through life, is like the Holy Sacrament carried in procession. This cipher of the Greek letters I H S, signifying *Iesous*, but interpreted in Latin as *In Hoc Signo* or as *Jesus Hominum Salvator* and often written in Gothic letters, can be analyzed in its primitive form into three elements—a vertical straight line, two vertical lines linked together, and a curved line—and thus contains a symbolism at once metaphysical, cosmological, and mystical; there is in it a remarkable analogy, not only with the name of *Allah* written in Arabic, which also comprises the three lines of which we have just spoken (in the form of the *alif*, the two *lams*, and the *hâ*), but also with the Sanskrit monosyllable *Aum*, which is composed of three *mâtrâs* (A U M) indicating a 'rolling up' and thereby a return to the Center. All of these symbols mark, in a certain sense, the passage from 'coagulation' to 'solution'" (*Stations of Wisdom*, pp. 131-132n). Symbols they remain, however, no single one of which manifests the Truth uniquely, for there is always more to the Name than a name.

authority seems to have acknowledged the saving efficacy of an invocation based upon the Name of the Father and employed by the followers of another religion, who *never* used the proper name of the Son. St Irenaeus writes that just as "all things are subject to the Name of our Lord [Jesus Christ], so must they also be [subject] to His [Name] who made and established all things by His Word", that is, the Father. "For this reason," he continues, "the Jews even now"—that is, during Irenaeus's time—"put demons to flight by means of this very adjuration, inasmuch as all beings fear the invocation of Him who created them."[42] Besides his own religion, Irenaeus knew of no other orthodox path except Judaism, but surely, given this ancient precedent, there is no reason for the Christian of our day to deny a like efficacy to the Name of *Allah.*

Yet a third point is this. Quite apart from the question of its proper or particular usage, the word "name" is often used in the Bible, not in reference to a specific person at all, but as a synonym for authority and power, above all that of God, and in the context of Acts 4, where the subject is the Divine saving presence that was embodied in Jesus, it is certainly this meaning that must be regarded as central. To say with St Peter that there is salvation in "no other name" is not to name Jesus uniquely; it is a way instead of underscoring His intrinsic Divinity. We Orthodox see this deeper meaning of the Name portrayed in many of our icons of Christ, where, inscribed within the nimbus surrounding His head, one finds not the proper name "Jesus", but the Greek words Ο ΩΝ, meaning "the One who is" and referring of course to the Name of God given to Moses on Horeb (Ex 3:14).[43]

Finally, there is a fourth reason for rejecting the claim that salvation is limited by the name itself "Jesus", and hence for a methodical detachment from the Person thus named, and it is a reason which Orthodox Christians, with their stress upon mystery and the way of negation, should be quick to understand. We have said that

42. *Against Heresies,* II.6; Vol. I of *The Ante-Nicene Fathers,* ed. Alexander Roberts and James Donaldson (Grand Rapids, MI: William B. Eerdmans, 1967), pp. 365-366. One wonders whether this means that the Jews of the late second century A.D. had retained the proper pronunciation of the *Tetragrammaton.*

43. The Fathers sometimes quote Psalm 46:10 in this connection to underscore the relationship between the Divine Name and the practice of *hesychia*: "Be still, and know that I AM God". Nikitas Stithatos comments that "this is the voice of the Divine Logos and is experienced as such by those who put the words into practice" ("On the Inner Nature of Things", *Philokalia,* Vol. IV, p. 109).

"Jesus" is only one of the names of God's Son, that the Father and the Holy Spirit have their own saving names, and that the word itself "name" connotes Divine Presence and power, regardless of the given form which this presence might take. But we must also remember that the ultimate Source of Divinity in the unknowable Godhead, however many names it might take in the world, *cannot* be named as It is in itself. Although rightly praised "by every name", says St Dionysius, It is finally best named "the Nameless One".[44] St Gregory Palamas, among many others, concurs: "The super-essential nature of God is not a subject for speech or thought or even contemplation," he writes, and hence "there is no name whereby it can be named, neither in this age nor in the age to come, nor word found in the soul and uttered by the tongue".[45]

It is still true, of course, that there is salvation in none other than the Name of Jesus, and the Hesychast is no less obliged than other Christians to accept and to honor this principle. But at the same time no Christian, least of all the aspiring Hesychast, should allow himself to forget that Jesus is not the only name of the Son, that the Son is not the only name of God, that God is not the only name of the Named, and that the Named is truly named by no name.

Picture Frames or Open Windows?

Bishop Kallistos has written that "the Jesus Prayer is fundamentally Christocentric. We are not simply invoking God," he asserts, "but our words are addressed specifically to Jesus Christ—to God incarnate, the Word made flesh, the second Person of the Holy Trinity, who was born in Bethlehem, truly crucified on Golgotha, and truly raised from the dead". He adds, with specific reference to the Sufi practice of *dhikr*, that "a religion such as Islam which rejects the incarnation cannot be invoking God in the same way as Hesychasm does", and he suggests that we should compare the invocatory method of prayer to a picture frame, while the specific name that one invokes in any given prayer may be likened to the image within that frame. "Despite the resemblances between the 'frame' of the Jesus Prayer and certain non-Christian 'frames'," Bishop Kallistos concludes, "we should never underestimate the uniqueness of the

44. *The Divine Names*, p. 54.
45. Quoted by Lossky, p. 37.

portrait within the 'frame'. Techniques are subsidiary; it is our encounter face to face, through the prayer, with the living person of Jesus that alone has primary value."[46]

With all due respect to the Bishop, however, our explorations in the previous sections of this chapter oblige me to ask whether what he has said is really true? Is it thus, and thus only, that one may engage in this prayer? The traditional teachings to which I have been calling your attention suggest otherwise, for the inner emptiness which the Christian aspirant is encouraged to seek and the inner plenitude of the Name which he is taught to invoke prove, if anything, that Hesychasm and Sufism are all but identical.[47] Indeed, it is precisely because of the often remarkable parallels between the teachings of certain Eastern Fathers and their counterparts in other religious traditions that Christian exoterists, including those of the East, are sometimes mistrustful of the Hesychast writers. The Orthodox scholar John Meyendorff, for example, voices his concern about what he calls the "individualistic and spiritualized tendency" of St Gregory of Sinai,[48] and much the same reservation is expressed, more forcefully, by the Catholic theologian Hans Urs von Balthasar, who complains that "the mystical teaching of Evagrius in its fully

46. Ware, "Praying with the Body", p. 31. Bishop Kallistos uses this same comparison in his contribution to the present volume, "How Do We Enter the Heart?" (Chapter 1); see above, p. 21.
47. The focus of this chapter is the spiritual path, but one may note in passing that the ultimate goal of these two traditions is described by their masters in remarkably similar terms (see the chapter in the present volume by Peter Samsel). It is impossible not to think of the maxim of Islamic mysticism that "the Sufi is not created" when St Gregory Palamas describes *theosis*, or deification, as "unoriginate (not only uncreated), indescribable, and supratemporal" and when he says that "those who attain it become thereby uncreated, unoriginate, and indescribable, although in their own nature they derive from nothingness" (*The Triads*, ed. John Meyendorff and trans. Nicholas Gendle [New York: Paulist Press, 1983], p. 86). St Gregory says that he is here following "the Divine Maximus", that is, St Maximos the Confessor, who tells us for his part that the supreme spiritual state involves 'the complete reversion of created beings to God. It is then that God suspends in created beings the operation of their natural energy by inexpressibly activating in them His Divine energy" ("First Century of Theology", *The Philokalia*, Vol. II, p. 123). Meanwhile Ibn Arabi teaches that "the final end and ultimate return of the gnostics . . . is that the Real is identical with them, while they do not exist" (*Futûhât al-Makkiyya*, II.512.9, quoted by William C. Chittick, *The Sufi Path of Knowledge: Ibn al-'Arabî's Metaphysics of the Imagination* (Albany, New York: State University of New York, 1989), p. 375.
48. *St Gregory Palamas*, p. 66.

developed consistency stands closer to Buddhism than to Christianity".[49] The criticism of Protestant writers often goes even further, of course, extending to the *via negativa* as such and thus to one of the distinguishing marks of the Eastern perspective in general. Luther was doubtless speaking for many others when he wrote that "Dionysius is most pernicious; he Platonizes more than he Christianizes".[50]

On the other hand, it is certainly true—and I have acknowledged this point already—that the writings of these same Fathers are at the same time strongly colored by a devotional attachment to Christ's Person; St Theodoros, whom I quoted earlier, is by no means unique in this respect. In fact, as one quickly discovers in reading the *Philokalia* and other traditional sources, even the most apophatic of Hesychast authors do not always practice what they preach, and the method of prayer which they follow and promulgate remains, not surprisingly, a largely bhaktic one. Schuon has written about "the unequal and often disconcerting phenomenon of average Sufism", a Sufism that confuses first principles with "the categories of an anthropomorphist and voluntaristic theology",[51] and we must in all honesty acknowledge the existence, in the Christian East, of what might be called by analogy an average Hesychasm, in which the absolute imprescriptibility of the Divine Essence and the operative rigor of a truly intellective detachment are both sacrificed to the needs of a more conventional piety.

My interests here, however, are not of the historical or textual kind. I am not asking the question how in fact most Eastern Christians have prayed, and my chief concern is not with how best to describe the spirituality disclosed in the surviving works of their major authorities, nor again with whether these writers should be praised or blamed. My sole interest is in discovering what is possible for the Christian seeker today, especially one who finds himself called to a path of knowledge and who seeks to understand the inner essence of religion, and with whether that Christian, without in any way denying the truth of his own tradition, may acknowledge the equal truth of a way not his own—perhaps even drawing from it

49. Quoted by McGinn, pp. 146-47.

50. "Babylonian Captivity", quoted by Karlfried Froehlich, "Pseudo-Dionysius and the Reformation of the Sixteenth Century", in Introduction III to *The Complete Works*, p. 44.

51. *Sufism: Veil and Quintessence*, trans. William Stoddart (Bloomington, IN: World Wisdom Books, 1981), p. 131.

an encouragement and nourishment for his own spiritual practice. I believe that he can, and the point of my remarks has been to indicate how the *hesychia* of the Christian East might help to point him in the right direction. Historically, of course, the Hesychast writers were not themselves concerned with these questions, and most of them would have been just as resistant as many other Christians to the claims of another religion, and hence to the possibility of an esoteric ecumenism. Nor is there is anything surprising in this, for as Schuon points out, "a man's spirituality cannot be held to depend on knowledge of a historical or geographical kind",[52] and in the case of the Fathers, even those who, like St John Damascene and St Gregory Palamas, had contact with Islam, it is far from certain whether they encountered Muslims of their own spiritual stature, with whom they could have joined in a truly metaphysical dialogue. Nevertheless, for the Christian today, who lives in such different circumstances, and who *does* know about the mystical paths of other religions, the teachings of the Hesychasts can serve as a means for deepening his participation in Christ, while at the same time providing the keys for inwardly transcending whatever limitations those teachers may have felt obliged to impose on themselves.

When as a young man St Gregory of Sinai was taken prisoner in a Turkish raid, I do not know where he may have gone or with what Muslims he may have spoken, or what his own spiritual aptitude may have been at the time, or why he entered the monastic life soon after being released from captivity. But when he tells me to "concentrate solely on the pure, simple, formless remembrance of Jesus",[53] I presume that he must have meant what he said, and that he is inviting me to enter into a method of invoking Christ's Name which does *not* involve thinking explicitly about the incarnation—about the One who was born in Bethlehem, truly crucified on Gol-

52. *The Transcendent Unity of Religions*, pp. 51-52. Schuon continues, "It can therefore be said that the universalism of initiates is virtual as to its possible application, and that it becomes effective only when circumstances permit or impose a determined application. In other words, it is only after contact with another civilization that this universalism is actualized, though there is, of course, no strict law governing this matter, and the factors which will determine the acceptance by such and such an initiate of any particular alien form may very greatly according to the case" (p. 52).
53. "On Stillness", p. 270n. He adds that God, "seeing your intellect so strict in guarding itself", will "Himself bestow pure and unerring vision upon it and will make it participate in God".

gotha, and truly raised from the dead. To be in-carnate, after all, is to be circumscribed by a form, and a formless *form* is a sheer contradiction. On the other hand, a formless *remembrance* is still a remembrance. There is no indication that I should stop invoking the Name, which continues to serve as a support for my concentration and as a vehicle of Divine saving power. But I must do so, it seems, in a way that is deliberately detached from all conceptual contents, and thus from my thoughts, not only about the particularities of the Son's earthly life, but even about His Person as such.

Similarly, when St Dionysius explains that "the wonderful 'name which is above every name'" (Phil 2:9) *is* the Name of "the Nameless One", of the "hidden Divinity which transcends [even] being",[54] I do not know whether he is speaking as a pseudonymous 5th century Syrian monk, or (as the Orthodox tradition tells me) as a disciple of St Paul's. What I *do* know is that for this same Paul, writing in Philippians 2, the "name which is above every name" is the Name of Jesus, and I must once again conclude, therefore, that within the initiatic context of an authentic Hesychast method the meaning of the word "Jesus" is not limited to the historical and individual order. St Dionysius adds strength to this conclusion: "Every affirmation regarding Jesus's love for humanity," he writes—and it is just such an affirmation that we find in the Jesus Prayer—"has the force of a negation pointing toward transcendence". For even though God is fully present in Jesus, "He is hidden even after this revelation, or, if I may speak in a more Divine fashion, is hidden even amid the revelation." The "mystery of Jesus" can thus "be drawn out by no word or mind. What is to be said of it remains unsayable; what is to be understood of it remains unknowable."[55]

If this is true, however, then clearly one's invocation of this Name need not—and, in the case of the Hesychast, *should* not—be combined with an exclusive focus upon the incarnate Person of Christ, but should be accompanied instead by a gradual detachment of the

54. *The Divine Names*, pp. 54, 49.

55. *The Letters* in *Pseudo-Dionysius: The Complete Works*, trans. Colm Luibheid (New York: Paulist Press, 1987), p. 264 (Letters Three and Four). In this respect, Schuon observes, the Name of Jesus is like all "Divine Names", which "have meanings that are particular because belonging to a revealed language and universal because referring to the Supreme Principle. To invoke a Divinity is to enunciate a doctrine; he who says 'Jesus' says implicitly that 'Christ is God'" (*Stations of Wisdom*, p. 132).

mind from all associations and categories, whether empirical or dogmatic in character. Without in any way denying the miraculous facts of Christ's life or the saving truths of Christological doctrine, the Christian pilgrim must make an effort to abstract from those facts to their essential meaning, and to look along these truths toward the Truth. For it is thus and thus only that, with Heaven's help, he may come at last to that dimensionless center where, in the words of St Hesychios, "the Heart sees the God of gods in its own depths"—a God who is no longer approached as a distinct object of consciousness, but who Himself (the saint adds) is both "the Seer and the Seen".[56] "I saw my Lord with the eye of the heart," echoes the Sufi saint Mansûr al-Hallâj. "I said, 'Who art Thou?', and He answered 'Thou'".[57]

According to the traditionalist author Marco Pallis, "the essential question to be asked" of any religion is whether it provides "the means for taking a man all the way in the spiritual life"—whether "the formal limits" are such as "to leave an open window looking towards the formless Truth, thus allowing for the possibility of its immediate or ultimate realization".[58] It must be admitted, unfortunately, that we Christians have tended to keep our shutters closed. Not of course that we are lacking in windows, but they are usually made of stained glass or painted on wood, coloring the beams they are designed to transmit, and most Christian authorities, content with their own devotional piety, have done very little to make the serious seeker aware that it is possible for a man to go outside into the fresh morning air.[59] Among the masters of the Christian East, however, one hears at least rumors of openings, and regardless of whether any given one of these saints was willing to look directly on the white light of the Truth, we find at least scattered hints in their writings as to how we might open a few windows for ourselves. The details of their practice are a subject for another time. How precisely to enunciate the invocation, and where to place it in the mind or the heart; how to

56. "On Watchfulness and Holiness", p. 185.

57. Quoted by William Stoddart, *Sufism: The Mystical Doctrines and Methods of Islam* (New York: Paragon House, 1985), p. 83. There could be no clearer evidence of Schuon's claim that while "dogmatically the divergence between Christianity and Islam is irreducible, metaphysically and mystically it is no more than relative" (*Christianity/Islam*, p. 104).

58. *The Way and the Mountain* (London: Peter Owen, 1991), p. 96.

59. One is reminded of Christ's chastisement of the Pharisees, who "have taken away the key of knowledge; you did not enter yourselves, and you hindered those who were entering" (Lk 11:52).

coordinate the repetition of the Name with a persevering effort to prescind from all thoughts; how to support this inner work by the rhythm of one's breathing or movement—these are important questions that I have not sought to address in this chapter. Nevertheless, enough has been said that we can begin at least glimpsing the essential elements of the Hesychast method, and what we find, I suggest, is that they mirror the instructions of the risen Lord Himself.

Thomas, as you will recall, jnanic patron of those seeking an immediate certitude, was told that he must be patient and begin by touching the form, truly taking hold of what God had revealed, for Jesus *is* the Son, and the Son *is* God, and God *is* the Named, and the Named *is* its Name, which Name, for the Christian, *is* "Jesus". As for Mary Magdalene, prototype of the *bhakta*, she was nonetheless warned against clinging, and thus against confusing the form with the Essence, for Jesus is *not* the only name of the Son, *nor* is the Son the only name of God, *nor* is God the only name of the Named, and the Named is truly named by *no* name.[60] Bishop Kallistos suggests that the method of invocatory prayer is only the picture frame of one's practice, and that it is the portrait within the Christian frame, Jesus Himself, to whom His followers must direct their undivided attention. But this, I believe, is not the best comparison. If we wish to follow the Hesychast path to the heart, it is Jesus who must be approached as the frame—the frame, not of a portrait, but a window. Seekers living in the Christian house must certainly not turn their backs on this window, supposing it to be too narrow to show them the Truth. But neither should they remain at a distance, as if they were admiring a favorite painting from across a gallery. They must take a step forward and lift up the sash, placing their head and shoulders inside its ample opening. What they shall see then, of course, is no longer the frame, but instead the bountiful emptiness of a mountain valley and across its verdant expanse, if they look carefully, the outlines of other houses with other windows not their own.

60. Whenever one is speaking of a manifestation of God's saving power, such and such an avataric name must be carefully distinguished from the Divine Name as such. Schuon observes that "the 'Name' in the Christian form—as in the Buddhist form and in certain initiatory branches of the Hindu tradition—is a name of the manifested Word, in this case the Name of 'Jesus', which, like every revealed Divine Name when ritually pronounced, is mysteriously identified with the Divinity" (*The Transcendent Unity of Religions*, p. 182).

Conclusions

Chapter 10

The Long Way Home

Huston Smith

We shall not cease from exploration
And the end of our exploring
Will be to arrive where we began
And know that place for the first time.

– T. S. Eliot

As the announcement for my part in this conference indicated, I think of my remarks as a sustained meditation on the quatrain from T. S. Eliot which serves as my lecture's epigraph. Right next to that epigraph I want to place a scientific finding that will serve as the controlling metaphor for my lecture. For if there can be sermons in stones, as Shakespeare tells us there were when the world was less distant from Eden, a time when (I quote his lines from *As You Like It*, II:1) there were "tongues in trees, books in the running brooks, sermons in stones and good in everything"—if, to resume my thought, there was a time when there were sermons in stones, is it not likely that in our scientific age we can find sermons in science? Chapter Five of my *Forgotten Truth* targeted a number of such sermons, and I want to add here another that has come to my attention since I wrote that book, for it provides a graphic metaphor for everything I shall be saying in this lecture.

Two decades or so ago the California Fish and Game Department in Humbolt County conducted an experiment relating to the instinct of salmon to return to their birthplace to breed. We all know that salmon swim upstream to breed near the places they were born, and this particular experiment was designed to determine how precise their homing instinct is. The control group in the experiment consisted of silver salmon that were born six miles from the Pacific Ocean in Lost Man Creek, which joins Redwood Creek before emptying into the ocean. In the same breeding season, some salmon were hatched in a breeding tank several miles from Lost Man Creek, and, duly marked to constitute the experimental group in the experiment, they were carried overland to the ocean in a tank truck. When the next mating season arrived, it was found that the salmon in the experimental group had managed to make their way back to the tank in which they were born. This was no easy feat, and it warrants describing.

To reach their birthplace these experimental salmon swam the 3½ miles up Redwood Creek and then branched off into Prairie Creek as did the control group. But when the control group turned left into Lost Man Creek where they were born, the experimental group continued 150 yards further up Prairie Creek, where they made a sharp right angle turn into a foot and a half wide culvert that runs under Highway 101. That culvert narrows to one foot in diameter on the other side of a storm drain, and several yards further on enters a concrete flume. Beyond that flume the salmon turned abruptly into a four inch drain which made two sharp right angle turns. The second of these shot straight up for 2½ feet where its mouth became the spill hatch for the tank in which these salmon had been born. The playing out of Eliot's quatrain here, "to arrive where we began", is obvious, but what comes to my mind is the closing line of a solo a high school classmate sang in a musical program our class put on in its senior year. "Safe at last, the harbor past, safe in my Father's arms, safe in my Father's arms."

With my epigraph from Eliot and my analogy of the homing salmon in place, I proceed now to speak straightforwardly. Why are we called to make this journey of human life? Why is it a long one? And what is the home we are headed for?

Why Are We on This Journey?

Perhaps the most familiar answer to this first question comes from the Sufis: "I [Allah] was a hidden jewel, and I wanted to be known." This first answer is couched in personal, dualistic terms and is easily understood. Life as we normally know it consists in give and take. Allah gives us life, and receives from us in return the gratitude we feel for the gift we have been given. As the Baltimore Catechism put it, the purpose of life is to know God and enjoy him forever.

A second answer to why we are on this journey derives from God's generosity. On first thought it would seem that God could have kept existence entirely to himself. Lacking nothing, completely sufficient in and to himself, why should he extend himself? But we quickly realize that this is not a possibility for God, for one of the Ninety-nine Beautiful Names of Allah is "the Generous". In the Buddhist tradition this cosmic generosity is epitomized in the dictum that there is no such thing as closed-fistedness with the Buddha. So *something* besides God—let us simply say his creation—must exist on pain of God's contradicting his nature. This too expresses the point in personal terms, for generosity is a virtue that applies to people as well as to God, though the essence of the virtue appears in non-dual metaphysics also, as when Plotinus speaks of the One as "that fountain ever on".

These two explanations for why we are on life's journey are, we might say, theological and present no difficulty to the understanding. The deepest reason for our presence here, however, is metaphysical, and it is demanding. It centers in the notion of infinity, and I was surprised that "the Infinite" is not listed as one of the Ninety-nine Beautiful Names of God as recorded in Victor Danner's book *The Islamic Tradition.* Since arriving at this conference however, Professor Nasr has assured me that the concept appears twice in the Ninety-nine Names; it was just that Professor Danner used English words that are cognate to "infinite" to translate them.

The Infinite is the one inescapable idea, because its alternative, finitude, implies a limit, a cut-off point, which the mind cannot accept as final because it would instinctively wonder what lies beyond it; an absolute boundary would be like a door with only one side, a contradictory concept. Prior to Plotinus, the West considered infinitude a privation, for it equated the infinite with the indefinite, which is shapeless and lacks form. India, by contrast, had from the beginning the notion of a positive Infinite, seeing it as All-possibility, including everything that could possibly exist, as in the classic Vedantic ternary, *sat, chit,* and *ânanda*: Infinite Being, Infinite Awareness, and Infinite Bliss.

I confess that I had considerable trouble with the notion of All-Possibility until, while I was visiting Dr Martin Lings in England a decade or so ago, he instructed me. In our conversation I had objected to the notion of All-Possibility on grounds that though we were sitting in his home conversing at that moment, *logically* it was altogether possible that at that moment I be back in my home instead of his—a genuine possibility that would now never be realized. In his characteristically gentle manner, Dr Lings simply asked me if I was cognizant of all the causes that went into our being together at that moment. He did not even have to complete the argument to the effect that, if I *were* aware of the full panoply of secondary causes, I would see that they precluded the possibility of our *not* being together at the moment; as I say, he did not have to complete the argument, because he picked up from my expression that I had already grasped the point. (In the words of Dylan Thomas, "Light dawns on secret lots,/When logics die/truth leaps through the eye.") Granted, All-Possibility opens onto the paradox of divine predestination and human freedom, but anyone who thinks that the Infinite will fit consistently into finite minds has not understood that not even the physical universe so fits. Niels Bohr put this definitively when he told us, "The opposite of a small truth is a small error, while the opposite of a great truth is another great truth."

If I may be excused for putting the matter somewhat flippantly, I can close this discussion of why we are *on* life's journey by saying that because the lives we are respectively leading are possible—here we are as proof—*someone* must fill each of our roles, and it might as well be us.

This said, I turn now to our journey's length.

Our Journey's Length

During the semester that Aldous Huxley served as Distinguished Professor of Humanities at M.I.T., I volunteered to be his social secretary, so to speak, for I wanted to spend as much time as possible in the company of his remarkable mind and spirit. One day as we were returning from lunch at the Faculty Club and laboring up the four flights of stairs to our respective offices, he began reciting Christina Rosetti's poem "Uphill".

> Does the road wind uphill all the way?
>   Yes, to the very end.
> Will the day's journey take the whole long day?
>   From morn to night, my friend.

When I got home that evening, I reached for my *Oxford Book of English Verse* and read the entire poem, which continues as follows:

> But is there for the night a resting place?
>   A roof for when the slow, dark hours begin.

May not the darkness hide it from my face?
You cannot miss the inn.

Shall I meet other wayfarers at night?
Those who have gone before.
Then must I knock, or call when just in sight?
They will not keep you waiting at that door.

Shall I find comfort, travel-sore and weak?
Of labor you shall find the sum.
Will there be beds for me and all who seek?
Yes, beds for all who come.

I turned back to that poem while I was preparing for this lecture and found that it fits the road we are all traveling so well that I shall spell out the connections.

Its title and opening stanza stake out the journey's difficulty. I speak of length, whereas Rosetti focuses on the steepness of the road, but the two come to the same thing. The second stanza asks whether there will be lodging along the way, "a roof for when the slow, dark hours begin", and in the context of this conference its affirmative answer points to Sufi *tarîqahs* on the one hand and the Christian Church on the other, for it is the point of these to provide "roofs" and "resting places" where we can find refreshment and restoration with our companions along the Path— "other way-fayers", as the third stanza of the poem calls them. The concluding stanza foretells our journey's end (the place of our beginning in Eliot's formulation), where "travel-sore and weak" we shall find beds for "all who seek/Yes, beds for all who come."

To my mind all this fits beautifully, but the title of my lecture presents one surd—that of persons who are struck down early in life. I think of my older brother whom I never knew, for he died in my father's arms on his second Christmas eve. My father, despairing in his grief, held him up to the decorated Christmas tree, hoping its beauty would afford the child a moment of pleasure. He extended an arm feebly toward a gilded bauble, but before his hand reached it he collapsed in my father's arms.

Less than two years old when he died, Wesley Moreland Smith, Jr did not live a long life, so it seems inappropriate to speak of his as a long journey to his heavenly home. I shall not enter into the mystery of why some of us are granted longer lives than others. All I shall say is that the word "long" in my title connotes difficulty, not span of years. And I will say right out loud that, New Age Aquarians notwithstanding, human life in its Christian fallenness and Islamic forgetful (*ghaflah)* state is inherently difficult. Keats was right when he said that there is no such thing as this world becoming an easy place to save one's soul in. I picked up somewhere that Martin Luther remarked toward the close of his life that he could count on the fingers of one hand the days of complete happiness that he could remember. It is easy for those of us who are gathered at this conference to forget life's difficulty, surrounded as we are by like-minded friends. Discussing important ideas on a beautiful campus where the autumn weather is at its best, it is easy to forget, not the "third world" but the *two*-thirds world, where hunger and epidemic disease are the rule of life. And we too, without exception, have trials to bear, as did Jesus and the Prophet Muhammad. An African spiritual reminds us that Jesus, too,

> walked this lonesome valley,
> He had to walk it by himself.
> Nobody else could walk it for him,
> He had to walk it by himself.

I come, finally, to the last word in my title, home.

Home Is Where the Heart Is

Nothing in this finite world is unambiguous, and when families run amuck homes can turn into prisons to escape from. But this does not mar the enduring icon of home as place of refuge, shelter, and rest—a haven of warmth where love and acceptance prevail. We all sense this so clearly that anything further I could say abstractly about the subject would amount to no more than wheel spinning, so I will speak concretely and personally to try to awaken some of your own memories of times when your homes meant the most to you.

First, when I was twelve years old I left my missionary home in a small town in rural China to enter an American boarding high school in Shanghai. I was up for the move; eager to enter the larger, exciting world that was opening up to me, I scarcely looked back over my shoulder as the barge pulled away from our town's dock on the canal. And during the week in my newfound home away from home I was happy—new friends to know and interesting things being learned. But for the first three weeks, on weekends when the pressures of classes and assignments were relaxed, I would go to the middle of the deserted athletic field, throw myself on the grass, bury my face in my arms, and cry my heart out in homesickness. My parents, my younger brother, our servants and their children who were our playmates, the comforting familiar haunts of childhood—those were all still there, and I was not with them in the only place I wanted to be on those afternoons. Three weekends, and it was all over, but the memory of that desperate homesickness will never leave me.

Christmas vacation brought a different experience of my childhood home, the experience of home as a desperately awaited destination. My father came to Shanghai to take me home, and the return trip was an ordeal. The hour-and-a-half on an unheated train to Soochow was not too bad, for at least we were out of the wind, but in the long wait on the boat dock the cutting wind began to get to us, as it did increasingly during the five hours on an open barge that took us up the canal to our hometown. We kept wiggling our toes and our fingers in our cheap cotton gloves to keep the circulation going as we counted the interminable hours, then minutes, until we would be home. When we finally did reach our town and then home, there was still the ordeal of soaking our feet in cold water in the hope of offsetting chill blains; but though painful, that ordeal was bearable, for at last we were *home*! A hot supper was awaiting us on the coal-burning kitchen stove, and the other stove in the house around which we happily huddled had taken the chill off the living and dining rooms. And we were already anticipating the hot water bottles that were warming the sheets of the beds we would soon collapse into.

The third childhood memory of home that I relate to strongly brings out the welcoming side of homecoming. Homecoming is not a benediction only to those who arrive; it is reciprocally a benediction to the homebodies who eagerly await their arrival.

The best Christmas sermon I have ever heard was during a retreat I was making at the Benedictine monastery in Collegeville, Minnesota. In it the homilist likened the Church's awaiting the anniversary of the Nativity to a child, his face pressed to the window on a dark winter's evening, who finally exclaims joyfully to the household, "Daddy's home!" My own parallel to that child's happiness concerns a dramatic homecoming of my own father.

In the dead of winter he had taken a launch across a thirty mile lake to conduct an evangelistic week in a village where, as missionaries used to say, Christ had never before been preached. During the week the temperature dropped precipitously, and when it came time for him to return the lake had frozen solid, blocking all traffic. We were worried, wondering if he was dressed warmly enough for the bitter cold, and more importantly how and when he would get home. Our worry deepened as the weekend progressed when suddenly, around ten o'clock Saturday night, the front door opened and he entered, looking to our startled eyes almost like an apparition. He had walked the thirty miles across the frozen lake. No father in the Parable of the Prodigal Son was more ecstatically grateful, overjoyed, and relieved to welcome home a son than were we that night to welcome home our father, and husband in our mother's case.

As I said as I began these three personal anecdotes, my intent in this section has been to try to *evoke* the sense of homecoming rather than speculate on what our final homecomings will be like. As to what it will be like, I shall content myself with reporting something I once heard our dear friend and mentor Professor Nasr say in a lecture. He said it is reported in the Islamic tradition that when one enters paradise, for three days the only word one is able to utter, over and over again, is the word "peace".

Coda

That was where the remarks I delivered at the conference ended, but as the title of the conference was "Paths to the Heart", I took it as more than coincidental that in the mail that was awaiting me on my return home, I found this instruction enclosed in one of the letters. It is Christian, but those of us who were at the conference will have no difficulty transposing it into Sufi idiom. It reads as follows:

> For one to five minutes, say this to the Holy Trinity in your heart:
>
> > At my baptism, Holy Trinity, You established Your throne room in my heart. You reside there now.
>
> For one to five minutes each, ask the Holy Trinity in your heart these questions. Do not try to answer the questions yourself. Ask the question, then pause listening for God's answer.

Holy Trinity, You sit on Your throne in my heart. What does that mean to you? (Listen for God's answer.)

Holy Trinity, You sit on Your throne in my heart. What does that mean to me? (Listen for God's answer.)

Holy Trinity, You sit on Your throne in my heart. What does that mean to your creation? (Listen for God's answer.)

Holy Trinity, You sit on Your throne in my heart. What does that mean to humanity, to every human being, to every person I encounter. (Listen for God's answer.)

For one to five minutes, thank the Holy Trinity for residing in your heart.

For one to five minutes, praise and glorify the Holy Trinity for residing in your heart.

Chapter 11

Panel Discussion

The final session of the conference was devoted to questions and answers and to an exchange among the speakers themselves, which included their responses to the events of September 11. Written questions had been submitted by members of the audience, and these were posed by the moderator, Professor Cutsinger. What follows is a somewhat modified version of that discussion.

James S. Cutsinger: Do Islam and Sufism believe in the sanctification of the human body as do Christianity and Hesychasm?

Seyyed Hossein Nasr: The answer is yes, absolutely yes. The Islamic rites involve the body and not only the mind; you have all seen the daily movement of prayers. In the practice of *tasawwuf*, the body has a very important role to play and is integrated, in the final analysis, into the heart's center, which in turn emanates throughout the body. So the sanctity, and sanctification, of the body play a very significant role in Islamic spirituality, and there is no dichotomy between body and soul, as developed in certain strands of Western Christianity, even in the general and traditional mainstream of Islamic thought and practice.

Cutsinger: How are *hesychia*, and Hesychasm in general, to be distinguished from quietism?

Bishop Kallistos Ware: Of course, the word *hesychia*, literally translated, means "quiet", and therefore "Hesychast" could be translated as "quietist". I deliberately and consistently avoid using that translation, however, because it seems to me that the seventeenth century quietist movement, associated with Michael of Molinos and Madame de Guyon and Fénelon, has its own specific character and is something distinct from Hesychasm. I am not an expert on quietism, but I understand that it contains two features which would not be characteristic of Hesychasm. First, in some quietist manuals, it is said that you can attain a state of sanctity which cannot thereafter be lost. Hesychasm does not teach that. Until the hour of our death, we are between hope and fear. It is always possible for us to fall away. We depend on the grace of God, for we know that, as human beings, we are weak. The second point is that quietism, according to some accounts that I have read, suggests that you are to be entirely passive. I do not think, in Hesychasm, there is the same emphasis upon passivity. Now it may be that the accounts of quietism that I have read are not accurate, but if those two points are true of quietism, they would not be true in the same way of Hesychasm.

Cutsinger: Does Sufism have an idea comparable to that of the *Bodhisattva* in Buddhism?

Nasr: The idea of the *Bodhisattva*, with all of the particular characteristics that it has, is of course unique to Buddhism. It does not exist in Christianity, Islam, Judaism, Zoroastrianism, Confucianism, or any other religion. However, there certainly exists, within Islam, all the mercy that flows from the Bodhisattvic nature. This is manifested in Islam in various ways, not only through the names of *Rahmân* and *Rahîm*, but also through the function of spiritual teachers, who must manifest that mercy and that grace within the community. It is also true that a deep concern for the whole of creation is a very basic Islamic teaching. Adam, when he was placed on earth as the *khalîfah t'Allah*, that is, the vicegerent of God on earth, was responsible for the whole of creation, and in fact the Quran addresses itself, not only to human beings, but also to the cosmos, to the world of nature. One third of the Quran concerns the non-human world; except for the *Tao Te Ching*, there is no sacred scripture which deals as much with God's creation as the Quran. This cosmic dimension of the Bodhisattvic nature, to which many contemporary Buddhist thinkers dealing with the environmental crisis are pointing, is certainly to be found in Islam. So I would say that the Bodhisattvic function exists in the Islamic universe, but all of the different aspects of a *Bodhisattva* are not united in a single person as they are in Buddhism.

Cutsinger: A Sufic text teaches that it is diabolical for the invoker to seek an identity outside of the invocation. Can Bishop Kallistos address this point in light of the Hesychast tradition?

Ware: I know of no Hesychast text which uses the word "diabolical' in this context. It is of course our aim, when we invoke the name of Jesus, that we should be gathered and concentrated, as far as possible, in the sense of the presence of Jesus Christ. The whole purpose of the discipline of repetition is to gather us together. We are fragmented, and we are scattered; this is part of our fallen condition. So indeed, the aim of the Jesus Prayer is to unify, and if a person was deliberately attempting to think about other things than the person of the Lord Jesus, that would defeat the aim of the prayer. However, we cannot, by a simple act of will, instantaneously overcome our condition of fragmentation. Our mind wanders. We continually suffer distracting thoughts. No spiritual teacher in Hesychasm would be particularly fierce with his disciples because their minds wandered. He would urge them simply to faithful patience and to persistence. When your mind wanders, you continue with the invocation; you bring it back to the center, back to the name of Jesus, which means to the person of Jesus. But your mind wanders again, and again you bring it back, without inner anger—inner violence will destroy the spirit of prayer—but patiently and faithfully. For this is our human condition, that we are continually distracted. I have heard someone define a saint as a person who is conscious of God all the time. My answer to that would be that not very many of us are saints.

Cutsinger: Ibn Arabi, it has been mentioned, speaks of "tasting" the Word. This sounds similar to the Christian Eucharist, the vehicle through which all Orthodox Christians participate in the communal life of Christ and the Church. Is there anything similar in Sufism?

Nasr: Whoever wrote this question, I think it is a very profound question. The Word is of course tasted and eaten in the Eucharist, within the Christian context. In the Sufi practice of invocation, and in Muslim prayer in general, as well as in the recitation of the Quran, which is the word of God, it is also "eaten" in a sense, because we always pronounce with our mouth, and this same organ of the body participates in both activities. It was Frithjof Schuon who wrote so beautifully that there are two fundamental functions for the mouth, to speak and to eat, and spiritually the two are closely related in various traditions. So there are certainly corollaries and parallels. As Professor Chittick pointed out, the word for "taste" in Arabic, *dhawq,* corresponds in a certain sense to the Latin word *sapiens,* which is derived in turn from the verb *sapere,* meaning "to taste", and it refers to the "tasting" of the wisdom contained in the word of God. When you invoke the Name of God, it does not mean that you are tasting to see whether that Name is sour or salty, but you are "tasting" the truth contained therein through direct experience. Tasting here means direct experience, and when the Sufis speak about tasted knowledge, it means precisely the kind of knowledge that we get when we taste, let us say, a spoonful of honey, which is very different from the description of honey that we read about in books, or the chemical analysis in chemistry texts. It is a direct form of knowledge to which they allude, and in the sacramental rites of Islam, which always concern the Word of God as contained in the Quran and thus the Names of God found in the Quranic revelation, there is that tasting, and in that sense it is very similar to the Eucharist in Christianity.

Cutsinger: Dr Shah-Kazemi, citing Kashani's *tafsîr* of the Quran, distinguished between the universal religion of "Islam" and Islam in the communal sense. According to the *religio perennis* as expressed in Islam, the gates of Paradise are open to all, Christians and Muslims alike, so long as they have faith in the spiritual foundation of Reality and embody that Reality through virtue. Is the Christian view of salvation for Muslims equally charitable?

Reza Shah-Kazemi: If the Christian speakers will pardon me, I have one small point on this question—small in the sense that it takes a very short time to express, but it is great in its magnitude. A good friend, after my talk, came to me and said that he found a tremendous similarity between certain Quranic verses that I had cited and a passage from the Acts of the Apostles. According to the Quran, "Those who believe, those who are Christians, those who are Jews, those who are Sabeans, and whosoever believes in God and the Day of Judgment and acts virtuously will get his reward from his Lord, no fear or grief shall be upon him". Similarly, in Acts 10:34-35, we find the following: "Then Peter addressed them: 'Truly I perceive that God shows no partiality, but in every nation any one who fears him and does what is right is acceptable to him.'" This is a remarkable parallel, and I thank the person very much who came to give me that. I do not want to take up time from the Christian response; I just wanted to let that be said.

Ware: Another text we should keep in mind is from the Prologue to the Gospel of John. John 1:9, speaking of the Divine *Logos* who is

Jesus Christ, describes Him as "the true light which illumines everyone who comes into the world." We believe, as Christians, that Jesus Christ is the Savior of the whole world, but we also believe that the light of Christ shines in the hearts of every human person. And if those who are not Christians live by the best that they know in their own tradition, I am fully confident that God will receive them, as I hope He will receive us Christians in His mercy.

Cutsinger: Must a Muslim transcend the exclusive emphasis on the Unity of God, adopting a somewhat Trinitarian view, in order to account of how the Nameless One, who is without qualification, can be seen talking with Adam?

Nasr: No. First of all, the Nameless One *qua* the "Nameless" would never speak to Adam. To have spoken to Adam means that the Nameless must have chosen a Name; in other words, It must have become involved in speech, and so there is already a paradox, a metaphysical paradox, in what is stated. But the point that I think the question is trying to bring out is whether Islam has to give up its absolute view of the Absolute, that is, the oneness of God as the center and axis of all of its belief, in order to understand the Christian perspective on God, man, and the universe. And my answer is no. I would apply in reverse what Vincent Rossi, my old friend, has said from the other side, from the Christian side. There are many people in the Christian world today who think that in order to have a deep dialogue with Judaism and Islam, the Christians have to put aside the dogmas of the Incarnation and the Trinity. I have been involved in religious dialogue for over forty years, and this has often happened. And I have asked what good this understanding does if the person I am talking to no longer represents traditional Christianity? The reverse also holds true for Islam. It would be really senseless for the sake of human understanding to undo God's message. I am totally opposed to any kind of ecumenism that is based on the reduction of the Divine forms and ways in which God has revealed Himself. The premise of this entire conference has been that Christians should accept the Trinitarian doctrine in a serious fashion while Muslims must cling to the doctrine of *tawhîd* or Unity, and that they then should try to understand each other on the spiritual plane. This is very different from a diluting on either side. In any case, the Muslim mind has no possibility of moving towards a Trinitarian doctrine. It is easier for the Christian mind, in which there is already the element of unity, although it is not much emphasized, to move towards a doctrine of Unity than for a Muslim to move towards the doctrine of a Trinity, which is incomprehensible to it on a popular or exoteric plane. On the metaphysical plane, of course, this has all been explained in the writings of the traditionalists, especially Frithjof Schuon. The doctrine of the Trinity, on a metaphysical plane, is in perfect accord with the doctrine of *tawhîd*, of Unity, and I for one have no qualm or difficulty about that whatsoever. But this agreement does not involve a change of perspective on the theological level, as this question seems to imply.

Cutsinger: The Quran implicitly recognizes Christ's uniqueness by calling Him, Him alone among all of the Prophets, the "Spirit of God" and in saying that He and His mother alone were born perfect and that He will come again at the end of time. Is this understanding of uniqueness, the uniqueness of Christ, sufficient for Christians who wish also to emphasize Christ's uniqueness?

Ware: The uniqueness of Christ, for me as a Christian, consists in the fact that He is the only begotten Son of God. Therefore the uniqueness refers first of all and fundamentally to the incarnation. Only once, according to Christian belief—only once in all the history of the human race—has God become man, in the sense that the second person of the Trinity was born according to the flesh from the Virgin Mary. That is a unique event, so the uniqueness of Christ refers first of all to the fact of the incarnation. Of course, there is another sense in which the word of God may be born in the soul of every believer, but this does not diminish the uniqueness of the event of Christ's birth in Bethlehem. Only once has God been born from a woman. So there, to me, is the uniqueness of Christ.

Cutsinger: Your Grace, this next question comes directly for you, and it is related to what you were just saying. Although, as Christians, we are always in the presence of the reality of the Trinity, must not an apophatic approach be applied to our formulations of the doctrine of this ever present reality? And, if so, will this apophatic approach not have some bearing on our interpretation of the Islamic insistence on the precedence of the Divine Unity?

Ware: On our Christian understanding, the dogmas of the faith, as defined by the seven Ecumenical Councils, are indeed true, but of course the eternal Truth of the transcendent God cannot be expressed in verbal formulae in an exhaustive fashion. The word "definition" means setting limits and is linked with the Latin word *finis,* meaning a limit or frontier, and the Greek term for a definition is *horos,* which is linked with our word "horizon", the limit beyond which you cannot see. So the definitions of the Church exclude certain false ways of thinking about God or Christ. They set a boundary in the sense of saying, Do not wander outside this fence. But as for the Mystery that lies within the boundaries, that can never be totally expressed in words. Therefore, it is true that for me as a Christian God is three in one, and therefore, for me as a Christian, it would be false to say that God is one and not three. And it would be false to say that God is four in one or five in one. These things are excluded. But what is meant by the Mystery of God as "three in one" cannot be fully expressed in words and can be discovered only through prayer. The fact, however, that definitions do not express the total truth does not mean that we lay them aside as provisional and transcend them. We never go beyond the definitions, but we never fully understand the Mystery which those definitions are safeguarding.

Cutsinger: When the Hesychasts are taught to lay aside all "thoughts", are they not being taught that in some sense they must lay aside "definitions" as well?

Ware: No, definitely not. But you can *believe* something without *thinking* about it all the time. So, the Hesychasts are taught that, when praying, they should have simply a sense of the presence of Christ. They do not formulate in their minds what precise remarks were made concerning the relation between *hypostasis* and *ousia,* and how these things are to be interpreted philosophically. They are not using their discursive reasoning to grasp these mysteries so far as they can be expressed philosophically. But you can believe something without thinking about it through your discursive reason, so the fact that you are not thinking about something does not mean that you have ceased to believe in it or that you think you have transcended it.

Vincent Rossi: In immersing myself in the early Hesychast fathers and, in particular, in St Maximus the Confessor and Dionysius the Areopagite, I have been led to make one or two observations that may be relevant and helpful here. My own observation is that the dogma of the Trinity has a function like a *koan,* in which the mind or the thoughts are supposed to be broken down in order for an experience to become manifest. So St Gregory the Theologian, for example, will say that anyone who tries to understand the one and the two and the three rationally—I am only paraphrasing—is liable to go into a frenzy, which is what seems to have been happening in some of our discussions. Professor Cutsinger poses the question, If you are asked to go beyond thought, then where is the Trinity? Well, according to St Maximus, the Trinity *is* beyond thought to begin with, and so there is no problem there; you are already beyond thought—thought simply does not work in that context. Furthermore, I would not be quite honest in this ecumenical setting if I failed to point out that in the Orthodox Hesychast tradition, going from the Cappadocians through Dionysius through Maximus through John of Damascus through Simeon to Gregory Palamas, there is a very clear sense that the Trinity functions as the basis, in part, for a criticism of the doctrine of Unity. One of the things that Dionysius and Maximus are doing when they teach the doctrine of the Trinity is being critical of Unity as a thought, or as a concept. Maximus insists that the Unity of God and the Trinity of God are on the same plane because he knows that as soon as you put them on different planes, you are in the realm of thought. But if you keep them on the same plane, you are messing up all thought—there is no way you can think that. There is, though, a way to enter into the Reality devotionally: with your mind and your heart enduring the remembrance of God in a spirit of devotion, keeping the Unity and the Trinity on the same plane, regardless of what you want to think about, regardless of how much your metaphysically oriented mind wants to put a hierarchy there. If you keep them on the same plane in a spirit of devotion, you may actually be able to remember God, and I think that this is what Maximus is all about.

Cutsinger: Turning now in a different direction, to a topic that has been very much on all of our minds, let me pose this question. Could the panelists elaborate further on the "hardening of hearts" which has led to the polarity of modernism and fundamentalism, specifically in light of the recent attacks on modernism by fundamentalism on September 11?

Shah-Kazemi: One of the most important developments arising out of this recent atrocity is the way in which moderate Muslims in the West and, to a lesser extent, in the rest of the Muslim world—but particularly in the West—have seen the danger of identifying Christians and Jews as the enemy. The otherness, the exclusivity, of the Islamic message is therefore becoming less of a dogma for them. Muslims who see themselves as living in the modern world, and who are at the same time trying to find some roots in their religion to cope with the problems in the modern world and the situations they are faced with, cannot escape the fact that their religion has indeed become hardened; it has become modernized in a way that prevents the spirituality of their tradition from enabling them to cope with their problems effectively. It is precisely put in the Quran that "their hearts were diseased, and We increased that disease". Many Muslims are now realizing that a hardening of the heart has taken place, namely, a turning away from the spiritual tradition followed by a turning towards religion as a source of ideology, thus intensifying that hardening process. To realize that this has happened, however, is to realize, at the same time as we are faced with this current crisis, that we are also faced with a tremendous possibility of opening, whereby the spiritual sources of the tradition can come forward. Frithjof Schuon has said that as soon as the esoteric essence of the religion is eclipsed or denied or ignored, what happens is a hardening of the exoteric form into a shell. A religion cannot live without the sap that gives it the spirituality without which it would suffocate and die. So I think that there is an opening in the midst of this crisis.

Nasr: This is such an important issue. I was in Egypt when this great tragedy occurred, and I have refrained from giving any public discourse until now. There is a delicate point to mention in response to this question. It must be said, first of all, that modernism came into the Islamic world in the eighteenth century. Parallel with it there grew a kind of puritanical movement, which finally led to the modern Salafiyyah-Wahhabi movement, which is the ideological background of these people who committed these horrendous acts. But had modernism not come into the Islamic world, that other movement would not have had the history that it has. It stood for a long time within Arabia itself in opposition to the onslaught of modernism. At the same time, as a Bedouin phenomenon in Najd, in the southern province of Arabia today, it was also opposed to the philosophical, intellectual, and mystical aspects of Islam—for which Najd was not known, to put it mildly. It was a little bit like the Taliban, who are Pashtu people from the villages of the Pashtu area of Afghanistan, and who suddenly appear on the scene, and people wonder why they do what they do. But in fact that is what they have been doing for the last thousand years, except they were not on the international scene: they did not run a country; they did not have political power. It was only in the twentieth century that the so-called reformists or *salafi*, to use the Arabic word, which means "going back to the beginning"—a kind of back to the Quran movement with a rather hardened, puritanical, and "Calvinistic" interpretation of Islam—it was only then that they gained political power, political power through oil, and of course through American interest in the oil of the Middle East, and especially Arabia. And a new factor set in, which everyone who thinks about this problem has to think about if you want to get to the deep-rooted causes of this crisis. It is also important to understand that the real critique of modernism in the Islamic world did not come from the Wahhabi movement; it came from Sufism. This is something which is getting all mixed up right now. In the nineteenth century, after the Napoleonic invasion of Egypt, even the class of *'ulamâ'*, that is, the religious scholars who were associated with the law, with the exoteric aspects of religion, became weakened *vis-à-vis* the onslaught of modernism. It was only the Sufis who resisted. It is not accidental that the most profound critique of the modern world, which came from the pen of René Guénon, came from the pen of a man who was a Shadhili Sufi living in Egypt, and who spent the last twenty years of his life in that area. This is very, very important to understand. The profound criticisms that have been given by Frithjof Schuon, René Guénon, Titus Burkhardt, and others of the very foundation of modernism must not be confused with what is going on right now. There is a tremendous confusion in the West between fundamentalist Islam, traditional Islam, and modernism. Fundamentalist Islam is not the same thing as traditional Islam, no more than is the fundamentalist Judaism that is wreaking havoc on the Middle East the same thing as traditional Judaism, and this is true of course in other religious frameworks. Fundamentalist Christians, some of them extremists, are not the same thing as traditional Christians who have been practicing their religion for centuries.

This very severe reaction we have seen by Muslim extremists who have come from the background of the Salafiyyah-Wahhabi movement, and who have now led the world to this disaster, must not be confused with the constant, but never violent, opposition of Sufism to modernism, as a philosophy, from the very beginning. And this must also not be confused with an attack on the other Abrahamic traditions. The attack against modernism is not the same thing as attacking Christianity and Judaism. Many people in the streets in the Islamic world might not be able to make this distinction, of course, because they think in religious terms; they think that the whole of the West is Christian. We wish that it were, but it is not! But they do not understand this. So in order to really understand the deep roots of this crisis, you must be able to make a distinction between these nuances, and you must understand, above all, what it is that has led the terrorists to these extremist positions. How can one clear the swamp? It is not enough to kill a few mosquitoes that give you West Nile Disease; you have to change the environment that creates the mosquitoes. And this, unfortunately, nobody wants to talk about. In the press and on the television, you have the same old chattering heads, who know very little about the Islamic world, the so-called experts, who are there for ideological purposes and who really mislead the American public in a remarkable way. The misinformation, and disinformation, that goes on at a tragic moment like this is extremely saddening. You really have to practice *hesychia* at the present moment in the middle of all this disinformation that clutters the space. But there is, as Dr Shah-Kazemi just said, also tremendous hope. Many people now are beginning to ask, "Well, what is this Islam that everybody is talking about?" And despite veil after veil of disinformation and malicious distortion, there is also I think a great deal of hope for making things better understood, and in this context I think that nothing is more important than the writings of the perennialist authors, especially people like Burckhardt, like Schuon, like Guénon. I think that they are going to have a very important role to play in the future, not only for America and the Middle East, but for the whole world.

Huston Smith: Of course we do not want to turn this conference into a political conference, but at the same time this is so deep that if we do not speak out the stones themselves will cry out. So having heard from my dear friend from the Islamic side, as an American, I just want to mention two facts which, in all the deluge and oceans of words, I have not heard in the public media. First, I suspect if one were to ask which major newspaper in history has ever been least read, the answer would be my local paper, *The San Francisco Chronicle,* on September 11. Why? Because it went to press before the Trade Buildings fell, but by the time it hit the homes and the streets, the buildings *had* fallen, and everybody listened to the television and the radio and nobody read the paper—except my wife, who is a marvelous research scholar in these respects. And on the front page of that paper, there was an article with a headline saying, "The War Goes On and On". But the war it was talking about was Vietnam, and it subject was the way in which agent green was still causing stillborn children and deformed children. I mention this just to say that my country has much, much to apologize for and to ask forgiveness for. My second observation is this. I happened to be a student at the University of Chicago when the first chain reaction, nuclear reaction, was, as we call it, a "success". And President Hutchins gave a speech with a striking title, which he had borrowed from a theologian: "The Good News of Damnation". And the point of his remarks was that if we take seriously enough damnation, we may mend our ways a little. I suspect that being toppled from the assumed position of the country that can "run the world" is, in the long run, probably a very good thing for America.

Ware: What I want to say fits with what has just been said by Professor Huston Smith. When a tragedy happens such as occurred on September 11, one's immediate reaction is to look for somebody to blame, and therefore to hate. That is a natural reaction, but it is also a very dangerous one. We fall into the trap of looking for someone responsible, a guilty person or group, whom we can then demonize, and we think in terms of "them" and "us", with a dichotomy and an opposition. But when a disaster such as happened on the 11th of September occurs, surely our true reaction should be to say, "I too am to blame. I too am responsible. I should not blame other people exclusively, but search my own heart." Surely the meaning, or one of the meanings, of what happened on September 11 is that we should all repent. If I had led a life of greater love and trust, would it have been exactly the same? You may say, "Yes, it would," but who knows, under the perspective of eternity, what all of us in this room have contributed in the world towards fear and alienation because of our own narrowness? Dostoevsky in *The Brothers Karamazov* speaks of a judge who has to condemn a man in the dock to a period of prison—this is from the "Discourses of Starets Zosima". Father Zosima says that the judge should reflect, "I too should be in the dock beside the prisoner. Sentence should be passed also on me, because I too am responsible for what he has done." So I think we have to say that we are all responsible, and that we should all repent.

Gray Henry: I would like to join the Bishop. My first reaction in recent days has been, "What is our government doing?" And then I thought of my own guilt. How long have I known about what we have been doing to the Iraqi people by denying them medicine? The hundreds of women and thousands of children that die daily, and I did nothing. I have been to conferences; I have listened to people who have been there on the ground; and I did nothing. Earlier this week, we had a conference in Louisville on the subject of Thomas Merton and Hesychasm, and this question came up; and at first I thought that it was interrupting the beautiful subject we were dealing with, inward prayer. But then I realized that we have all been told over and over to love and pray for our enemies, but many of us have never had such a chance. Everyone on that panel spoke to the question in such a way that I was deeply moved. I wonder whether the Bishop, who was also in Louisville, could say something about what we decided on the subject of loving and praying for our enemies.

Ware: I do not wish to add to what you have just said, except to say that Christ constantly speaks of loving enemies. He would not have mentioned it so often if it was not important, and he would not have mentioned it so often if it was not difficult.

Rossi: I would like to get back to the original question and to Professor Nasr's answer, which I think is very crucial. The purpose of the question was to try to understand what is going on in the Islamic world at the present moment, and what can we trust. And I think that Professor Nasr's answer is extremely important, and all I have to do to add to it is to ask a further question. Strictly from my own reading, is it not fair to say that throughout Islamic history and throughout the Islamic world, whenever Sufism has had a chance to have some kind of influence, its influence has always been a moderating one?

Nasr: By and large, yes, but I want to add one proviso to this. There were times in the history of Islam when the Islamic world was invaded, such as the Mongol invasion, or the Italian invasion of Libya, in which the Sufi orders participated along with the rest of society in the defense of the country. The most recent example, of course, is what happened in the Soviet Union during seventy years of Soviet rule in Central Asia, and what has happened in Caucasia during the last five to ten years, when one of the Sufi orders, the Naqshbandiyyah order, has had a very important role to play. But one thing you could say definitely is that throughout the whole of Islamic history, the organized Sufi orders have never participated in any offensive moves, militarily speaking. This has never been seen even once. So yes, by and large, the influence of Sufism has always been moderating. It is interesting that Jalal al-Din Rumi, whose father had to flee the Mongol invasion, and who lost his homeland as a boy of twelve years old—and who was then brought to Mecca and Medina, and then settled in eastern Anatolia, where he died in Konya—is the most universalist of all Sufi writers, writing so much about the universality of the truth, of religion, and the love for Christians. He actually had many Christian disciples, and when he died, both Jewish and Christian rites were held for him. What we see is that his horrendous experience, family-wise, had no effect whatsoever on the moderating influence he had within Anatolia with regard to the relationship between Muslims and Christians.

Shah-Kazemi: I just wanted to continue those comments, and to mention a very important example of the way in which Sufism responded to imperialism in the Algerian context. Professor Nasr mentioned Libya and Chechnia, but in Algeria we have the example of a Sufi saint, the Emir Abd al-Qadir al-Jazairi, who fought against the French. In the 1830s and 40s, the French had resorted to a kind of "scorched earth" policy in Algeria, and during that time the ears of Arabs were regarded as trophies by the French. The French soldiers would cut off ears, and they would be given rewards for the number of Arab heads that they could produce. It was a barbaric time, and when the Emir was asked, "What do we do in return?", he said, "When you capture a French soldier, you bring him to me, and if he complains of ill treatment, you will receive yourself a punishment of ten blows on the soles of your feet." When he was finally defeated and when he was taken to Paris, among the people who came to him in droves to pay their respects were the French officers whom he had treated so well and who knew what their people were doing to the Algerians. Later this same man, the Emir Abd al-Qadir, was exiled to Damascus, and in Damascus he was responsible for saving, it is estimated, two to three thousand Christians at the time of the Civil War between the Druzes and the Christians. He was insistent that the Christians had absolutely nothing to do with the conflict, that they were non-combatants, and that their immunity must be respected according to the *shari'ah*. But he was ignored. Damascus was attacked, and the Christians were on the verge of being massacred, when the Emir took them personally first to his home, and then, when he realized the extent of the attack, to the Citadel of Damascus, where he assembled a few soldiers that were under his command and defended these people. His biographer, Churchill, wrote that this was an amazing scene: thousands of Christians, and their delegations and their families, were being defended; the Bride of Christ, he said, was being defended by a descendent of the Prophet. And Shamil, the great warrior from Chechnia, wrote to him and said, "How happy I am to live in a time when the *sunnah* of the Prophet is being really implemented by someone like you, who knows when to fight, when not to fight, and when to defend those who have a right to be defended." What the Emir was putting into practice is an extremely important Quranic principle, one which completely undermines the ideological edifice that was raised by the people who perpetrated the attacks on the innocents in New York and Washington. It says very clearly in the Quran, "Let not hatred of a people cause you to deal with them unjustly. God does not love those who are unjust." This is an extremely important verse. However much hatred and rage there may be in the Muslim world, the Quran does not allow the Muslim to act unjustly. And justice in war means that you fight only combatants, and that you do not make war against those who have no guilt or have no malicious intent towards you. Also in the Quran is the "peace verse", which clearly says that if your enemy inclines to peace, you should incline also to peace. The Quran says that you do not have any warrant against those who do not fight you for your religion. It also says, "God does not forbid you from making peace with those who do not fight you on account of your religion, who do not persecute you." I just want to make this point in relation to the Emir Abd al-Qadir, because here we have a wonderful combination of the highest spirituality—in Damascus, at the tomb of Ibn Arabi, he wrote his famous *Mawaqif*, which is one of the most esoteric interpretations of the Quran and the *hadîth* we have, based on Ibn Arabi, but in a sense more esoteric than Ibn Arabi himself—with a genuine compassion toward people of a different religion. So we have in this figure a real *mujâhid*, who exemplifies the real concept of *jihad*: one who is a warrior inwardly, first of all, who fights the *jihâd* within himself, and who has love and compassion for those who are defenseless, whether Christian or Jew or anyone else, and who is willing to lay his life down for them, in keeping with the verse which I cited in my paper. It is not just mosques, but churches, cloisters, synagogues—all places wherein the name of God is "oft mentioned"—which the Muslim is obliged by the Quran to defend with his life, if necessary.

Father John Chryssavgis: I am just so glad all this has been brought up. I do not think that we are politicizing when we address these concerns. The events of September 11 cannot help but be at the center of this conference, and what this conference is about. Professor Nasr remarked, in the discussion which followed his address, that we cannot do good unless we are good, and we have heard from Bishop Kallistos that the saint is the one who is conscious of God all of the time. But there is a flip side to this picture. The desert tradition tells me that I do not know whether I am doing more for my brother when I pray for him, or when I offer him a plate of beans. I do not think the issue here is offering beans, and yet there are clearly other ways of doing something for my brother. There is a spiritual depth to doing good as much of the time as we can in order to become good all the time, and not only to being aware of God as much of the time as we can in order to become aware of Him all the time—a spirituality "bottoms up", if you like. God will continue to do His work in Heaven. We need to do our work here, to knock down barriers that we have set up, and that work, that activity, is not secular or merely political. It is deeply spiritual.

Cutsinger: There was a final question that I had been asked to pose. How can we bring away from this conference something of the spirit of unity and friendship that we have found? But I think that we have already had any number of good answers to that. Please join me in thanking our panelists.

Contributors

KALLISTOS WARE is Spalding Lecturer in Eastern Orthodox Studies at Oxford University, Bishop of Diokleia in the Orthodox Archdiocese of Thyateira and Great Britain, and a monk of the Monastery of St John the Theologian in Patmos. He is the author of *The Orthodox Church* (1963; revised 1993), *Eustratios Argenti: A Study of the Greek Church under Turkish Rule* (1964), and *The Orthodox Way* (1979; revised 1995); a translator of the *Philokalia, The Festal Menaion,* and *The Lenten Triodion*; and co-editor of the journal *Sobornost.*

GRAY HENRY lectures and writes on the spirituality of the world's sacred traditions and has published in this field for many years. Founder and trustee of the Islamic Texts Society and former director of Quinta Essentia Publications, she currently directs Fons Vitae Press and is a consulting editor for *Parabola.*

SEYYED HOSSEIN NASR is University Professor of Islamic Studies at George Washington University. The author of over thirty books and three hundred articles, he is a former president of Aryamehr University in Iran, and the founder and first president of the Iranian Academy of Philosophy. He has delivered a number of major lectureships around the world, including the Gifford Lectures in Scotland and Cadbury Lectures in England. His publications include *Ideals and Realities of Islam* (1966), *Sufi Essays* (1972), *Knowledge and the Sacred* (1981), and *Religion and the Order of Nature* (1996).

WILLIAM C. CHITTICK is a professor in the Department of Comparative Studies at the State University of New York, Stony Brook. Among his publications are *The Sufi Path of Love: The Spiritual Teachings of Rumi* (1983), *The Psalms of Islam* (1988), *The Self-Disclosure of God: Principles of Ibn al-'Arabî's Cosmology* (1998), *Sufism: A Short Introduction* (2000), and *The Heart of Islamic Philosophy: The Quest for Self-Knowledge in the Teachings of Afdal al-Dîn Kâshânî* (2001).

VINCENT ROSSI is Director of Education for the American Exarchate of the Jerusalem Patriarchate of the Orthodox Church. He also serves as the U.S. Director of the U.K.-centered Religious Education and Environment Program. Author of two books and nearly a hundred articles on theology, spirituality, and the environment, he was the founder and for twelve years the editor of the journal *Epiphany*.

JOHN CHRYSSAVGIS is Professor of Theology and former Dean at Holy Cross Greek Orthodox School of Theology. He is the author of several books and numerous articles on Orthodox spirituality, including *Ascent to Heaven* (1989), *The Desert is Alive* (1994), *The Way of the Fathers* (1998), and *Soul Mending: The Art of Spiritual Direction* (2000).

REZA SHAH-KAZEMI is a Research Associate at the Institute of Ismaili Studies in London. His publications include *Paths to Transcendence: Spiritual Realization according to Shankara, Ibn Arabi, and Meister Eckhart* (forthcoming), and he is currently working on a new English translation of the Imam Ali's *Nahj Al-Balagha.*

PETER SAMSEL holds a doctorate in physics and is an independent scholar living in upstate New York.

JAMES S. CUTSINGER is Professor of Theology and Religious Thought at the University of South Carolina and Secretary for the Foundation of Traditional Studies. His publications include *The Form of Transformed Vision: Coleridge and the Knowledge of God* (1987), *Advice to the Serious Seeker: Meditations on the Teaching of Frithjof Schuon* (1997), and *Reclaiming the Great Tradition: Evangelicals, Catholics, and Orthodox in Dialogue* (1997).

HUSTON SMITH is Thomas J. Watson Professor of Religion and Distinguished Adjunct Professor of Philosophy, Emeritus, Syracuse University. His many books include *Forgotten Truth: The Common Vision of the World's Religions* (1976), *Beyond the Post-Modern Mind* (1989), and *Why Religion Matters: The Fate of the Human Spirit in an Age of Disbelief* (2001), as well as the classic study *The World's Religions.* His discovery of Tibetan multiphonic chanting was lauded as "an important landmark in the study of music", and his film documentaries of Hinduism, Tibetan Buddhism, and Sufism have all won international awards.